Delia Smith's
Winter Collection

Comfort Food

Illustrations by
Flo Bayley

Random House
NEW YORK

DEDICATION

To everyone at *The Magazine,*
THANK YOU FOR YOUR PATIENCE

This book is published to accompany the BBC television series entitled
Delia Smith's Winter Collection, which was first broadcast in October 1995.
Executive Producer: Frances Whitaker
Produced and directed by Trevor Hampton

Originally published in Great Britain by BBC Books, an imprint of BBC
Worldwide Publishing, in 1995.

Library of Congress Cataloging-in-Publication Data

Smith, Delia.
[Winter collection]
Delia Smith's winter collection / illustrations by Flo Bayley.
p.   cm.
"Accompany the television series entitled Delia Smith's winter collection,
which was first broadcast in October 1995."
ISBN 0-375-50024-3
1. Cookery. 2. Winter.   I. Delia Smith's winter collection (Television
Program)   II. Title.
TX714.S5888   1997
641.5′64—dc21   97-13564

Random House website address: http://www.randomhouse.com/

Printed in the United Kingdom
Butler & Tanner Ltd
9   8   7   6   5   4   3   2
First U.S. Edition

BOOK DESIGN BY DEBORAH KERNER

Illustrations by Flo Bayley
All photographs by Peter Knab, except the following:
Jean Cazals (page 93), Tony Heathcote (page 56),
Norman Hollands (pages 129; 196–97), Kevin Summers (pages 17; 32;
80; 84; 116; 120–21; 136–37; 156; 216–17).

My thanks to Mary Cox, Catherine Calland, Lulu Grimes and Tamsin Burnett-Hall for
their help with the recipe testing, photography and TV series. To Jane Houghton for
coordinating the book and to Diana Hughes, Aggie MacKenzie and Eirwen Hughes for
their help with the production. My thanks also to Kevin Summers, Norman Hollands, Jean
Cazals and Tony Heathcote for allowing me to include their splendid photographs from
Sainsbury's *The Magazine,* and a special thanks to Peter Knab, who beautifully
photographed the rest of this book.

Contents

Introduction

EVER SINCE I WAS A SMALL CHILD I HAVE FELT A SENSE OF MAGIC IN THE CHANG-
ing seasons. For me this sense of change and the fact that nothing ever remains quite
the same gives our everyday life that joyful quality of anticipation. Having said that, I
can envisage nods of agreement when it comes to spring or summer . . . but winter?
Perhaps a few furrowed brows?

The truth is that winter has every bit as much charm as the other seasons for me:
the dazzling splendor of autumnal colors and Keats' as yet unmatched description of
mists and mellow fruitfulness, the stark emptiness of bare branches against the winter
skies, and always the very special pale winter light.

Yes, there will be cold and gray days and long dark nights, but surely it is in winter that food comes into our lives with an even sharper focus—because it's then that we
all need to be warm, cozy and comforted. In winter, cooking and eating are a much
more serious affair—and here in the following pages I have attempted to offer what I
hope is a strong case for reviving this idea.

I have an instinct (no more) that perhaps our current preoccupation with
healthy eating has eclipsed what I consider to be a very health-giving joy of more traditional cooking, of eating gathered around a table enjoying conversation, good food
and good wine.

Okay. Excesses of anything are unhealthy. I'm not suggesting you eat Steak and
Kidney Pudding followed by Fallen Chocolate Soufflé every day, but what I am saying
is let's not completely lose sight of our heritage: puddings steaming merrily on the
stove, the smell of home baking and the evocative aroma and the sound of a roast sizzling in the oven after a long frosty walk. Then there's that glorious anticipation of
something braising long and slow while at the same time all its wonderful flavors are
being gently imparted.

I could of course go on and on, but now it's over to you—and hopefully as you
read and try the recipes you too will share my enthusiasm and joy in all that winter
cooking has to offer.

CHAPTER ONE

Warming Up: The Soup Collection

ALTHOUGH THERE ARE SOME DELIGHTFUL SUMMER VERSIONS, IT'S DURING the winter months that soups really come into their own. Steaming bowls of something fragrant and homemade are not just psychologically warming, they're physically warming too. Like nothing else hot soup really does give you an inner glow right down to the chilliest fingers and toes. So it's been essential for me to find and put together a very special collection of homemade winter soups to begin this book. If I'm honest I was apprehensive at the prospect of doing this as, looking back over the years, I seemed to have already made every soup in existence. But what I want people to know is that the whole subject of food and cooking never loses its fresh edge; new ideas are always popping up through travel, friends and discovering new ingredients. And the result is nine of the best soups I've ever tasted—I know you won't be disappointed!

Most of the following recipes have two dimensions. First, on their own they are good for large family meals along with good bread, cheese and salad. Secondly, with the addition of an interesting garnish, you have something a little more special for entertaining.

Stocks are now available in cans from supermarkets, but if you need a large quantity these can be expensive. Powdered vegetable stock, gluten-free, is usually available from health food shops and is an excellent cupboard standby. For those who do not have my other books, here's how to make vegetable stock and chicken stock— either of which can be used for the soups in this chapter—and a choice of croutons.

Quick Vegetable Stock

*1 stalk celery, cut in half and split
    lengthwise
2 small carrots, split in half lengthwise
2 small onions, sliced
2 bay leaves*

*12 black peppercorns
1 small bunch parsley stalks and
    celery leaves
Salt
2½–3¾ cups cold water*

Simply place all the ingredients in a saucepan, cover it with a lid, bring everything to the boil, and boil briskly for 30 minutes. After that, strain, discarding the vegetables, and the stock is ready for use.

Chicken Giblet Stock

*1 set of chicken giblets (or see Note)
1 stalk celery, cut in half and split
    lengthwise
2 small carrots, split lengthwise
2 small onions, sliced
2 bay leaves*

*12 black peppercorns
1 small bunch parsley stalks and
    celery leaves
Salt
1 quart cold water*

Place the giblets and the rest of the ingredients in a saucepan, cover and bring to the boil. Boil it briskly for 1 hour, then strain, discarding the giblets and vegetables.

NOTE: *If you can't get hold of chicken giblets, use a couple of chicken wing tips instead.*

Croutons

Serves 4

2 ounces bread, cut into small cubes   *1 tablespoon olive oil*

Preheat the oven to 350°F.

Just place the cubes of bread in a bowl together with the oil, and stir them around so that they get an even coating. Then arrange them on a baking sheet.

Bake them on the high rack in the oven for 10 minutes or until they are crisp and golden. One word of warning: Do use a kitchen timer for this operation because it's actually very hard to bake something for just 10 minutes without forgetting all about it. I have baked more batches of charcoal-colored croutons than I care to remember! Then allow them to cool, and leave them on one side until the soup is ready or store them in a screw-top jar.

Garlic Croutons

Follow the recipe above, only this time add 1 crushed clove of garlic to the bowl along with the olive oil and cubes of bread.

Parmesan Croutons

For this you place the oil and cubes of bread in a small bowl, stir them around until the oil is soaked up, then sprinkle in 1 tablespoon of freshly grated Parmesan. Stir the cubes around to coat them in that as well, then spread them on the baking sheet and bake as above.

Chickpea, Chili and Cilantro Soup

Serves 4–6

This has decidedly Mexican overtones. It isn't too hot and spicy but the presence of the chili does give it a nice kick, and the flavor and texture of chickpeas is perfect for soup.

1½ cups dried chickpeas, soaked overnight in twice their volume of cold water
1 tablespoon coriander seeds
1 tablespoon cumin seeds
½ stick butter
6 large cloves garlic, finely chopped
2 small red chilies, halved, seeded and chopped
1 teaspoon ground turmeric

Grated zest of 1 lemon
½ cup fresh cilantro stalks and leaves separated
Salt and freshly ground black pepper
1 cup crème fraîche
2–3 tablespoons lemon juice

FOR THE GARNISH:
1 mild large red or green chili, seeded and cut into very fine hairlike shreds

You will also need a large saucepan of about 3 quarts capacity.

First of all drain the chickpeas in a colander, rinse them under cold water, then place them in the saucepan with 1½ quarts of boiling unsalted water. Then bring them up to simmering point, put a lid on and cook them very gently for about 1 hour or until the chickpeas are absolutely tender and squashy.

While they're cooking prepare the rest of the soup ingredients. The coriander and cumin seeds should be dry-roasted in a small preheated skillet for 2–3 minutes, then crushed with a mortar and pestle. After that melt the butter in the skillet, add the crushed spices along with the chopped garlic and chilies and cook over a low heat for about 5 minutes. Now add the turmeric; stir and heat that gently before removing the skillet from the heat.

As soon as the chickpeas are tender, drain them in a colander placed over a bowl to reserve the cooking water. Transfer the chickpeas to a blender together with a couple of ladles of cooking water and purée them until fine and smooth. Now add the lemon zest, cilantro stalks and spices from the skillet along with another ladleful of cooking water and blend once more until fine and smooth.

Next everything needs to go back into the saucepan with the rest of the reserved cooking water. Bring it all up to a gentle simmer, give it a good stir, season with the salt and pepper, then simmer gently for a further 30 minutes. All this can be done in advance, then when you're ready to serve the soup reheat very gently without letting it come to the boil. Stir in half the crème fraîche and the lemon juice, taste to check the seasoning, then serve in hot soup bowls with the rest of the crème fraîche swirled in and scatter with the shredded chili and cilantro leaves as a garnish.

NEXT PAGE: ROASTED PUMPKIN SOUP WITH MELTING CHEESE (SEE PAGE 14)

Roasted Pumpkin Soup
with Melting Cheese

Serves 6

The lovely thing about pumpkin is that it has a really velvety texture in soup, and if it's oven-roasted before you add it to the soup, it gives an unusual nuttiness to the flavor. Just before serving, add little cubes of quick-melting cheese like Gruyère or fontina. Then finding little bits of half-melted cheese in the soup that stretch up on the spoon is an absolute delight. (See photograph on pages 12–13.)

1 pumpkin, weighing 3–3½ pounds	To Serve:
1 tablespoon peanut oil	4 ounces Gruyère or fontina, cut into ¼-inch dice
Salt and freshly ground black pepper	
¼ stick butter	6 teaspoons crème fraîche
1 large onion, finely chopped	2 ounces Gruyère or fontina, coarsely grated
3¾ cups vegetable or chicken stock	
2 cups whole milk	Croutons (see page 10)
Freshly grated nutmeg	Chopped flat-leaf parsley

You will also need a solid baking sheet that won't buckle in the high heat, and a saucepan of about 5 quarts capacity. Preheat the oven to 475°F.

Begin by cutting the pumpkin in half through the stalk, then cut each half into 4 pieces again and scoop out the seeds using a large spoon. Then brush the surface of each section with the oil and place them on the baking sheet. Season with salt and pepper, then pop them on the high rack of the oven to roast for 25–30 minutes or until tender when tested with a skewer.

Meanwhile melt the butter in a large saucepan over high heat, add the onion, stir it, and when it begins to color around the edges, after about 5 minutes, turn the heat down. Let it cook gently without a lid, stirring from time to time, for about 20 minutes.

Then remove the pumpkin from the oven and leave it aside to cool. Now add the stock and the milk to the onion, and leave them with the heat turned low to slowly come up to simmering point. Next scoop out the flesh of the pumpkin with a sharp knife and add it to the stock together with a seasoning of salt, pepper and nutmeg. Then let it all simmer very gently for about 15–20 minutes.

Next the soup should be processed to a purée. Because there's a large volume of soup, it's best to do this in two batches. What you need to do is process it until it's smoothly blended, but as an extra precaution it's best to pass it through a sieve as well in case there are any unblended fibrous bits. Taste and season well, then when you're ready to serve the soup reheat it gently just up to simmering point, being careful not to let it boil.

Finally, stir in the diced cheese, then ladle the soup into warm soup bowls. Garnish each bowl with a teaspoonful of crème fraîche and scatter with the grated cheese, a few croutons as well, if you like them, and a sprinkling of parsley.

Polish Beet Soup

The beet is either loved or hated—mostly the latter I suspect, because in England people have a surfeit of it doused in strong vinegar. But its lovers know of its earthy charm and delicious but distinctive flavor. It makes wonderful soup, and this one is Polish in origin and especially good. Although the soup is a dazzling color, you won't want your hands to match it, so it's best to wear gloves while you're handling it!

FOR THE STOCK:
½ tablespoon oil
6 ounces uncured side of pork cut in cubes
1 large carrot, cut in chunks
1 medium onion, roughly chopped
1 quart water
1 bay leaf
A handful of parsley stalks
Salt and freshly ground black pepper

FOR THE SOUP:
1½ pounds uncooked beets, whole but
*   with stalks removed*
Salt
1 tablespoon flour, mixed to a paste with
*   ¼ stick butter*
⅔ cup sour cream
2 tablespoons lemon juice

You will also need a large saucepan of about 3 quarts capacity.

First of all you need to make a stock: Heat the oil in a large saucepan and when it's really hot, brown the pieces of pork, carrot and onion, keeping the heat high so they turn brownish-black at the edges. This is important because it gives the stock a good flavor.

When you're happy with the color (after about 6 minutes) add the water, bay leaf and parsley stalks, followed by a good seasoning of salt and freshly ground pepper. As soon as it begins to simmer turn the heat down and let it simmer very gently without a lid for 40 minutes. After that strain it through a sieve into a bowl, throw out the stock ingredients and rinse the saucepan to use again.

While the stock is cooking you can deal with the beets. Place them in another saucepan, add enough boiling water to just cover, then add salt. Put on a lid and simmer gently for 40 minutes or until tender when pierced with a skewer. After that drain off the water, then cover the beets with cold water to cool them down. As soon as they're cool enough to handle, take off the skin. Now reserve one medium beet for the garnish and cut the rest into cubes. Transfer them to the saucepan in which you made the stock, add the stock, bring to simmering point, cover and simmer gently for 20 minutes.

Now, using a slotted spoon, transfer the beets to a blender or food processor. Switch on the motor and while it's running add the flour-and-butter paste and the soup stock followed by ⅓ cup of sour cream. When it's all blended pour it back into the saucepan, add the lemon juice, taste to check the seasoning and reheat very gently, without letting it come to the boil. Grate the reserved beet on the fine side of the grater. Then serve the soup in warmed soup bowls, swirl in the remaining sour cream and scatter the grated beet on top as a garnish. For entertaining, croutons (see page 10) made with pumpernickel bread would be a good addition.

Curried Parsnip and Apple Soup
with Parsnip Crisps

Serves 6

T his is such a lovely soup. The sweetness of the parsnips is sharpened by the presence of the apple, and the subtle flavor of the spices comes through beautifully. If
you're entertaining, the soup can be enhanced by some crunchy parsnip crisps sprinkled over as a garnish (see opposite).

1 heaping teaspoon coriander seeds
2 teaspoons cumin seeds
6 cardamom pods, seeds only
3 tablespoons butter
1 tablespoon peanut oil
2 medium onions, chopped
2 cloves garlic, chopped

2 teaspoons ground turmeric
2 teaspoons ground ginger
1½ pounds young parsnips
1 quart good-flavored stock (see page 9)
Salt and freshly ground black pepper
1 medium Rome apple

You will also need a large saucepan of about 3 quarts capacity.

Begin by heating a small skillet and dry-roasting the coriander, cumin and cardamom
seeds—this is to toast them and draw out their flavor. After 2–3 minutes they will
change color and start to jump in the pan. Then crush them finely with a mortar and
pestle.

Next heat the butter and oil in a saucepan until the butter begins to foam, then
add the onions and gently soften for about 5 minutes before adding the garlic. Let that
cook along with the onions for another 2 minutes, then add all the crushed spices
along with the turmeric and ginger, stir and let it all continue to cook gently for a few
more minutes while you peel and chop the parsnips into 1-inch dice. Add the parsnips
to the saucepan, stirring well, then pour in the stock, season with salt and pepper and
let the soup simmer as gently as possible for 1 hour without putting on a lid.

After that remove it from the heat, then purée in the blender if possible; if not,
use a food processor and then a sieve—or even just a sieve, squashing the ingredients
through using the bowl of a ladle. After the soup has been puréed return it to the
saucepan, taste to check the seasoning, then when you're ready to serve reheat very
gently. While that's happening, peel the apple and as the soup just reaches simmering
point grate the apple into it. Be careful to let the soup barely simmer for only 3–4 minutes. Serve in hot soup bowls garnished with parsnip crisps.

Parsnip Crisps

1 medium to large parsnip
(10–12 ounces)

½ cup peanut oil
Salt

First peel the parsnip and then slice it into rounds as thinly as you possibly can, using a sharp knife. Now heat the oil in a 10-inch skillet until it is very hot, almost smoking, then fry the parsnip slices in batches until they are golden brown, about 2–3 minutes (they will not stay flat or color evenly but will twist into lovely shapes). As they're cooked remove them with a slotted spoon and spread them out on paper towels to drain. Sprinkle lightly with salt. If you like you can make these in advance as they will stay crisp for a couple of hours.

Black Bean Soup with Black Bean Salsa

Serves 4–6

This soup is simply stunning, one you'll want to make over and over again. Black beans don't have a strong flavor of their own but they do carry other flavors superbly, while at the same time yielding a unique velvety texture. If you forget to soak the beans overnight, bring them up to the boil for 10 minutes and then presoak them for three hours. Serving salsa with soup makes a clever contrast of the cold refreshing textures of the vegetables and the hot lusciousness of the soup.

1½ cups dried black beans
2 tablespoons olive oil
3 ounces pancetta or smoked bacon, finely chopped
1 large onion, finely chopped
1 large clove garlic, crushed
½ cup finely chopped carrot
½ cup finely chopped rutabaga
½ cup or ½ bunch cilantro stalks, finely chopped and leaves reserved for the salsa
1 teaspoon cumin seeds
1 teaspoon Tabasco sauce
1 quart chicken stock
Juice of ½ lime (keep other ½ for the salsa)

Salt and freshly ground black pepper

FOR THE SALSA:
2 large tomatoes, not too ripe
⅔ cup cooked beans (see directions)
1 small red onion, finely chopped
1 green chili, seeded and chopped
Cilantro leaves reserved from above
½ tablespoon extra virgin olive oil
Juice of ½ lime
Salt and freshly ground black pepper

TO SERVE:
1 heaping tablespoon crème fraîche

⟋ You will also need a large saucepan of about 3 quarts capacity.

It's best to start the soup the night before by throwing the beans into a pan and covering them with approximately twice their volume of cold water. Next day, drain them in a colander and rinse them under cold running water and set aside. Now take the saucepan and heat the 2 tablespoons of olive oil. As soon as it's really hot, add the chopped pancetta and cook for about 5 minutes. Then turn the heat down to medium, stir in the onion, garlic, carrot, rutabaga and cilantro stalks and continue to cook for another 10 minutes with the lid on, stirring everything once or twice.

While that's happening heat a small skillet over medium heat, then add the cumin seeds and dry-roast them for 2–3 minutes until they become very aromatic, begin to change color and start to dance in the skillet. At that point remove them from the skillet and crush them to a coarse powder with a mortar and pestle. Add this to the vegetables along with the drained beans, Tabasco sauce and stock (but no salt at this stage), then bring everything up to a gentle simmer for about 1½ hours with the lid on. It's very important to keep the simmer as gentle as possible, so you might need to use a heat diffuser here.

When the time is up, use a slotted spoon to remove ⅔ cup of the beans; rinse and drain them in a sieve and reserve them for the salsa. Now you need to purée the soup, and the best way to do this is in a blender—if not, a processor and a sieve will do or even just a sieve. When the soup is puréed, return it to the saucepan, add the lime juice, season with salt and pepper and it's now ready for reheating later when you want to serve it.

To Make the Salsa

Pour boiling water over the tomatoes, leave them for 1 minute, then slip the skins off, cut them in half and gently squeeze each half in your hand to remove the seeds. After the seeds are removed, chop the tomatoes into a small dice and place them in a bowl along with the reserved beans, finely chopped red onion, green chili, cilantro leaves and extra virgin olive oil. Then add the juice of half a lime, some salt and freshly ground black pepper and leave it aside for about 1 hour for the flavors to mingle and be absorbed.

To serve the soup, reheat it very gently, being careful not to allow it to come to the boil, as boiling always spoils the flavor of soup. Serve in warm soup bowls, adding a spoonful of crème fraîche and an equal portion of salsa sprinkled over the surface.

If you're entertaining and really want to have some fun, make this soup *and* the Tuscan White Bean Soup on page 22, and serve them together with one or other of the garnishes. All you do is reheat both soups, then using two ladles pour both ladlefuls into the warmed bowls simultaneously, one from the left, the other from the right. It looks a treat (see photograph on page 20) and makes a lovely contrast. Any leftover soup can be frozen.

NEXT PAGE: BLACK BEAN SOUP AND
TUSCAN WHITE BEAN SOUP (SEE PAGE 22)

Smoked Haddock Chowder with Poached Eggs

Serves 4

S moked haddock makes a very fine soup, and this I've adapted from a famous version invented in Scotland, where it is called Cullen skink. If you add poached quails' eggs to the soup this makes a delightful surprise as you lift up an egg on your spoon. For a main-course meal you could use poached hens' eggs to make it more substantial. Either way it is lovely served with brown bread and butter.

1¼ pounds undyed smoked haddock, cut into 4 pieces
2¼ cups milk
2¼ cups water
Freshly ground black pepper
1 bay leaf
3 tablespoons butter

1 medium onion, finely chopped
¼ cup flour
Salt
1 tablespoon lemon juice
8 quails' eggs (or 4 hens' eggs)
1 tablespoon chopped flat-leaf parsley

You will also need a large saucepan of about 3 quarts capacity, and 4 warmed shallow soup bowls.

Start off by placing the haddock pieces in a large saucepan, pour in the milk and water, season with pepper (but no salt yet) and add the bay leaf. Now gently bring it up to simmering point and simmer very gently for 5 minutes before taking it off the heat and pouring it all into a bowl to soak for 15 minutes.

Meanwhile, wipe the saucepan with paper towels and melt the butter, add the chopped onion and let it sweat very gently without browning for about 10 minutes. By that time the haddock will be ready, so remove it with a slotted spoon (reserving the liquid) to a board, discard the bay leaf and peel off the skin.

Next stir the flour into the pan to soak up the juices, then gradually add the fish cooking liquid, stirring after each addition. When that's all in, add half the haddock, separated into flakes.

Now pour the soup into a blender or food processor and blend thoroughly. After that pass it through a sieve back into the saucepan, pressing any solid bits of haddock that are left to extract all the flavor. Discard what's left in the sieve, then separate the remaining haddock into flakes and add these to the soup. Taste it now and season with salt, pepper and lemon juice and leave to one side to keep warm.

Now poach the eggs: Pour boiling water straight into a medium-sized skillet and place over a heat gentle enough for there to be the merest trace of bubbles simmering on the bottom of the skillet. Break the 8 quails' eggs (or 4 hens' eggs) into the water and let them cook for just 1 minute. Then remove the skillet from the heat and let the quails' eggs stand in the water for 3 minutes (or the hens' eggs for 10 minutes), after which time the whites will be set and the yolks creamy. Use a slotted spoon and a wad of paper towels underneath to remove the eggs, place 2 quails' eggs (or 1 hen's egg) in each warmed soup bowl, ladle the soup on top and serve sprinkled with the chopped parsley.

Tuscan White Bean Soup
with Frizzled Shallots and Pancetta

Serves 4

*I*f you look down the list of ingredients here you might be forgiven for thinking this doesn't sound very exciting. Yet Italian cannellini beans transformed into a soup are just wonderful, both in texture and in flavor. The other essential ingredients are fresh herbs and the best Italian extra virgin olive oil you can lay your hands on. (See photograph on page 20.)

1⅓ cups dried cannellini beans
⅓ cup extra virgin olive oil
1 large onion, chopped
2 large cloves garlic, crushed
1 stalk celery, chopped
1 good sprig each of parsley, thyme
  and rosemary

1 bay leaf
Freshly ground black pepper
1 quart chicken stock
Salt
Juice of ½ lemon

⌒ You will also need a saucepan of about 3 quarts capacity.

First of all you need to soak the beans in twice their volume of cold water overnight or, failing that, use the same amount of cold water, bring them up to the boil, boil for 10 minutes and leave them to soak for 2 hours.

When you're ready to make the soup, heat half of the olive oil in the saucepan and gently soften the onion in it for 5 minutes. Then add the garlic and continue to cook gently for about 1 minute. After that add the drained beans, celery, herbs, bay leaf and black pepper, but no salt at this stage. Now pour in the stock and stir well. As soon as it reaches a gentle simmer put a lid on and keep it at the gentlest simmer for 1½ hours, stirring it from time to time. When the time is up, check that the beans are tender and if not continue to cook them for a further 15–30 minutes.

When the beans are ready, season with salt, purée the soup in a blender or process it and pass it through a sieve (or simply sieve all the soup). When you are ready to serve the soup, reheat gently without letting it come to the boil and add the lemon juice, check the seasoning and add the remaining olive oil just before serving. While you're reheating the soup, make the garnish (recipe follows).

Frizzled Shallots
and Pancetta Garnish

3 ounces thinly sliced pancetta or bacon
3 tablespoons olive oil

4 shallots, finely sliced
into rings

Roll the pancetta or bacon strips into a cigar shape, then with a sharp knife cut them into fine shreds, which you then need to separate out. Now heat 2 tablespoons of the olive oil in a large skillet over high heat, and when the oil is hot and shimmering add the shallots and fry them for 3–4 minutes, stirring occasionally so they don't stick to the bottom of the pan. When they are crisp and golden brown lift them onto crumpled paper towels to drain, using a slotted spoon.

Now heat the remaining tablespoon of olive oil in the same pan and fry the pancetta over a high heat for about 2 minutes until they too are golden and crunchy. Drain on paper towels, then serve a little of the shallots and pancetta on the soup as it goes to the table. If you want to make the garnish in advance you can refrizzle both in a hot skillet just before serving.

Libyan Soup with Couscous

Serves 6

This recipe first appeared in *The Food Aid Cookery Book*, published in 1986. Its contributor Mary El-Rayes has kindly given me permission to reprint it here. It's the perfect soup to serve on a cold winter's day with pita bread warm from the oven.

1 heaping teaspoon coriander seeds
1 heaping teaspoon cumin seeds
2 tablespoons oil
1 large onion, chopped
2 cloves garlic, crushed with 1 teaspoon
   sea salt with a mortar and pestle
1 heaping teaspoon ground allspice
2 heaping teaspoons mild chili powder
6 ounces finely chopped raw lamb, leg
   steak or similar
½ cup tomato paste
1 green chili, seeded and chopped
2 teaspoons superfine sugar

3¾ cups water
2½ cups good lamb stock
⅔ cup dried chickpeas, soaked overnight
   in twice their volume of cold water
Salt
⅓ cup couscous
1 tablespoon chopped fresh parsley
1 tablespoon chopped fresh mint

TO SERVE:
Lemon wedges
Pita bread

You will also need a large saucepan of about 3 quarts capacity with a tight-fitting lid.

Begin by preheating a small skillet over medium heat, then add the coriander and cumin seeds and dry-roast them for about 2–3 minutes, moving them around the skillet until they change color and begin to dance. This will draw out their full spicy flavor. Now crush them quite finely with a mortar and pestle.

Next heat 1 tablespoon of the oil in the saucepan and gently cook the onion until soft and lightly browned, about 5–6 minutes, then add the crushed garlic and let that cook for another 2 minutes. After that add the crushed spices, allspice and chili powder and stir them into the juices in the pan. Now transfer all this to a plate and keep it aside while you heat the remaining tablespoon of oil in the same pan until it's very hot. Then add the pieces of lamb and brown them, quickly turning them over and keeping them on the move.

Turn the heat down and now return the onion-and-spice mixture to the pan to join the meat, adding the tomato paste, chopped chili and superfine sugar. Stir everything together, then add the water and stock. Give it all another good stir then drain the soaked chickpeas, discarding their soaking liquid, and add these to the pan. Give a final stir then put a lid on and simmer as gently as possible for 1 hour or until the chickpeas are tender.

When you're ready to serve the soup taste it, add some salt, then add the couscous, parsley and mint and take the pan off the heat. Put the lid back on and let it stand for 3 minutes before serving in hot soup bowls. Serve with lemon wedges to squeeze into the soup and some warm pita bread.

FRENCH ONION SOUP (SEE PAGE 26)

French Onion Soup

Serves 6

There are few things more comforting than making a real French Onion Soup—slowly cooked caramelized onions that turn mellow and sweet in a broth laced with white wine and cognac. The whole thing is finished off with crunchy baked croutons of crusty bread topped with melted, toasted cheese. If ever there was a winter stomach warmer, this is surely it! (See photograph on page 25.)

FOR THE CROUTONS:
1 tablespoon olive oil
1–2 cloves garlic, crushed
French bread or baguettine, cut into
    1-inch diagonal slices

FOR THE SOUP:
2 tablespoons olive oil
½ stick butter
1½ pounds onions, thinly sliced

2 cloves garlic, crushed
½ teaspoon granulated sugar
1 quart good beef stock
1¼ cups dry white wine
Salt and freshly ground black pepper
2 tablespoons cognac (optional)

TO SERVE:
6 large or 12 small croutons
8 ounces Gruyère, grated (2 cups)

Preheat the oven to 350°F.

You will also need a heavy-bottomed saucepan or flameproof casserole of 3 quarts capacity and an ovenproof tureen or soup bowls.

First make the croutons—begin by drizzling the olive oil on a large, solid baking sheet, add the crushed garlic and then, using your hands, spread the oil and garlic all over the baking sheet. Now place the bread slices on top of the oil, and turn over each one so that both sides have been lightly coated with the oil. Bake for 20–25 minutes till crisp and crunchy.

Next place the saucepan or casserole on high heat and melt the oil and butter together. When this is very hot, add the onions, garlic and sugar, and keep turning them from time to time until the edges of the onions have turned dark—this will take about 6 minutes. Then reduce the heat to its lowest setting and leave the onions to carry on cooking very slowly for about 30 minutes, by which time the bottom of the pan will be covered with a rich, nut-brown, caramelized film.

After that, pour in the stock and white wine, season with salt and pepper, then stir with a wooden spoon, scraping the bottom of the pan well. As soon as it all comes up to simmering point, turn down the heat to its lowest setting, then go away and leave it to cook very gently, without a lid, for about 1 hour.

All this can be done in advance, but when you're ready to serve the soup, bring it back up to simmering point, taste to check for seasoning—and if it's extra-cold outside, add a couple of tablespoons of cognac! Warm the tureen or soup bowls in a low oven and preheat the broiler to its highest setting. Then ladle in the hot soup and top with the croutons, allowing them to float on top of the soup.

Now sprinkle the grated Gruyère thickly over the croutons and place the tureen or bowls under the broiler until the cheese is golden brown and bubbling. Serve immediately—and don't forget to warn your guests that everything is very hot!

CHAPTER TWO

Warm Salads, Hot Starters and Supper Dishes

WINTER SALADS HAVE BECOME MUCH MORE POPULAR IN RECENT YEARS, mainly due to the improving quality of imported salad vegetables. There was a time when these were limp and tasteless, but now they're getting better and better all the time. For instance, in England our Fenland Celery Growers move their whole operation to Spain during the winter to provide us with crisp and crunchy celery all year round. There is also a dazzling array of salad leaves constantly winging their way to us from around the world, not to mention fresh herbs and an enormous choice of vinegars and oils.

What is also helpful in winter is the current fashion for warm salads, where some of the ingredients are warm or even hot but the crisp fresh texture of the salad is retained. Most of the hot starters included in this chapter can double up as supper dishes serving fewer people.

If you are entertaining you may like to consider other starters elsewhere in the book. There are dishes that translate easily from lunch to evening meal in almost every chapter: Try Linguini with Mussels and Walnut Parsley Pesto (page 66), Fillets of Sole Véronique (page 49), Oven-Baked Wild Mushroom Risotto (page 101), Red Onion Tarte Tatin (page 94), Roasted and Sun-Dried Tomato Risotto (page 99), Warm Roquefort Cheesecake with Pears in Balsamic Vinaigrette (page 92), Crêpe Cannelloni with Spinach and Four Cheeses (page 89), Mashed Black-Eyed Beancakes with Ginger Onion Marmalade (page 104).

Pan-Roasted Italian Onions with San Daniele Ham and Shaved Pecorino

Serves 4 as a starter

I first tasted this at one of my favorite London restaurants, Le Caprice, and loved it so much I asked for the recipe, which the chefs Mark Hix and Tim Hughes very kindly gave me. It is really one of the nicest first courses I have ever had. San Daniele is available from specialty food shops, but if you can't get hold of it use thinly sliced Parma ham. And the same applies to the sheep's cheese Pecorino, which can be replaced by Parmigiano-Reggiano.

¼ cup extra virgin olive oil
12 ounces flat Italian onions or shallots, peeled
1 teaspoon brown sugar
1 teaspoon fresh thyme leaves
Salt and freshly ground black pepper

¼ cup balsamic vinegar
6–8 ounces San Daniele ham, thinly sliced
4 ounces aged Pecorino Romano
Coarsely crushed peppercorns

Begin by heating the olive oil in a heavy-bottomed saucepan, stir in the onions or shallots, cover and cook over medium heat for 5 minutes. After that add the brown sugar, thyme leaves, the salt and pepper and 2 tablespoons water. Cover the pan and cook slowly over low heat—stirring the onions from time to time to prevent them from sticking to the bottom of the pan—for about 30–35 minutes, or until the liquid caramelizes slightly and the onions are soft, with a little color.

After that, add the balsamic vinegar to the pan, stir well, then remove it immediately from the heat and allow the onions to cool. (If you want to prepare this part in advance you can store them at this stage in an airtight jar in the fridge.)

Just before you are ready to serve, preheat the oven to 350°F and place the onions in a shallow, covered casserole for 15 minutes. After that arrange them on a plate with a little of the balsamic dressing spooned over. Lay the ham over the onions and use a potato peeler to shave the Pecorino over it. Now spoon a little more of the dressing around the plate and sprinkle some crushed black pepper over the cheese. Serve with country bread and some good butter.

Baked Eggs in Wild Mushroom Tartlets

Serves 6 as a starter

It's quite a long time since I made a large quiche or tart for entertaining. I feel that individual tarts are prettier and more practical, and people seem to enjoy them. This recipe, with a base of a concentrated mixture of fresh mushrooms and dried porcini, is a delight coupled with a softly baked egg and crisp pastry. (See photograph on page 32.)

FOR THE PASTRY:
¼ stick butter, softened
1⅓ cups flour, sifted
½ cup finely grated Parmesan
   (Parmigiano-Reggiano)

FOR THE FILLING:
1 ounce dried porcini mushrooms
¾ stick butter
2 small red onions, finely chopped
2 cloves garlic, chopped

6 ounces button mushrooms
6 ounces portobello mushrooms
Sea salt and freshly ground black pepper
2 teaspoons lemon juice
1 heaping tablespoon chopped fresh
   parsley
6 large eggs
⅓ cup freshly grated Parmesan
   (Parmigiano-Reggiano), for sprinkling over the tarts

You will also need 6 tart tins with removable bottoms (4-inch base diameter, ½ inch deep)
and a 5½-inch plain pastry cutter.

Begin by placing the porcini in a bowl. Pour ¾ cup boiling water over them and leave to soak for 30 minutes.

Now make the pastry. This can easily be done in a food processor or by rubbing the butter into the flour and stirring in the grated Parmesan and sufficient water (approximately 3 tablespoons) to mix to a soft but firm dough. Place the dough in a plastic bag and leave in the fridge for 30 minutes to rest. This pastry will need a little more water than usual as the cheese absorbs some of it.

For the filling, heat ½ stick of the butter in a heavy-bottomed skillet, add the onions and garlic and fry until they are soft and almost transparent (about 15 minutes). While that's happening, finely chop the button and portobello mushrooms. When the porcini have had their 30 minutes' soaking, place a sieve over a bowl and strain them into it, pressing to release the moisture. You can reserve the soaking liquid and freeze it for stocks or sauces if you don't want to throw it out.

Then chop the porcini finely and transfer them with the other mushrooms to the skillet containing the onions. Add the remaining ¼ stick of butter, season with the sea salt and pepper and cook till the juices of the mushrooms run, then add the lemon juice and parsley. Raise the heat slightly and cook the mushrooms without a lid, stirring from time to time to prevent them from sticking, until all the liquid has evaporated and the mixture is of a spreadable consistency. This will take about 25 minutes.

While the mushrooms are cooking, preheat the oven to 400°F. Now roll out the pastry to a thickness of ⅛ inch and cut out 6 rounds, rerolling the pastry if necessary.

Grease the tart tins with a little melted butter and line each with the pastry, pushing it down from the top so the pastry will not shrink while cooking. Trim any surplus pastry from around the top and prick the base with a fork. Now leave this in the fridge for a few minutes until the oven is up to temperature.

Now place the tart tins on a solid baking sheet and bake on the middle rack of the oven for 15–20 minutes until the pastry is golden and crisp. Remove them from the oven and reduce the temperature to 350°F.

Divide the filling between the tarts, making a well in the center with the back of a spoon. Then break an egg into a saucer or a small ramekin, slip it into the tart and scatter a little Parmesan over the top. Repeat this process with the other five tarts and return them to the oven for 12–15 minutes until they are just set and the yolks are still soft and creamy. Serve immediately, because if they wait around the eggs will go on cooking.

Spaghetti alla Carbonara

Serves 2 as a supper dish

This is my favorite, and the very best version I know of the great classic Italian recipe for pasta with bacon and egg sauce. This is one that is made using authentic ingredients: pancetta (Italian cured bacon, which has a wonderful flavor) and Pecorino Romano (a sheep's cheese), which is sharper than Parmesan. However, if you can't get either of these ingredients it's still marvelous made with regular sliced bacon and Parmigiano-Reggiano.

8 ounces spaghetti	¼ cup crème fraîche
1½ tablespoons extra virgin olive oil	Freshly ground black pepper
5 ounces pancetta, sliced or cubed	
2 large eggs plus 2 extra yolks	TO SERVE:
½ cup finely grated Pecorino Romano	Extra grated Pecorino Romano

First of all take your largest saucepan and fill it with at least 2 quarts of hot water and then put it on the heat to come up to simmering point, adding salt and a few drops of olive oil. As soon as it reaches simmering point add the spaghetti and stir it once, then time it for 8 minutes exactly. (Some pasta might need 10 minutes, so follow the instructions on the package.)

Meanwhile, heat the olive oil in a skillet and fry the pancetta until it's crisp and golden, about 5 minutes. Next, whisk the eggs, yolks, cheese and crème fraîche in a bowl and season generously with black pepper. Then when the pasta is cooked, drain it quickly in a colander, leaving a little of the moisture still clinging. Now quickly return it to the saucepan and add the pancetta and any oil in the pan, along with the egg-and-cream mixture. Stir very thoroughly so that everything gets a good coating—what happens is that the liquid egg cooks briefly as it comes into contact with the hot pasta.

Serve the pasta on really hot deep plates with some extra grated Pecorino.

Warm Lentil Salad
with Walnuts and Goat Cheese

Serves 4

I think we should all be eating more legumes, so the more recipes that include them the better. In this warm salad, I've chosen the tiny black-gray Puy lentils, but the green or brown variety will work just as well, given slightly less cooking time.

1 tablespoon extra virgin olive oil
⅓ cup walnuts, roughly chopped
1 small red onion, finely chopped
1 large clove garlic, crushed
1⅛ cups Puy lentils
1 bay leaf
1 heaping teaspoon fresh thyme leaves, chopped
Salt
½ bunch arugula
4 ounces firm goat cheese

FOR THE DRESSING:
1 large clove garlic
1 teaspoon sea salt
2 teaspoons ground mustard
2 tablespoons balsamic vinegar
2 tablespoons walnut oil
¼ cup extra virgin olive oil
Freshly ground black pepper

First you need to cook the walnuts. To do this, heat the oil in a medium-sized saucepan and when it's hot, lightly fry the chopped walnuts for about 1 minute. Then remove them with a slotted spoon to a plate and keep them aside for later.

Now to the oil left in the pan, add the onion and crushed garlic and let these cook and soften for about 5 minutes. After that, stir in the lentils, bay leaf and thyme and make sure they all get a good coating with oil. Next add 1¼ cups of boiling water, but don't add any salt—just put a lid on, turn the heat down to a gentle simmer and let the lentils cook for 30–40 minutes or until they're tender and all the liquid has been absorbed. You really need to bite one to test if they're done.

While the lentils are cooking you can prepare the dressing. Use a mortar and pestle to crush the garlic with the salt until it's creamy, then add the mustard and work that into the garlic paste. After that, whisk in the balsamic vinegar, followed by the oils. Then season well with freshly ground black pepper.

As soon as the lentils are cooked, add salt to taste. Empty them into a warm serving bowl and while they're still hot, pour the dressing over. Give everything a good toss and stir, then crumble the goat cheese all over and add the arugula torn in half. Give everything one more toss and stir, and serve immediately with the walnuts scattered over.

BAKED EGGS IN WILD MUSHROOM TARTLETS (SEE PAGE 30)

Blinis with Smoked Salmon, Crème Fraîche and Dill

Serves 8 as a starter

*B*linis originated in Russia and are traditionally made with buckwheat flour, but I find them better and lighter if made with a mixture of white bread flour and buckwheat. Buckwheat is available in health food shops and some supermarkets, but if you can't get hold of it you can replace it with whole wheat flour. (See photograph on pages 36–37.)

1 teaspoon salt	*2 large eggs*
½ cup buckwheat flour	*3 tablespoons butter*
1⅓ cups white flour	
1 package active dry yeast	*FOR THE TOPPING:*
2¼ cups crème fraîche (reserve 1¼ cups	*1 pound smoked salmon*
for the topping)	*Reserved 1¼ cups crème fraîche*
1 cup milk	*A few dill sprigs*

Begin by sifting the salt, buckwheat flour and bread flour together into a large roomy bowl and then sprinkle in the yeast. Pour 1 cup of the crème fraîche into a measuring cup and add 1 cup milk to bring it up to the 2-cup level. Place this in a small saucepan and warm it gently—it must only be slightly warm, as too much heat will kill the yeast. Next separate the eggs, reserving the whites until later; add the yolks to the milk, mix them in with a whisk and after that pour everything into the flour mixture. Whisk everything until you have a thick batter, then cover the bowl with a clean cloth and leave it in a warm place for about 1 hour—this can simply be a matter of placing the bowl in another large bowl filled with warm water.

After 1 hour the batter will be spongy and bubbly. Now beat the egg whites until they form stiff peaks and gently fold them into the batter. Cover with the cloth again and leave as before for another hour.

When you're ready to make the blinis, begin by melting the butter in a heavy-bottomed skillet, then tip the melted butter out into a cup and use it—with the help of a tightly rolled wedge of paper towel—to brush the pan all over as you make each blini. To do this keep the pan on medium heat and add 1½ tablespoons of batter (1 tablespoon goes in first then another ½ tablespoon on top)—it won't spread out much and the underneath sets as soon as it touches the pan. This amount should give you a blini approximately 4 inches in diameter.

Don't worry at this stage if it looks too thick; it isn't, it's just light and puffy. After 40 seconds, no longer, flip the blini over and give it just 30 seconds on the other side. Transfer it to a wire rack and repeat, brushing the pan with butter each time. This mixture should give you 24 blinis.

When all the blinis are made and have cooled, wrap them in foil parcels, with six laid out flat in each one. To serve, preheat the oven to 275°F and place the foil parcels on the high rack for 10 minutes.

Serve the blinis on warm plates, giving each person two to start with, and top with slices of smoked salmon, about 2 ounces per person, add a tablespoon of very cold crème fraîche on the side of the plate and garnish with sprigs of fresh dill.

NOTE: *Any unused blinis can be warmed and served for breakfast with honey or jam. They also freeze very well if left in the foil parcels and can be reheated in the oven, as above, after defrosting. If you want to serve blini canapés, these are made in the same way with teaspoonfuls of the mixture. Cook them for about 15 seconds on each side. Then reheat, as above, and top with smoked salmon, crème fraîche and dill.*

NEXT PAGE: BLINIS WITH SMOKED SALMON, CRÈME FRAÎCHE AND DILL

Camembert Croquettes
with Fresh Date and Apple Chutney

Serves 6 as a starter

Ripe Camembert is essential for this recipe, so plan ahead and buy a Camembert that will be ready to use roughly on its expiration date. I keep mine in the garage or in the trunk of a car, which is cool enough in the winter, though you have to warn people about the smell!

1 small carrot
½ small onion
½ stalk celery
1¼ cups milk
A pinch or blade of mace
1 bay leaf
6 peppercorns
3 tablespoons butter
⅓ cup plus 1 tablespoon flour
9 ounces round, ripe unpasteurized
*   Normandy Camembert, chilled*

Peanut oil for frying

FOR THE COATING:
1 tablespoon flour, seasoned
2 large eggs
2 tablespoons milk
3 cups fine white breadcrumbs

TO SERVE:
6 flat-leaf parsley sprigs

You will also need 6 half-cup, 2¾-inch- diameter straight-sided ramekins and some plastic wrap.

First of all peel and roughly chop the vegetables and place them in a saucepan with the milk, mace, bay leaf and peppercorns. Bring everything up to simmering point, then turn the heat off and leave to infuse for 30 minutes.

After that strain the milk into a pitcher, using a sieve and pressing the vegetables with the back of a spoon to extract all the juices. Now rinse and dry the saucepan and, over medium heat, melt the butter in it, then add the flour and, using a wooden spoon, stir briskly until the mixture has turned a pale straw color.

Now add the milk a little at a time and switch to a whisk, whisking vigorously after each addition until you have a very thick, glossy mixture. Then take the pan off the heat and allow it to cool slightly.

While the mixture is cooling you can deal with the cheese—although it needs to be ripe, it makes life a lot easier if it has been chilled. So all you do is cut the Camembert in half and, using a small sharp knife, peel it carefully, paring the skin away from the cheese. After that, add the cheese to the sauce in smallish pieces and give it all a really good mixing to combine it as thoroughly as possible. Then leave it aside for 10 minutes or so to cool.

Meanwhile, prepare the ramekins. The easiest way to do this is to lightly oil each one, then take pieces of plastic wrap about 8 inches long and lay them across the center of each ramekin. Then, using a clean pastry brush, push the plastic wrap into the ramekins all around the edges—it doesn't matter if it creases. Now divide the cheese mixture among the ramekins and press it in evenly. Fold the surplus plastic wrap over the top, smooth it out, then place them in the fridge for several hours, but preferably overnight.

The croquettes can be coated with the egg and breadcrumbs in advance, provided that you keep them well chilled afterward. Sprinkle the seasoned flour onto a piece of parchment paper, then lightly beat the eggs and milk together and spread the breadcrumbs out on a plate. Also, have another flat plate on hand.

Now all you do is unfold the plastic wrap and flip each croquette onto the flour and lightly coat it on all sides. Next dip it in the beaten egg, then in the breadcrumbs, shaking off any surplus. Now return it to the egg and then back again to the breadcrumbs. This double coating gives good protection while the croquettes are cooking.

When the croquettes are coated, if you're not cooking them immediately, put them on the flat plate and return them to the fridge, uncovered. When you're ready to cook them, have some crumpled paper towels spread out on a plate and then heat up enough peanut oil to just cover the bottom of a solid skillet. The oil needs to be really hot, so test it by dropping in a little cube of bread and if it turns golden in 30 seconds the oil is ready. Now fry the croquettes for about 2 minutes on each side and transfer them to paper towels to drain while you fry the rest. You need to take some care here not to overcook them—it's okay for little bits to ooze out of the sides, but if you leave them in too long they tend to collapse. Serve as soon as possible after they are cooked. Garnish with sprigs of parsley and the chutney alongside.

Fresh Date and Apple Chutney

⅓ teaspoon allspice berries
2 whole cloves
2 small Granny Smith apples
3 ounces fresh pitted dates (or dried if
   fresh not available)

3 tablespoons balsamic vinegar
2 shallots, roughly chopped
A pinch of cayenne pepper

This chutney is best made a couple of hours in advance. First, using a mortar and pestle, crush the spices to a fine powder. Quarter and core the apples, but leave the peel on, then cut each quarter into 8.

Place the apples, dates and all the rest of the ingredients in a food processor, give it all a good whirl to start, then use the pulse action to chop everything evenly. Then transfer everything into a serving bowl, cover with plastic wrap and chill before serving.

Apple and Cider Salad
with Melted Camembert Dressing

Serves 6 as a starter or 2 as a light lunch

When I wrote the *Summer Collection* I felt I'd got Caesar salad as perfect as it could be, but then I ate so many Caesar salads that I began to get bored. If this has happened to you too, then let me tell you that this makes an absolutely brilliant alternative, especially in the winter months. It does need ripe Camembert, but if you don't live near a supplier, a supermarket Camembert will have an expiration date that shows when it will have fully ripened, so you can gauge the best time to make the salad. The piquancy of the apple combined with cheese is absolutely superb.

*1 quantity of Garlic Croutons
(see page 10)*

*FOR THE DRESSING:
9 ounces round, ripe unpasteurized
    Normandy Camembert, chilled
½ cup crème fraîche*

*FOR THE SALAD:
1 head romaine lettuce
½ bunch arugula
1 medium apple (such as Granny Smith
    or Braeburn)
1–2 tablespoons dry cider (if
    Camembert isn't quite ripe)*

First make the Garlic Croutons. Then prepare the dressing—cut the cheese in half and use a small, sharp knife to peel it carefully like a potato, paring the skin away from the soft cheese. Place the cheese in a small saucepan. Next measure in the crème fraîche but don't heat it until just before you are going to serve the salad.

When you're ready, mix the salad leaves together, breaking up the larger ones into manageable pieces, and arrange the salad on the serving plates. Slice the apple, leaving the skin on, and put the slices in a small bowl, then sprinkle on a little of the cider—just enough to cover the slices. After that, pat them dry and arrange over the salad leaves.

Now place the saucepan over a gentle heat and blend the cheese and crème fraîche together for about 3–4 minutes—using a small balloon whisk—until the mixture is smooth. If the cheese is very ripe and runny, you may not need to add the rest of the cider, but if the center is less ripe, you will need to add it to keep the mixture smooth. The main thing is to melt the cheese just sufficiently for it to run off the whisk in ribbons, while still retaining its texture. Don't allow the cheese to overheat or it may go stringy—it needs to be melted rather than cooked.

Next, using a small ladle, pour the dressing equally over the salad and finish with a scattering of croutons. Alternatively, you can hand the dressing around the table and let your guests help themselves.

NOTE: *You can, if you want to, prepare the dressing ahead, then just gently melt it again before serving.*

APPLE AND CIDER SALAD WITH MELTED CAMEMBERT DRESSING

Rillettes of Duck with Confit of Cranberries

Serves 6 as a starter

This is one of my favorite starters: a terrine of tiny shreds of tender, succulent duck melded together like a pâté, then served with the dazzling depth of color and sharpness of a confit of cranberries to counteract the richness. It's very simple to make and instead of serving it as a starter you could, as I did recently, offer it as a lunch for three people with a green salad and some slightly chilled Beaujolais. Magnificent!

1 duck, cut into quarters, approximately 4–5 pounds, or buy it quartered with the bones in
1 teaspoon salt
1 tablespoon chopped fresh thyme leaves
½ teaspoon ground mace
2 cloves garlic, chopped
15 black peppercorns

15 juniper berries
1 cup dry white wine

TO GARNISH:
A few thyme sprigs
2 or 3 bay leaves
Peppercorns and juniper berries
A few whole cranberries
1 bunch watercress

You will also need a 2-pint terrine or loaf pan.   Preheat the oven to 400°F.

Begin by placing the duck quarters on a rack in a shallow roasting pan, pierce them with a skewer, sprinkle salt on the skins then place them on the high rack of the oven and leave them for 1 hour. Then remove them from the oven and drain off all the fat from the roasting pan into a bowl. The fat is excellent for cooking, so hang on to it.

Now place the duck quarters in a solid ovenproof casserole or saucepan, and sprinkle in the thyme, mace and garlic. Then use a mortar and pestle to crush the peppercorns and juniper berries coarsely, and add these as well. Next pour in the wine, bring everything up to simmering point, then turn the heat down to the gentlest simmer possible and leave it like that for 2 hours.

After that pour off all the liquid into a bowl and reserve it, then have ready the terrine or loaf pan. Take a quarter of duck, place it on a board and simply strip away the skin and bones, which will part very easily from the flesh. Then, using either two forks or just your hands, shred the pieces of duck flesh as finely as possible, and pack them into the terrine. When you have repeated this with the other duck quarters, press all the shreds of meat down very firmly into the terrine, then pour in all the cooking juices (there's no need to strain them).

Lastly decorate the surface with the thyme sprigs, bay leaves, peppercorns, juniper berries and a few whole cranberries. Then as soon as it's cool put a lid on the terrine or cover with foil and place in the fridge until needed. You can make it well in advance as it will keep for about three days.

Serve the terrine with thick slices of toasted bread, garnish with sprigs of watercress and spoon some cranberry confit (recipe follows) onto the plate, saving some to pass around separately.

Confit of Cranberries

4 cups fresh cranberries
½ cup granulated sugar
2 cups red wine

2 tablespoons best-quality red wine
vinegar
Grated zest and juice of 1 orange

To make the confit, place the cranberries in a saucepan with the rest of the ingredients. Bring the mixture up to a very gentle simmer, give it all a good stir and let it barely simmer without a lid for about an hour, stirring from time to time. What you end up with is a concentrated mass of glazed cranberries that tastes absolutely wonderful. Remove it from the heat, leave to cool, then spoon it into a serving bowl and cover until needed.

NOTE: *Cranberry confit provides the perfect balance of sharpness for rich game dishes as well as this terrine. If you were serving it with a hot game dish, you might even like to gently reheat it, but it's excellent cold.*

Homemade Mayonnaise

H omemade mayonnaise made by the traditional method is unbeatable. First a couple of tips: (a) use a small bowl with a narrow base—a 2½-cup mixing bowl is ideal—and (b) place the bowl on a damp towel so it will remain steady and leave your two hands free, one to drip the oil, the other to hold the mixer.

2 large egg yolks
1 clove garlic, crushed
1 heaping teaspoon ground mustard
1 teaspoon salt

Freshly ground black pepper
1¼ cups peanut oil
1 teaspoon white wine vinegar

First of all put the egg yolks into a bowl, add the crushed garlic, mustard, salt and a little freshly ground black pepper. Mix all of these together well. Then, holding the peanut oil in a pitcher in one hand and an electric handheld mixer in the other, add 1 drop of oil to the egg mixture and beat it in.

However stupid it may sound, the key to a successful mayonnaise is making sure each drop of oil is thoroughly beaten in before adding the next drop. It won't take all day, because after a few minutes—once you've added several drops of oil—the mixture will begin to thicken and go very stiff and lumpy. When it gets to this stage you need to add the teaspoon of vinegar, which will thin the mixture down.

Now the critical point has passed, so you can then begin pouring the oil in a very, very thin but steady stream, keeping the mixer going all the time. When all the oil has been added, taste and add more salt and pepper if it needs it. If you'd like the mayonnaise to be a bit lighter, at this stage add 2 tablespoons of boiling water and beat it in.

Mayonnaise only curdles when you add the oil too quickly at the beginning. If that happens, don't despair. All you need to do is put a fresh egg yolk into a clean bowl, add the curdled mixture to it (drop by drop), then continue adding the rest of the oil as though nothing had happened.

The mayonnaise should be stored in a screw-top jar in the bottom of the fridge, but for no longer than a week.

HOMEMADE MAYONNAISE

Prawn Cocktail 2000

Serves 6

This recipe is part of my sixties revival menu. In those days it used to be something simple but really luscious, yet over the years it has suffered from some very poor adaptations, not least watery prawns and inferior sauces. So here, in all its former glory, is a starter quite definitely fit for the new millennium!

2 pounds large prawns (or jumbo shrimp) in their shells (see directions)

FOR THE SAUCE:
1 quantity of Homemade Mayonnaise (see page 45)
½ tablespoon Worcestershire sauce
A few drops Tabasco sauce
½ tablespoon lime juice
2 tablespoons ketchup (preferably organic)

Salt and freshly ground black pepper

1 head crisp-hearted lettuce, such as romaine
½ bunch (or 1 ounce) arugula leaves
1 ripe but firm avocado
Cayenne pepper
1 lime, cut into 6 wedges

The very best version of this is made with prawns (either fresh or frozen in their shells) that you have cooked yourself. Failing that, buy the large cooked prawns in their shells, or if you can only get shelled prawns cut the amount to 1 pound. To prepare them: If frozen put them in a colander and allow to defrost thoroughly at room temperature for about 1 hour. After that heat a large solid skillet or wok and dry-fry the prawns for 4–5 minutes until the gray turns a vibrant pink. As soon as they're cool, reserve 6 in their shells for a garnish and shell the remainder. Then take a small sharp knife, make a cut along the back of each shelled prawn and remove any black thread. Place the prawns in a bowl, cover with plastic wrap and keep in the fridge until needed.

To make the cocktail sauce, prepare the mayonnaise and add it to the rest of the sauce ingredients. Stir and taste to check the seasoning, then keep the sauce covered with plastic wrap in the fridge until needed.

When you are ready to serve, shred the lettuce and arugula fairly finely and divide them among 6 stemmed glasses, then peel and chop the avocado into small dice and scatter this in each glass among the lettuce. Top with the prawns and the sauce, sprinkle a dusting of cayenne pepper on top and garnish with 1 section of lime and 1 unpeeled prawn per glass. Serve with brown bread and butter.

Warm Poached Egg Salad
with Frizzled Chorizo

Serves 4

This makes a fun starter for four people, or a zappy light lunch or supper dish for two. For poaching you need very fresh eggs, so watch the expiration date on the carton when you buy them and, to be absolutely sure, pop them into a glass measuring cup filled with cold water. If the eggs sit horizontally on the bottom they're very fresh. A slight tilt is acceptable, but if they sit vertically your supplier's dates are in doubt.

Chorizo is a spicy Spanish pork sausage made with paprika. At specialty food shops you can also buy *chorizo piccante*, a spicier version, which gives the whole thing a wonderful kick.

1 quantity of croutons (see page 10), plus
   1 tablespoon hot paprika
4 very fresh large eggs
3 ounces assorted green salad leaves
3 tablespoons extra virgin olive oil
6 ounces chorizo sausage, skinned and
   cut into ¼-inch cubes

1 medium onion, finely chopped
2 cloves garlic, finely chopped
1 red bell pepper, seeded and chopped
   small
3 tablespoons dry sherry
1½ tablespoons sherry vinegar
Salt and freshly ground black pepper

First make the croutons by following the basic recipe, but sprinkle the paprika over the bread cubes before the olive oil.

When you're ready to make the salad, start with the eggs. A useful way to poach 4 eggs without any last-minute hassle is to pour boiling water straight from the kettle into a medium-sized skillet. Place it over a heat gentle enough for there to be the merest trace of bubbles simmering on the bottom of the skillet. Now carefully break the 4 eggs into the water and let them cook for just 1 minute. Then remove the skillet from the heat and leave the eggs in the hot water for 10 minutes, after which time the whites will be set and the yolks creamy.

Now arrange the salad leaves on 4 plates. Then, in another skillet, heat 1 tablespoon of the olive oil until it's very hot, then add the chorizo; cook for 2–3 minutes then add the onion, garlic and bell pepper. Keeping the ingredients on the move and turning down the heat if it gets too hot, cook for about 6 minutes until the ingredients are toasted around the edges. Now add the sherry, sherry vinegar and the remaining 2 tablespoons of olive oil to the pan. Let it all bubble a bit and season with salt and pepper.

To remove the eggs from the first skillet, use a slotted spoon with a wad of paper towels underneath to absorb the moisture. Place them centrally on the salad leaves on the serving plates, pour the warm chorizo dressing over everything, and finally sprinkle on the croutons. We eat this with olive bread to mop up the juices—a wonderful accompaniment.

NOTE: *If you like you can make this with red wine and red wine vinegar or white wine and white wine vinegar for a little variety.*

CHAPTER THREE

Seafood in Winter

I WOULDN'T BE AT ALL SURPRISED IF FISH BECAME *THE* FOOD FOR THE twenty-first century. Fish has just about everything going for it: What other food can you think of that provides first-class protein, is low in fat and calories yet at the same time cooks faster than almost anything else? While I was researching and preparing this chapter, I actually made a personal vow to include much more fish in my daily cooking routine, not least because it's so quick. You can provide such a great variety of interesting and up-to-the-minute supper dishes in as little as 10 minutes—and very few fish dishes take longer than half an hour.

One of the reasons it all got so much easier is that although, sadly, the local fishmonger is an endangered species, fish in supermarkets has taken on a whole new dimension in that it has become far more accessible, and a great deal of the tedious work once involved in its preparation has been removed. Fish nowadays comes cleaned and gutted, boned and filleted and sometimes even skinned. Also with supplies now coming in from all corners of the world and at all times of the year, there is a far wider choice than ever. So for a more varied and interesting diet without too much work, let's all vow to eat more fish!

Fillets of Sole Véronique

Serves 2 as a main course or 4 as a starter

This famous French classic has always been a favorite of mine and, as it has somehow been neglected on restaurant menus, I think it's time for a revival. Personally I love to serve it with the grapes well chilled, which beautifully complements the warm rich sauce. However, if you prefer you could add the grapes to the fish before it goes under the broiler, so they would be warmed through.

3 ounces Muscat-type grapes
2 Dover or lemon sole, about 12–16
  ounces each, filleted and skinned
Salt and freshly ground black pepper
1 heaping teaspoon chopped fresh
  tarragon

¾ cup Chambéry vermouth or dry
  white wine
1 tablespoon butter
2 tablespoons flour
⅔ cup heavy cream

You will also need an ovenproof serving dish.

First peel the grapes well in advance by placing them in a bowl and pouring boiling water over them. Leave them for 45 seconds, then drain off the water and you will find the skins will slip off easily. Cut the grapes in half, remove the seeds, then return them to the bowl and cover and chill in the refrigerator until needed.

When you are ready to start cooking the fish, begin by warming the serving dish and have a sheet of foil ready. Then wipe each sole fillet and divide each one in half lengthwise by cutting along the natural line, so you now have 8 fillets. Season them with salt and pepper and roll each one up as tightly as possible, keeping the skin side on the inside and starting the roll at the narrow end. Next put a faint smear of butter in the bottom of a medium-sized skillet and arrange the sole fillets in it. Then sprinkle in the tarragon followed by the vermouth.

Now place the pan on medium heat and bring it up to simmering point. Cover, then poach the fillets for 3–4 minutes, depending on their thickness. While the fish is poaching preheat the broiler to its highest setting.

Meanwhile take a small saucepan, melt the butter in it, stir in the flour to make a smooth paste and let it cook gently, stirring all the time, until it has become a pale straw color. When the fish is cooked transfer the fillets to the warmed dish, cover with foil and keep warm.

Next boil the fish-poaching liquid in its pan until it has reduced to about a third of its original volume. Stir in the cream and let that come up to a gentle simmer, then gradually add this cream-and-liquid mixture to the flour-and-butter mixture in the small saucepan, whisking it in well until you have a thin, creamy sauce. Taste and season with salt and freshly ground black pepper.

Pour the sauce over the fish and pop it under the preheated broiler (about 4 inches from the source of the heat) and leave it there for approximately 3 minutes, until it is glazed golden brown on top. Serve each portion on warmed serving plates, garnished with grapes.

Luxury Fish Pie with Rösti Caper Topping

Serves 4–6

This is a perfect recipe for entertaining and wouldn't need anything to go with it other than a simple green salad. The fish can be varied according to what's available as long as you have 2¼ pounds in total.

FOR THE FISH MIXTURE:
⅔ cup dry white wine
1¼ cups fish stock
1 bay leaf
Salt and freshly ground black pepper
1½ pounds halibut
½ stick butter
⅓ cup plus 1 tablespoon flour
2 tablespoons crème fraîche
6 cornichons (continental gherkins), drained, rinsed and chopped
⅓ cup chopped fresh parsley
½ tablespoon chopped fresh dill

8 ounces sea scallops, including the coral, cut in half
4 ounces uncooked shrimp, thoroughly defrosted if frozen, shelled

FOR THE RÖSTI CAPER TOPPING:
2 pounds round white or red potatoes, even-sized if possible
1 tablespoon salted capers or capers in brine, drained, rinsed and dried
½ stick butter, melted
½ cup finely grated sharp Cheddar

You will also need a baking dish about 2 inches deep of 3 pints capacity, well buttered.

Preheat the oven to 425°F.

First of all, prepare the potatoes by scrubbing them, but leaving the skins on. As they all have to cook at the same time, if there are any larger ones, cut them in half. Then place them in a saucepan with enough boiling, salted water to barely cover them and cook them for 12 minutes after they have come back to the boil, covered with the lid. Strain off the water and cover them with a clean dishcloth to absorb the steam.

Meanwhile, heat the wine and stock in a medium-sized saucepan, add the bay leaf and some salt and pepper; then cut the fish in half if it's a large piece, add it to the saucepan and poach the fish gently for 5 minutes. It should be slightly undercooked.

Then remove the fish to a plate, using a slotted spoon, and strain the liquid through a sieve into a bowl.

Now rinse the pan you cooked the fish in, melt the butter in it, whisk in the flour and gently cook for 2 minutes. Then gradually add the strained fish stock little by little, whisking all the time. When you have a smooth sauce turn the heat to its lowest setting and let the sauce gently cook for 5 minutes. Then whisk in the crème fraîche, followed by the cornichons, parsley and dill. Give it all a good seasoning and remove it from the heat.

To make the rösti, peel the potatoes and, using the coarse side of a grater, grate them into long shreds into a bowl. Then add the capers and the melted butter and, using two forks, lightly toss everything together so that the potatoes get a good coating of butter.

Now remove the skin from the halibut and divide it into chunks, quite large if possible, and combine the fish with the sauce. Next, if you're going to cook the fish pie more or less immediately, all you do is add the raw scallops and shrimp to the fish mixture, then spoon it into a well-buttered baking dish. Sprinkle the rösti on top, spreading it out as evenly as possible and not pressing it down too firmly. Then finally scatter the cheese over the surface and bake on the high rack of the oven for 35–40 minutes.

If you want to make the fish pie in advance, this is possible as long as you remember to let the sauce get completely cold before adding the cooled halibut and raw scallops and shrimp. When the topping is on, cover the dish loosely with plastic wrap and refrigerate it until you're ready to cook it. Then give it an extra 5–10 minutes' cooking time.

Fried Herring Fillets with a Lime Pepper Crust

Serves 2

For me the humble herring, once the food of the poor, is a great delicacy with all the gutsy flavors of fresh sardines but lots more juicy flesh. Now they can be bought boned and filleted and are cooked in moments. This recipe is probably the fastest in this chapter. The lime and pepper crust is fragrant and slightly crunchy. Squeeze lots of lime juice over before you start eating—it cuts through the richness perfectly.

2 teaspoons mixed peppercorns
2 limes
1 tablespoon flour

2 herring fillets weighing 6–7 ounces each
2 tablespoons olive oil
Salt

First of all crush the peppercorns with a mortar and pestle—not too fine, so they still have some texture. Then grate the zest of the limes and add half of it to the peppercorns, then add the flour. Mix them all together and spread the mixture out on a flat plate. Wipe the herrings dry with paper towels and coat the flesh side with the flour-pepper mixture. Press the fish well in to give it a good coating—anything left on the plate can be used to dust the skin side lightly.

Now in your largest skillet, heat the oil until it is very hot and fry the herrings flesh side down for about 2–3 minutes. Have a peek by lifting up the edge with a spatula—it should be golden. Then turn the fish over onto the other side and give it another 2 minutes, and drain on crumpled parchment or paper towels before serving. Serve sprinkled with salt, the rest of the lime zest and the limes cut into quarters to squeeze over.

Roasted Fish Topped
with Sun-Dried Tomato Tapenade

Serves 6

his is quite simply a fantastic recipe—it takes no time at all but has the kind of taste that makes people think you have spent hours in the kitchen. And another of its great virtues is that, apart from the fish itself and fresh basil leaves, the whole thing is made from pantry ingredients. (See photograph on pages 52–53).

FOR THE TAPENADE:
1½ cups pitted black olives in brine,
*   drained and rinsed, or 6 ounces*
*   bought loose*
1 bunch basil leaves
1 cup sun-dried tomatoes, drained, but
*   reserve the oil*
1 heaping teaspoon (about 36) green
*   peppercorns in brine, rinsed and*
*   drained*
2 large cloves garlic

One 2-ounce tin anchovies including the
*   oil*
⅔ cup capers, drained and pressed
*   between double layers of paper towels*
3 tablespoons oil from the tomatoes
Freshly ground black pepper

6 tail-end pieces of cod or haddock
*   weighing 6–7 ounces each, skin*
*   removed*
Salt and freshly ground black pepper

Preheat the oven to 400°F.

Begin by reserving 6 whole olives and 6 medium basil leaves from the above ingredients, then all you do to make the tapenade—which can be made 2 or 3 days in advance—is place all the ingredients in a food processor and blend them together to a coarse paste. It's important not to overprocess; the ingredients should retain some of their identity, as shown in the photograph (see pages 52–53).

When you're ready to cook the fish, wipe the fillets with paper towels, season with salt and pepper, then fold them by tucking the thin end into the center and the thick end on top of that so you have a neat, slightly rounded shape. Place the fish on an oiled baking sheet, then divide the tapenade mixture equally among them, using it as a topping. Press it on quite firmly with your hands, then lightly roughen the surface with a fork. Dip the reserved basil leaves in olive oil and place one on the top of each piece of fish, following that with an olive. Now place the baking sheet on the high rack in the oven, bake the fish for 20–25 minutes, and serve immediately.

PREVIOUS PAGE: ROASTED FISH TOPPED
WITH SUN-DRIED TOMATO TAPENADE

Pepper-Crusted Monkfish
with Red Bell Pepper Relish

Serves 4

Filleted monkfish can be quite pricey, but there is no waste with head or bones. It has a lovely firm, meaty texture, and I think this particular recipe would be a superb choice for someone who wants to cook something quite special but has very little time. The pieces of fish are coated with crushed mixed peppercorns and this simplest of sauces not only tastes divine but looks amazingly colorful in contrast to the fish.

FOR THE RED BELL PEPPER RELISH:
1 tablespoon olive oil
2 medium red bell peppers, seeded and cut into strips
2 medium tomatoes, skins removed (canned Italian tomatoes would be fine)
1 large clove garlic
3 anchovy fillets, chopped
Salt and freshly ground black pepper

1 tablespoon balsamic vinegar

2 pounds monkfish (off-the-bone weight)
3 tablespoons mixed peppercorns
4 tablespoons flour, seasoned with 1 teaspoon salt
⅓ cup olive oil

Watercress or fresh cilantro sprigs to garnish

Begin the relish by heating the oil in a medium-sized saucepan. When it's really hot add the strips of pepper and toss them around, keeping them on the move so they get nicely toasted and browned at the edges. Then add the tomatoes, the whole garlic clove and the chopped anchovies. Give it all a good stir, put a lid on and, keeping the heat at its lowest possible setting, let the whole thing stew gently, stirring once or twice, for 25 minutes or until the peppers are soft. Then whirl everything to a coarse purée in a blender or food processor. Taste and season with salt and freshly ground pepper, then empty into a serving bowl and stir in the balsamic vinegar. It is now ready for serving and can be made in advance.

To cook the fish first cut it into small rounds about ¾ inch thick. Crush the peppercorns with a mortar and pestle—or using the end of a rolling pin in a small bowl—to a fairly coarse texture, then combine them with the flour.

Next heat the oil until very hot in a good solid skillet. Dip each piece of fish in the flour-and-peppercorn mixture, pressing them gently on all sides to get an even coating. Now fry the fish in 2 batches, for about 2–3 minutes on each side, until they're tinged nicely brown. Keep the first batch warm while you cook the second.

Serve garnished with watercress or fresh cilantro sprigs, and the sauce passed around separately.

Smoked Haddock
with Spinach and Chive-Butter Sauce

Serves 4

My thanks to top chef and dear friend Simon Hopkinson for this superb recipe, which he cooked for me at his restaurant Bibendum one day for lunch—and had invented that day! Now, thanks to his generosity, all of us can make and savor what has become one of my very favorite fish recipes.

FOR THE SAUCE:
1 ½ sticks butter, melted
3 large egg yolks
Salt and freshly ground black pepper
1 tablespoon lemon juice
¼ cup chopped fresh chives

4 pieces smoked haddock, approximately
*   6 ounces each, skinned and boned*

1 ¼ cups milk
Freshly ground black pepper

FOR THE SPINACH:
¼ stick butter
2 pounds fresh spinach, picked over,
*   trimmed and thoroughly rinsed*
1 teaspoon salt
Freshly ground black pepper

First you need to make the sauce: Place the butter in a small saucepan and let it melt slowly. Meanwhile blend the egg yolks and seasoning in a blender or food processor.

Then turn the heat up and when the butter reaches the boil, pour it into a measuring cup and start to pour this very slowly into the blender in a thin trickle, with the motor running, until all the butter is added and the sauce is thickened. Then, with the motor still switched on, slowly add the lemon juice. Then keep the sauce warm by placing it in a bowl over some hot water.

To cook the fish, place it in a skillet, pour in the milk, add some freshly ground black pepper, then bring it all up to a gentle simmer. Cover and poach for 6–7 minutes. While that is happening, cook the spinach: Melt the butter in a large saucepan and pile the spinach in with the salt and some freshly ground black pepper. Put the lid on and cook it over medium heat for 2–3 minutes, turning it all over halfway through. Quite a bit of water will come out, so what you need to do then is drain the spinach in a colander and press down a small plate on top to squeeze out every last bit of juice. Cover with a cloth and keep warm.

When the haddock is ready divide the spinach among 4 warm serving plates and place the haddock pieces on top. Now just add a little of the poaching liquid (about 2 tablespoons) to the sauce and whisk it in along with the chives, then pour the sauce over the haddock and spinach and serve immediately.

SMOKED HADDOCK WITH SPINACH AND CHIVE-BUTTER SAUCE

Parmesan-Coated Fish
with Walnut Romesco Sauce

Serves 4

This method of cooking fish with a light dusting of flour and grated Parmesan is excellent, but to make it even more special serve it with a Romesco sauce made with walnuts. The advantage of Romesco is that you can make it well ahead; it's always served at room temperature, so keep it in the fridge and remove it about 1 hour before serving.

FOR THE SAUCE:
¾ cup extra virgin olive oil
3 large cloves garlic
2 green chilies, halved and seeded
⅓ cup chopped walnuts
3 ripe plum tomatoes, skins removed
Salt and freshly ground black pepper
2 tablespoons balsamic vinegar

2 tablespoons flour
Salt and freshly ground black pepper

½ tablespoon finely grated Parmesan
(Parmigiano-Reggiano)
¼ cup milk
4 6-ounce thick fish fillets (cod,
haddock, monkfish or halibut),
skin removed
¼ stick butter
1 tablespoon oil

FOR THE GARNISH:
A few flat-leaf parsley sprigs

To make the sauce, take a good solid skillet and heat 1 tablespoon of the oil over medium heat, then lightly sauté the whole garlic cloves for about 3 minutes or until they feel softened and have turned golden. Then add the chilies and walnuts and continue to cook for another 2 minutes.

Now put them into a processor, then return the skillet to a high heat and when the oil begins to smoke cut the tomatoes in half lengthwise and place them in the hot pan cut side down. Keep the heat high and cook the tomatoes until they are charred and blackened all over—this will take about 1½–2 minutes on each side.

Next add the tomatoes to the processor or blender, turn it on to a low speed and add the rest of the oil in a slow, steady stream. The sauce will then begin to thicken and assume the consistency of mayonnaise. After that add some salt and pepper, then transfer the sauce to a bowl and stir in the balsamic vinegar. Cool, cover with plastic wrap and chill until needed. But let it come back to room temperature before serving.

When you're ready to cook the fish, mix the flour, seasoning and cheese together on a plate and pour the milk into a shallow dish. Now wipe and dry the fish with paper towels. Then dip each piece first into the milk and then into the flour mixture, making sure it's well coated and that you shake off any surplus.

Next heat the butter and oil in a large skillet and as soon as it's really hot cook the fish for 2–3 minutes on each side, depending on its thickness. The coating should be golden brown, and as soon as it's cooked remove the fillets carefully with a spatula to warm serving plates.

Serve with a little of the sauce spooned over, and garnish with the parsley. A nice accompaniment to this would be Puy lentils (see page 82).

Oven-Baked Mackerel Stuffed with Pesto Mash

Serves 4

It takes only one word to describe this recipe—wow! It's simply one of the best fish recipes ever. Easy to make and such a divine combination of flavors, it can also be prepared in advance, so all you have to do is just pop it in the oven, then make a salad and a nice lemony dressing. One important point, though: Buy fresh pesto, available from most supermarkets (it's not quite the same with bottled pesto).

12 ounces red potatoes, peeled and cut into evenly sized pieces
½ cup fresh pesto
6 scallions, finely chopped, including the green parts
Salt and freshly ground black pepper
About 1½ slices brown bread, cubed
1 tablespoon rolled oats

Four 10-ounce very fresh mackerel, heads removed
A little olive oil

To Serve:
Lemon quarters
A few flat-leaf parsley sprigs

You will also need a solid baking sheet, approximately 16 × 12 inches, lined with foil and brushed with a little olive oil.

Preheat the oven to 400°F.

First cook the potatoes in boiling salted water for 20 minutes. Test them with a skewer and, when they're absolutely tender, drain them well. Leave them in the saucepan and cover with a dishcloth to absorb some of the steam. Next add all but 1 tablespoon of the pesto to the potatoes, then use an electric mixer to mash them—start with a slow speed to break them up, then go on to high until you have a smooth, lump-free purée. Now fold in the scallions and taste to check the seasoning. Add salt and pepper if needed.

Next make the topping for the fish by dropping cubes of bread into a processor or blender with the motor switched on, then follow with the rolled oats until everything is uniformly crumbled.

To prepare the fish, wipe them inside and out with paper towels, lay them on the foil-lined baking sheet and make 3 diagonal cuts about 1 inch in depth all along the top side of the mackerel. Spoon the pesto mash into the body cavities, pack it in neatly, then fork the edges to give some texture. Now brush the surface of the fish with olive oil, scatter it with the crumbs and finally add ½ tablespoon of olive oil to the remaining pesto and drizzle it over the crumbs using a teaspoon.

Now it's ready for the oven: Bake for 25 minutes on the high rack, then serve with lemon quarters and sprigs of flat-leaf parsley.

NEXT PAGE: SEARED SPICED SALMON STEAKS WITH BLACK BEAN SALSA (SEE PAGE 61)

Seared Spiced Salmon Steaks
with Black Bean Salsa

Serves 6

Everyone I know who has eaten this has loved it. The black bean salsa looks very pretty alongside the salmon and provides a marvelous contrast of flavors and textures, and what's more the whole thing is so little trouble to prepare.

6 salmon steaks, 5–6 ounces each
3 large cloves garlic
2 teaspoons rock salt
1½-inch piece of gingerroot, grated
Grated zest of 2 limes (reserve the juice for the salsa)
A good pinch of ground cinnamon
A good pinch of ground cumin
2 tablespoons light olive oil
½ bunch fresh cilantro leaves (reserve 6 sprigs and finely chop the remainder)
Freshly ground black pepper

FOR THE SALSA:
⅔ cup dried black beans, soaked overnight in twice their volume of cold water
1¼ cups ripe but firm, skinned, seeded and finely chopped tomatoes
1 red chili, seeded and finely chopped
½ bunch cilantro leaves, finely chopped
1 medium red onion, finely chopped
1 tablespoon extra virgin olive oil
Juice of the limes reserved from the salmon recipe
½ teaspoon salt

You will also need a baking sheet that won't buckle under the heat.

A few hours before you want to cook the salmon, wipe each of the steaks with damp paper towels and remove any visible bones using tweezers. Place the salmon on a plate, then, with a mortar and pestle, crush the garlic cloves and rock salt together until you have a creamy purée. Now add the grated ginger, lime zest, cinnamon, cumin, 1 tablespoon of olive oil and the chopped cilantro, and a good grind of black pepper. Mix everything together and spread a little of this mixture on each salmon steak. Cover with plastic wrap and set aside for the flavors to develop and permeate the salmon.

To make the salsa, rinse the beans in plenty of cold water, put them in a saucepan with enough water to cover, bring to the boil and boil rapidly for 10 minutes. Then reduce the heat and simmer the beans for 30 minutes until tender. Drain and allow them to cool completely before adding all the other ingredients. Then leave them covered for several hours to allow the flavors to develop.

When you're ready to cook the salmon, preheat the broiler to its highest setting. Brush the baking sheet with the remaining olive oil and put it under the broiler to heat up. When the broiler is really hot, remove the baking sheet using an oven mitt, and place the salmon pieces on it. They will sear and sizzle as they touch the hot metal. Position the tray 3 inches from the heat and broil them for 7 minutes exactly. Use a kitchen timer as the timing is vital. Remove them when the time is up and use a sharp knife to ease the skins off. Transfer to warm plates and garnish with sprigs of cilantro. Serve immediately with the black bean salsa.

Salmon Coulibiac

Serves 6

*T*his is one of the best fish pies ever invented. It's perfect for entertaining as it can all be made well in advance and popped into the oven just before you serve the first course. Serve it cut in slices, with a large bowl of mixed leaf salad tossed in a sharp lemony dressing, and pass around some Foaming Hollandaise sauce. Or you can simply melt some butter with an equal quantity of lemon juice and serve it with that.

¾ stick butter
½ cup white basmati rice
1 cup fish stock
1¼-pound salmon tail fillet, skinned
Salt and freshly ground black pepper
1 medium onion, finely chopped
1½ cups small button mushrooms,
   finely sliced
1½ tablespoons chopped fresh dill
1 teaspoon lemon zest

2 tablespoons fresh lemon juice
2 large eggs, hard boiled (7 minutes
   from simmering), roughly chopped
¼ cup chopped fresh parsley
One 14-ounce package of ready-rolled
   fresh puff pastry

TO FINISH:
¼ stick unsalted butter, melted
1 egg, lightly beaten

You will also need a good solid baking sheet, 16 × 12 inches, and a lattice cutter.

Preheat the oven to 350°F.

First melt ¼ stick of the butter in a medium-sized saucepan and stir in the rice. When the rice is coated with butter, add the stock and a little salt and bring it up to simmering point, then stir well and cover with a lid. Cook the rice for 15 minutes exactly, then take the pan off the heat, remove the lid and allow it to cool.

As soon as the rice is cooking, take a sheet of buttered foil, lay the salmon on it and add some seasoning. Then wrap it up loosely, pleating the foil at the top and folding the edges in. Place it on a baking sheet and pop it in the oven for just 10 minutes—the salmon needs to be only half cooked. After that remove it from the oven, open the foil and allow it to cool.

While the salmon and the rice are cooling, melt the remaining ½ stick of butter in a small saucepan and gently sweat the onion in it for about 10 minutes until it softens. After that add the sliced mushrooms and half the dill, then carry on cooking gently for another 5 minutes. After that stir in the lemon zest and juice and some salt and freshly ground black pepper, and allow this mixture to cool.

Next take a large bowl and combine the salmon, broken up into large flakes, the hard-boiled eggs, the remaining dill and half the parsley. Season with salt and freshly ground black pepper. Next, in another bowl, combine the rice mixture with the onion-mushroom mixture and the rest of the parsley, season this too.

Now for the pastry. What you need to do here is take it out of its package, unfold it and place it lengthwise on a lightly floured surface, then using a tape measure, roll the pastry into a 14-inch square. Now cut it into 2 lengths, one 6½ inches and one 7½ inches.

Lightly brush the baking sheet and surface of the pastry with melted butter and lay the narrower strip of pastry on it. Then spoon half the rice mixture along the center, leaving a gap of at least 1 inch all the way around. Next spoon the salmon mixture on top of the rice, building it up as high as possible and pressing and molding it with your hands—what you're aiming for is a loaf-shaped mixture. Then lightly mold the rest of the rice mixture on top of the salmon and brush the 1-inch border all around with beaten egg.

Next take the lattice cutter and run it along the center of the other piece of pastry, leaving an even margin of about 1 inch all around. Brush the surface of the pastry with the remaining melted butter, then very carefully lift this and cover the salmon mixture with it. The idea here is not to let the lattice open too much as you lift it, because it will open naturally as it goes over the filling. Press the edges together all around to seal, then trim the pastry so that you're left with a ¾-inch border. Now using the back edge of a knife, "knock up" the edges of the pastry, then crimp it all along using your thumb and the back of the knife, pulling the knife toward the filling each time as you go around. Alternatively, just fork it all around.

When you're ready to cook the coulibiac raise the oven temperature to 425°F and brush the surface of the pastry all over with beaten egg and any remaining butter. And, if you feel like it, you can reroll some of the trimmings and cut out little fish shapes to decorate the top. Now place the coulibiac onto the high rack of the oven and bake it for 20–25 minutes until it's golden brown. Remove it from the oven and leave it to rest for about 10 minutes before cutting into slices and serving with the sauce.

NOTE: *Provided everything is cooled thoroughly first you can make the coulibiac in advance. Cover it with plastic wrap and leave in the fridge until you want to cook it.*

Foaming Hollandaise

2 large eggs, separated
Salt and freshly ground black pepper
½ tablespoon white wine vinegar

½ tablespoon lemon juice
1 stick salted butter

To make the sauce, begin by placing the egg yolks in a food processor or blender together with some salt, switch on and blend them thoroughly. In a small saucepan heat the vinegar and lemon juice till the mixture simmers, then switch the processor on again and pour the hot liquid onto the egg yolks in a steady stream. Switch off.

Now in the same saucepan melt the butter—not too fiercely: It mustn't brown. When it is liquid and foaming, switch on the processor once more and pour in the butter, again in a steady thin stream, until it is all incorporated and the sauce has thickened. Next, in a small bowl, whisk the egg whites until they form soft peaks and then fold the sauce, a tablespoon at a time, into the egg whites and taste to check the seasoning. When you've done that it's ready to serve, or it can be left till later and placed in a bowl over barely simmering water to gently warm through.

Foil-Baked Salmon Served with English Parsley Sauce

Serves 4

Now that farmed salmon is plentiful and available all year round, we can all enjoy luxury fish at affordable prices. However, this recipe works equally well using cod cutlets, halibut or other firm white fish. Another luxury—perhaps because of its sheer rarity nowadays—is a classic parsley sauce, so simple but so delightfully good.

FOR THE PARSLEY SAUCE:
2 cups milk
1 bay leaf
1 slice onion, ¼ inch thick
1 blade mace
A few chopped parsley stalks
10 black peppercorns
3 tablespoons flour
3 tablespoons butter
1 cup finely chopped fresh parsley
1 tablespoon light cream

1 teaspoon lemon juice
Salt and freshly ground black pepper

4 salmon steaks (approximately 6 ounces each)
A few parsley stalks
4 small bay leaves
4 slices lemon
Salt and freshly ground black pepper
2 tablespoons dry white wine

You will also need a solid baking sheet.

To make the sauce, place the milk, bay leaf, onion slice, mace, parsley stalks and peppercorns in a saucepan. Bring everything slowly up to simmering point, then pour the mixture into a bowl and leave it aside to get completely cold.

Meanwhile, to prepare the salmon, take a sheet of foil large enough to wrap all the fish steaks in and lay it over a shallow baking sheet. Wipe the pieces of salmon with paper towels and place on the foil. Then place the parsley stalks, a bay leaf and a slice of lemon over each steak, and season with salt and pepper. Finally, sprinkle the wine over, bring the foil up either side, then pleat it, fold it over and seal it at the ends.

When you need to cook the salmon, preheat the oven to 350°F and bake the salmon on the high oven rack for 20 minutes exactly. Then, before serving, slip off the skin, using a sharp knife to finis a cut and just pulling it off all around.

When you're ready to finish the sauce, strain the milk back into the saucepan, discarding the flavorings, then add the flour and butter and bring everything gradually up to simmering point, whisking continuously until the sauce has thickened. Now turn the heat down to its lowest possible setting and let the sauce cook for 5 minutes, stirring from time to time. When you're ready to serve the sauce, add the parsley, cream and lemon juice. Taste and add seasoning, then transfer to a warm pitcher to pour over the fish at the table.

Gratin of Mussels
with Melted Camembert

Serves 6 as a starter

I first sampled this concept in Normandy, where the Camembert was used as a topping for oysters. Then back home, I discovered it goes superbly well with mussels too.

1 tablespoon olive oil
1 shallot, chopped
1 clove garlic
2 pounds mussels, cleaned and prepared
¾ cup dry white wine
Salt and freshly ground black pepper

FOR THE TOPPING:
9 ounces slightly underripe Normandy
   Camembert, rind removed, cut into
   small cubes
1 cup fresh breadcrumbs
⅓ cup finely chopped fresh parsley
2 cloves garlic, finely chopped
Salt and freshly ground black pepper

You will also need a baking sheet measuring 12 × 16 inches.

First you need to deal with the mussels: Heat the olive oil in a large pan, add the shallot and garlic and cook these over a medium heat for about 5 minutes or until they're just soft. Now turn the heat up high and add the prepared mussels along with the wine and some salt and pepper. Put on a tight-fitting lid, turn the heat down to medium and cook the mussels for about 5 minutes, shaking the pan once or twice, or until they have all opened. When the mussels are cooked pull away the top shells and discard them. Arrange the mussels sitting on their half shells on a baking sheet. Then put ½ teaspoon of strained mussel juice into each shell.

For the topping, place a cube of Camembert on top of each mussel. Then, in a bowl, combine the breadcrumbs, parsley, garlic and a seasoning of salt and pepper and sprinkle this mixture on top.

When you are ready to finish the mussels, preheat the broiler to its highest setting for at least 10 minutes, then place the tray of mussels fairly close to the heat source and don't go away. You need to watch them like a hawk. It will only take about 3–4 minutes for the cheese to melt and turn golden brown and bubbling. Serve immediately with lots of crusty bread.

Linguini with Mussels
and Walnut Parsley Pesto

Serves 2

For me, mussels are still a luxury food that cost very little money. I don't think anything can match their exquisite, fresh-from-the-sea flavor. In this recipe every precious drop of mussel juice is used, which gives a lovely, concentrated flavor. Now that mussels come ready cleaned and prepared, it makes the whole thing very simple and easy: All you have to do is put them in cold water, then pull off any beardy strands with a sharp knife, use the mussels as soon as possible and discard any that don't close tightly when given a sharp tap.

FOR THE PESTO:
2 tablespoons olive oil
⅛ cup walnuts, chopped
1 cup curly parsley leaves
1 clove garlic
Salt and freshly ground black pepper

1 tablespoon olive oil
1 shallot, chopped

1 clove garlic, chopped
2 pounds mussels, cleaned and
  prepared
¾ cup dry white wine
Salt and freshly ground black pepper
6 ounces linguini or other pasta

TO SERVE:
⅓ cup chopped fresh parsley

First prepare the pesto: Select a large pan that will hold the mussels comfortably, then in it heat 1 tablespoon of olive oil and sauté the walnuts in the hot oil to get them nicely toasted on all sides—this will take 1–2 minutes. Place the walnuts and any oil left in the pan into a blender or food processor and add the parsley, garlic, the remaining tablespoon of oil and seasoning, then blend everything to make a purée.

Next you need to deal with the mussels: Heat the olive oil in the same pan that you sautéed the walnuts in, add the shallot and chopped garlic and cook these over a medium heat for about 5 minutes or until they're just soft. Now turn the heat up high and add the prepared mussels along with the wine and some salt and pepper. Put on a tight-fitting lid, turn the heat down to medium and cook the mussels for about 5 minutes, shaking the pan once or twice, or until they have all opened.

During those 5 minutes bring another large pan of salted water up to the boil. Then, when the mussels are cooked, remove them from the heat and transfer them to a warm bowl using a slotted spoon and shaking each one well so that no juice is left inside. Keep 8 mussels aside still in their shells, for a garnish. Then remove the rest from their shells and keep them warm, covered with foil in a low oven.

Then place a sieve lined with cheesecloth over a bowl and strain the mussel liquid through it. This is very important as it removes any bits of sand or grit that get lodged in the shells.

Now it's time to pop the pasta into the boiling water and put a timer on for 8 minutes (some pasta might need 10 minutes, so follow the instructions on the package). Then pour the strained mussel liquid back into the original saucepan and fast-boil to reduce it by about one third. After that turn the heat to low and stir in the pesto.

Now add the shelled mussels to the pesto sauce and remove from the heat. As soon as the pasta is cooked, quickly strain it into a colander and divide it between two hot pasta bowls. Spoon the mussels and pesto over each portion, add the mussels in their shells and scatter the chopped parsley over all. Serve absolutely immediately with some well-chilled white wine. Yummy!

CHAPTER FOUR

Poultry and
the Game Season

SOMETHING THAT I'VE DISCOVERED SINCE I LAST WROTE ABOUT GAME IN THE *Christmas* book is the changing face of venison. Naturally lean with a low fat content, it has quite rightly come to be regarded as a fashionably healthy meat, and in Britain it is reared in natural herds that roam free in parklands.

Thus the emotive question of inhumane animal rearing does not apply. Because the farmed herds are controlled—which means they are culled at the right season and at the right age—we no longer have to introduce to the cooking pot some tough and veteran trophy of the hunter that needs weeks of marinating to tenderize the flesh and has an overpowering gamey flavor. Instead, and in increasing quantities, we have tender, lean meat with a very good flavor. And it is for these reasons that I've included some new venison recipes in this chapter.

The same thing more or less could be said of pheasants, which in my part of Suffolk range well and truly free (often in our garden). There's nothing to beat a well-roasted pheasant, but it *does* have to be young and tender and I must admit to having had one occasionally which turned out tough and dry. That problem shouldn't occur here because the recipes in this chapter are for alternative ways of cooking them—poaching and pot roasting.

Roast Duck with Sour-Cherry Sauce

Serves 4

Τhis is a very old favorite of mine, quite nostalgic really because it was one of the first things I learned to cook when I started washing up in a restaurant. Now all these years afterward it suddenly has taken on a whole new dimension with the arrival of dried sour cherries and some very high-quality sour-cherry jams that are now available.

1 large duck, approximately 6 pounds in weight
Salt and freshly ground black pepper
2 cups red wine

⅓ cup pitted dried sour cherries
12 ounces sour-cherry jam (with a high fruit content)
Watercress

You will also need a good solid roasting pan and either a roasting rack or a large piece of crumpled roasting foil. Preheat the oven to 425°F.

The most important thing to remember when you're roasting a duck is that if you like the skin really crisp it must be perfectly dry before it goes in the oven. This means if you buy it with any kind of plastic wrapping on, remove it as soon as you get it home, dry the duck thoroughly with paper towels and leave it in the fridge without covering, preferably for a day or so before you want to cook it.

When you're ready to cook the duck place it on a rack or on some crumpled foil in a roasting pan. Prick all the fleshy parts with a skewer, as this allows some of the fat to escape, and season it well with salt and freshly ground black pepper. Now pop it onto the highest rack of the preheated oven and give it 30 minutes' initial cooking time, then reduce the heat to 350°F and continue to roast the duck for a further 2 hours. From time to time during the cooking remove the pan from the oven and drain off the fat into a bowl. Don't be alarmed at the amount of fat; it is quite normal, and if you keep it to use later it makes wonderful roast potatoes.

Fifteen minutes before the end of the cooking time measure the wine into a bowl and add the cherries to presoak. Then take 1 tablespoon of the jam and pass it through a sieve. Remove the duck from the oven, brush it all over with the sieved jam to make a glaze, then return it to the oven for another 15 minutes.

After that, remove the duck to a carving board and let it rest for 10 minutes. Meanwhile spoon off any excess fat from the roasting pan, then place it over direct heat, and stir in the wine and soaked cherries, scraping all the bottom and sides of the pan to incorporate all the crusty bits. Turn the heat up and let it bubble and reduce to about two-thirds of its original volume, then add 4 tablespoons of sour-cherry jam. Whisk the jam in and let it bubble and reduce for a couple of minutes more. Then carve the duck simply by using a very sharp knife to cut it into 4 sections, then pull each section away from the backbone. Spoon some of the sauce over each portion, garnish with watercress and pass the rest around the table.

N O T E : *This might seem a long time to cook duck, but it's essential if you like it really crispy.*

Chicken Breasts
with Wild Mushroom and Bacon Stuffing and Marsala Sauce

Serves 4

T his is a very simple way to deal with four boneless chicken breasts. The use of wild porcini mushrooms combined with the beautifully rich flavor of Marsala wine in the sauce turns them into something quite unusual and special.

½ ounce dried porcini mushrooms
¼ stick butter
3 ounces pancetta or sliced bacon
1 medium onion, finely chopped
1 large clove garlic, crushed
1 heaping teaspoon chopped fresh sage
　　leaves
2 cups portobello mushrooms, finely
　　chopped
A grating of nutmeg
Salt and freshly ground black pepper
4 boneless, skinless chicken breasts, each
　　weighing about 5 ounces

FOR THE SAUCE:
1 teaspoon oil
Reserved pancetta or bacon
1 shallot, chopped
3 cremini mushrooms, finely sliced
1 teaspoon chopped fresh sage leaves
½ tablespoon flour
Soaking liquid from porcini
⅔ cup dry Marsala
Salt and freshly ground black pepper

You will also need 4 squares of foil measuring approximately 10 inches.

First you need to soak the porcini mushrooms, so pop them into a bowl, pour ⅔ cup of boiling water over them and leave them to soak for 20 minutes. After that strain them in a sieve placed over a bowl and squeeze every last bit of liquid out of them because you are going to need it for the sauce.

Now melt the butter in a good solid skillet, finely chop the pancetta and cook half of it in the hot butter until golden and crisp, and remove it to a plate. Then add the chopped onion to the pan and fry that gently for about 5 minutes to soften.

While that is happening, chop the strained porcini finely and add these to the skillet along with the garlic, sage and finely chopped portobello mushrooms, a little nutmeg and the cooked pancetta. Stir well to get everything coated with the oil, then, as soon as the juices start to run out of the mushrooms, reduce the heat to very low and let everything cook gently without covering until all the juices have evaporated and all you have left is a thick mushroom paste. This will take about 30 minutes in all. After that remove it from the heat, taste and season well with salt and freshly ground black pepper, then allow it to get completely cold.

Now take each of the chicken breasts and remove the silvery sinew from the back. Fold back the fillet, making a deeper cut if necessary, so that it opens out almost like a book. Season the chicken and spread a quarter of the mushroom mixture over it, fold back the flap and then roll it up lengthwise like a Swiss roll. When they are all filled, lay each chicken breast on a lightly buttered piece of foil. Wrap each in its foil, folding over the ends to seal. At this stage the parcels should be chilled for at least an hour to firm up.

When you're ready to cook them, preheat the oven to 450°F. Place the chicken parcels on a baking sheet and cook for 20 minutes. Then remove them from the oven and allow them to rest, still in the foil, for 10 minutes before serving.

While the chicken is cooking you can make the sauce. First add the oil to the skillet in which you cooked the mushroom filling, then gently fry the remaining pancetta and shallot for about 5 minutes, then add the sliced mushrooms and chopped sage, stir and continue to cook for about 1 minute, by which time the juices of the mushrooms will begin to run. Next stir in the flour to soak up the juices, then gradually add the porcini soaking liquid, followed by the Marsala and a good seasoning of salt and freshly ground black pepper. Keep stirring until it bubbles and thickens, then turn the heat down and add a spoonful more of Marsala if you think it's too thick. Now let the sauce cook very gently for about 20 minutes.

To serve, unwrap each parcel onto a plate and cut each one into 4 pieces—at an angle to show the stuffing. Then pour the sauce over each one and serve immediately.

Moroccan Baked Chicken
with Chickpeas and Rice

Serves 4

*C*hicken pieces simmered with chickpeas, bell peppers and olives in a saffron-flavored rice with cilantro and lemons—hope you like it. Chicken Basque was such a huge hit in the *Summer Collection* because, I imagine, everything needed for a meal for four people was cooked in one large cooking pot with no extra vegetables needed. This has meant I have been under a lot of pressure to produce a recipe that could match it. So to a flourish of trumpets here it is. (See photograph on pages 72–73.)

⅔ cup dried chickpeas
2 teaspoons cumin seeds
1 tablespoon coriander seeds
½ teaspoon saffron threads
2 small thin-skinned lemons
1 4-pound chicken, jointed in 8 pieces
   (or you could use a package of
   8 drumsticks and thighs)
Salt and freshly ground black pepper
2 large yellow bell peppers
2 large onions

2 tablespoons olive oil
1 bunch cilantro
3 cloves garlic, chopped
2 fresh chilies, halved, seeded and
   finely chopped
1 cup brown basmati rice
1¼ cups chicken stock
⅔ cup dry white wine
½ cup pitted black olives
½ cup pitted green olives

You will also need a wide, shallow flameproof casserole with a domed lid, about 9 inches in diameter. Failing that, use any flameproof casserole of about 3 quarts capacity.

Preheat the oven to 350°F.

There are two ways to deal with chickpeas. The easiest is to pop them into a bowl, cover them with cold water and leave them overnight or a minimum of 8 hours. But if it slips your mind, what you can do is place them in a saucepan, cover them with cold water and bring them up to the boil for 10 minutes. Then turn off the heat and let them soak for 3 hours. Either way, when you want to start making this recipe, the chickpeas need to be simmered for 20 minutes.

    While they're simmering, place a small skillet over medium heat, add the cumin and coriander seeds and toss them around in the hot skillet for about 2–3 minutes or until they start to dance and change color. Then remove the seeds to a mortar and pestle, crush them coarsely and transfer them to a plate. Next crush the saffron threads to a powder with the mortar and pestle, then squeeze out the juice of 1 of the lemons and add it to the saffron, stirring well.

PREVIOUS PAGE: MOROCCAN BAKED CHICKEN
WITH CHICKPEAS AND RICE

Then prepare the chicken by seasoning the joints with salt and pepper, and slice the bell peppers in half, remove the seeds and pith and cut each half into 4 large pieces. The onions should be sliced roughly the same size as the bell peppers. Now heat 1 tablespoon of the olive oil in the flameproof casserole and when it's really hot, brown the chicken pieces on all sides—don't overcrowd the pan; it's best to do it in 2 batches, 4 pieces at a time.

After that remove the chicken pieces to a plate, then add the second tablespoon of oil and turn the heat to its highest setting. When the oil is really hot add the bell peppers and onions and cook them in the hot oil, moving them around until their edges are slightly blackened– this should take about 5 minutes—then turn the heat down. Strip the cilantro leaves from the stalks, wrap them in a piece of plastic wrap and keep them in the fridge. Then chop the cilantro stalks finely and add these to the bell peppers and onions along with the garlic, chilies, crushed spices, chickpeas and rice, giving everything a good stir to distribute all the ingredients.

Season well with salt and pepper, then combine the lemon-and-saffron mixture with the stock and wine, pour it all into the casserole and stir well. Cut the remaining lemon into thin slices and push these well into the liquid. Now scatter the olives in and finally place the pieces of chicken on top of everything. Cover with a tight-fitting lid and place in the preheated oven for 1 hour or until the rice and the chickpeas are tender. Then just before serving scatter the cilantro leaves on top, and serve immediately on warmed serving plates.

Traditional Roast Stuffed Chicken
with Cranberry, Sage and Balsamic Sauce

Serves 8

When roasting a chicken the skill is to ensure that the meat is not dry, but juicy and succulent. Placing a pork-based stuffing inside the chicken ensures that the pork juices provide a kind of internal basting. Most of it is placed around the breast end, which is potentially the driest, with a small amount tucked inside so the flavors can permeate the meat. At the same time the bacon juices do the same from the outside. You can help the process by basting the chicken at least three times during the cooking.

Two 4-pound free-range chickens with
   giblets

FOR THE STUFFING:
4 ounces fresh white bread, crusts
   removed
1 tablespoon fresh parsley
1 heaping tablespoon fresh sage leaves
1 dessert apple, cored and quartered
1 small onion, quartered
Chicken livers from the giblets
8 ounces ground pork or pork sausage
   meat

¼ teaspoon ground mace
Salt and freshly ground black pepper
12 slices smoked bacon
¾ stick butter, softened
Salt and freshly ground black pepper
Chicken Giblet Stock (see page 9)
2 tablespoons flour

FOR THE SAUCE:
½ cup jellied cranberry sauce
1½ tablespoons balsamic vinegar
½ tablespoon chopped fresh sage
Salt and freshly ground black pepper

Preheat the oven to 375°F.

First of all the chickens need to be stuffed. If you have a food processor, then making stuffing is easy; all you do is switch the motor on, add the pieces of bread and process to crumbs, then add the parsley, sage leaves, apple and onion quarters and process till everything is finely chopped. Next trim the chicken livers (use the rest of the giblets for stock—see page 9), rinse under cold water and pat them dry. Then add them together with the sausage meat, mace and seasoning. Give a few pulses in the processor or until it is all thoroughly blended. Remove the stuffing with a spatula, then place in a plastic bag and store in the fridge until it is needed.

To stuff the chickens, you begin at the neck end, where you'll find a flap of loose skin: Gently loosen this away from the breast and you'll be able to make a triangular pocket. Pack about one third of the stuffing inside as far as you can go and make a neat round shape on the outside. Then tuck the neck flap under the bird's back and secure it with a small skewer. Repeat with the other chicken, then divide the stuffing you have left and place a small amount in each body cavity.

Now place the chickens side by side in a large solid roasting pan. Divide the butter in half and simply smear it over each chicken, using your hands and making sure you don't leave any part of the surface unbuttered.

Season the chickens all over with salt and freshly ground pepper, then arrange 6 slices of the smoked bacon, slightly overlapping, in a row along each breast (I like to leave the rind on the bacon for extra flavor, but you can remove it if you prefer).

Place the chickens in the oven on the center rack and cook them for 1¾ hours (i.e., 20 minutes to the pound plus 10–20 minutes extra). The chickens are cooked when the thickest part of the leg is pierced with a skewer and the juices run clear. It is important to baste the chickens at least 3 times during the cooking; the juices mingled with the bacon fat and butter help to keep the flesh succulent.

During the last basting (about half an hour before the chickens are cooked), remove the crisped bacon slices and keep them warm. If they are not crisp, leave them around the chicken to finish off. For the final 15 minutes of the cooking, turn up the heat to 425°F, which will give the skin that golden crispness.

When the chickens are cooked it is important to leave them in the warm kitchen (near the oven) covered in foil for 30 minutes, which will allow them to relax. This is because when a chicken is cooking all the juices bubble up to the surface (if you look inside the oven you can actually see this happening just under the skin), and what relaxing does is allow time for all those precious juices to seep back into the flesh. It also makes it much easier to carve.

You can make the sauce and the gravy while the chickens are relaxing—all you do to make the sauce is combine everything in a small saucepan by whisking over a gentle heat until the cranberry sauce has melted. Then pour the sauce into a serving pitcher and leave till needed (it doesn't need reheating—it's served at room temperature).

Next make the giblet gravy using the giblet stock on page 9. When you have spooned off the excess fat from the roasting pan and only the dark juices are left, work about 2 tablespoons of flour into these juices over a low heat. Now, using a balloon whisk, whisk in the giblet stock bit by bit, until you have a smooth gravy. Let it bubble and reduce a little to concentrate the flavor, and taste and season with salt and pepper. Pour it into a warm gravy boat and pass it around separately.

Poached Pheasant with Celery

Celery has a wonderful affinity with poultry and game, and the two have often appeared together in English recipes over the centuries. This recipe is what I would call old-fashioned comfort food. It has the purest of flavors, as the juices from the pheasant and celery combine to make a wonderful, light creamy sauce. (See photograph on page 80.)

1 pheasant (or guinea fowl or small
    chicken), dressed weight about 1
    pound 6 ounces
1 bunch of celery
10 small shallots, about 1 inch
    in diameter

FOR THE STOCK:
Celery trimmings
1 quart water
The trimmings from the bird
1 large onion, halved
2 thyme sprigs
2 stalks parsley
A few peppercorns
1 large carrot, chopped into chunks

1 bay leaf
2 rosemary sprigs
1 teaspoon salt

FOR THE SAUCE:
1½ tablespoons butter
3 tablespoons flour
¼ cup heavy cream
Salt and freshly ground black pepper

FOR THE GARNISH:
Peanut oil
1 egg white
About 10 celery leaves, reserved
½ tablespoon flour, seasoned

You will also need a large saucepan with a tight-fitting lid, of approximately 2 quarts capacity.

Begin by making the stock for the sauce. First of all remove any tough outer stalks of the celery, and trim the root minimally but leave most of the bottom on. Then cut the tops off the celery about 3 inches up from the bottom and set aside the base half, reserving about 10 of the prettiest leaves for later. Next rinse the other stalks from the top half, chop them roughly and place them in a saucepan.

Now add all the other stock ingredients along with the wings of the pheasant. Pheasant wings can be removed very easily—all you do is insert a small knife at the point where the wing is attached to the bone, push your thumb into the incision and feel the little ball-and-socket joint, then use the knife again to cut the ball away from the socket. Repeat with the other wing, then bring everything up to simmering point, and simmer for 30 minutes.

Meanwhile, cut the lower part of the celery in half vertically (including the bottom), then into quarters and finally into eighths. Rinse the sections carefully, keeping them attached to the bottom. Now peel the shallots.

When the stock has had its 30 minutes, place a large sieve over a bowl, line it with a single sheet of paper towel and strain the stock through it, then return the strained stock to the saucepan. Season the pheasant and lower it into the liquid. Bring it very gently up to simmering point, then put a lid on and let it simmer for 20 minutes.

After that add the shallots and time it for a further 15 minutes, then add the celery and give the whole thing another 15 minutes. After that remove the pheasant to a dish and use a slotted spoon to transfer the vegetables to join it. Cover everything with foil and keep warm.

To make the sauce, boil the liquid left in the pan without a lid until it has reduced to approximately 1¼ cups, or a third of the original. Then, once again, line the sieve with a single sheet of paper towel, place it over a bowl and give the stock a final straining. Next melt the butter in a small saucepan, adding the flour and cooking it (stirring all the time) until the mixture turns a pale straw color—this takes 3–4 minutes. Then, starting off with a wooden spoon and finishing with a whisk, add the stock gradually and whisk until you have a smooth, glossy sauce. Simmer the sauce very gently for 5 minutes. Add the cream and check the seasoning. Then make the garnish.

Heat up ½ inch of peanut oil in a shallow pan. Whisk the egg white till just frothy, then dip the celery leaves first in flour, shaking off the surplus, then in the egg white and briefly fry them in the hot oil for about 10 seconds till pale gold. Then drain them on a paper towel.

To serve the pheasant: Put the bird on its back, take a sharp knife and run the blade down the breastbone and along the wishbone, keeping as close to the bone as you can. Using the knife as a lever, gently pull the breast away from the frame. Now insert your fingers along the rib cage and you'll find you can ease the leg and thigh away from the bone. Trim the bits of skin off, and repeat with the other side. Now cut each half in half again and serve them on warmed plates with the vegetables, the sauce poured over and garnished with the celery leaf fritters.

Venison Steaks
with Cranberry Cumberland Sauce

Serves 2

T his is a perfect meal for two for a special occasion, and it has the added bonus of being superfast. For Cumberland sauce red-currant jelly is traditionally used, but when it's made with cranberry jelly, as it is here, it has a new, deliciously different dimension.

FOR THE SAUCE:
Zest and juice of ½ large orange
Zest and juice of ½ small lemon
4 tablespoons jellied cranberry sauce
1 teaspoon freshly grated gingerroot
2 teaspoons ground mustard
¼ cup port

FOR THE STEAKS:
1 tablespoon peanut oil
2 venison steaks, about 7–8 ounces each
½ tablespoon crushed peppercorns
2 medium shallots, finely chopped
Salt

Make the sauce way ahead of time—preferably a couple of hours or even several days ahead—so there is time for the flavors to develop. With a sharp knife shred the orange and lemon zest into really fine hairlike strips, about ½ inch long. Then place the cranberry sauce, ginger and mustard in a saucepan, add the zest and the orange and lemon juice, and place it over medium heat. Now bring it up to simmering point, whisking well to combine everything together, then as soon as it begins to simmer turn the heat off, stir in the port and pour it into a pitcher to keep till needed.

When you're ready to cook the steaks, heat the oil in a medium-sized, heavy-bottomed skillet. Dry the venison thoroughly with paper towels, then sprinkle and press the crushed peppercorns firmly over both sides of each steak. When the oil is smoking hot, drop the steaks into the pan and let them cook for 5 minutes on each side for medium (4 minutes for rare and 6 minutes for well done).

Halfway through add the shallots and move them around the pan to cook and brown at the edges. Then 30 seconds before the end of the cooking time pour in the sauce—not over but around the steaks. Let it bubble for a minute or two, season with salt, and then serve the steaks with the sauce poured over. A garnish of watercress would be nice, and a good accompaniment would be small baked potatoes and a mixed-leaf salad.

POACHED PHEASANT WITH CELERY (*SEE PAGE 78*)

Broiled Chicken with Lemon, Garlic and Rosemary Served with Puy Lentils

Serves 2

*T*his recipe is for the stressed, overworked men and women who still want to eat real food when they finally get home. All you do is shove the chicken in the marinade, go off to have a nice relaxing shower, followed by something that includes the sound of ice tinkling on glass, and then when you're finally ready for supper it will only take about 40 minutes. On the other hand, if you have time, marinate it for longer or even the night before.

2 boneless chicken breasts, 6 ounces
   each, skin on
1 medium red onion, halved
2 bay leaves, snipped in half
1 tablespoon fresh rosemary leaves,
   bruised and finely chopped
1 clove garlic, crushed
Grated zest of 1 lemon
¼ cup fresh lemon juice
¼ cup extra virgin olive oil
Salt and freshly ground black pepper

FOR THE LENTILS:
½ red onion (see left)
½ tablespoon extra virgin olive oil
¾ cup Puy lentils
1 cup water or red or white wine
1 rosemary sprig
Salt and freshly ground black pepper

TO GARNISH:
Flat-leaf parsley sprigs

You will also need 2 bamboo skewers, which should be soaked in water while the chicken is marinating.

Begin by cutting each chicken breast into 5 evenly sized pieces and place these in a bowl. Then cut one half of the onion into quarters and separate into layers, adding them to the chicken, along with the rest of the ingredients. Now give everything a good mixing, cover with a cloth and go away and leave it for at least half an hour.

When you're ready to cook the chicken, preheat the broiler to its highest setting and set the broiling pan 5 inches from the element. Next see to the lentils. Just chop the other half of the onion finely, heat the oil in a medium-sized saucepan, fry the onion for about 5 minutes, then stir in the lentils, making sure they get a good coating of oil. Then add the water or wine and sprig of rosemary, but no salt. Put on a lid and let the lentils simmer gently for about 30–40 minutes until the liquid has been absorbed.

To cook the chicken thread the pieces on the skewers, putting half a bay leaf first, then a piece of chicken, then a piece of onion, finishing with the other half of the bay leaf. Then, keeping the skin side of the chicken pieces upward, lay the skewers on the broiler rack with a dish underneath to catch the juices. Season them well, then broil for 20 minutes, turning once and basting with the marinade juices once or twice. When the chicken is ready, taste and season the lentils with salt and a little freshly ground black pepper, and arrange them on warm serving plates. Slide the chicken, onion and bay leaf off the skewers between the prongs of a fork, then spoon the warm basting juices over everything. Garnish with flat-leaf parsley and serve with the lentils and a green salad.

Pot-Roasted Venison
with Shrewsbury Sauce

Serves 4

As the title suggests this is a warming, fragrant and very inviting supper dish that will do wonders to cheer up the long winter nights. Serve it with clouds of fluffy mashed potatoes, which will absorb the sublimely good sauce. You can, if you wish, use beef instead of venison, in which case I would choose brisket or round rump roast and cook it for 2½ hours.

2 pounds boneless tied venison roast
Salt and freshly ground black pepper
1 tablespoon peanut oil
1 tablespoon butter
1 small carrot, chopped
1 small onion, chopped
A few thyme sprigs
1 bay leaf
*½ bottle (375 ml) red wine, something
    light like Beaujolais*
A grating of nutmeg

FOR THE SAUCE:
¼ cup good-quality red-currant jelly
2 tablespoons Worcestershire sauce
1 tablespoon butter, softened
1 tablespoon flour
2 teaspoons ground mustard
1–2 tablespoons lemon juice
Salt and freshly ground black pepper

You will also need a flameproof casserole, with a tight-fitting lid, that will hold the meat comfortably.

First wipe the venison with paper towels and season the surface with salt and freshly ground pepper. Now heat up the oil and butter together in the casserole and, when it is foaming hot, add the meat to brown on all sides, with the carrot and onion alongside it to brown as well. When everything is browned add the thyme, bay leaf, wine, nutmeg and seasoning. Bring this up to a very gentle simmer and cover with a lid. (If the lid is not really tight place a sheet of foil under it and press down firmly to seal it.)

Give the meat an initial cooking time of 30 minutes. Then turn it over in the liquid so it will cook to an even color, and give it a further 30 minutes. After that remove the meat to a warm plate, cover it with foil and keep warm.

Now to make the sauce. Place a sieve over a bowl and strain the liquid through it, pressing the vegetables to extract their juices, then discard them. Next pour the liquid back into the casserole, boil it up and let it reduce slightly. Then add the red-currant jelly and Worcestershire sauce and whisk it very thoroughly to dissolve the jelly. Now mix the softened butter, flour and mustard together to a paste and whisk this, in small pieces, into the sauce so that it thickens slightly and takes on a glossy appearance.

Now add 1 tablespoon of the lemon juice, adding more if needed; taste and check the seasoning. Simmer the sauce gently for 3–4 minutes, then carve the venison and serve with the sauce spooned over.

Pot Roast of Pheasant
with Shallots and Caramelized Apples

Serves 4–6

This is a superb way to cook pheasants and would make an excellent alternative Christmas lunch for four people. The pheasants are first browned and flamed in Calvados (apple brandy) and then are slowly braised in cider.

1 tablespoon butter
1 tablespoon oil
2 pheasants (or guinea fowl)
Salt and freshly ground black pepper
12 shallots
2 fresh thyme sprigs
1 bay leaf
3 tablespoons Calvados (or brandy)
2 pints apple cider

1 heaping teaspoon flour and 1 heaping
*   teaspoon butter mixed to a paste*

FOR THE CARAMELIZED APPLES:
3 tablespoons butter, melted
3 medium apples (such as Granny
*   Smith or Braeburn), unpeeled,*
*   quartered and sliced in half*
½ cup granulated sugar

You will also need a flameproof casserole in which 2 pheasants can sit comfortably.

Start off by heating the butter and oil together in a heavy skillet, then brown the pheasants until they're a good golden color all over. Then place them, breasts uppermost, in the casserole and season them well. Then brown the shallots in the butter and oil remaining in the skillet and add these to the pheasants along with the thyme and bay leaf.

Next pour the Calvados into a small saucepan and warm it gently, then ignite with a match. When it is alight, pour the flaming Calvados all over the pheasants. The alcohol will burn off, leaving just the beautiful essence to flavor the birds. Now pour in the cider and bring everything up to a very gentle simmer, put a tight lid on and let the pheasants braise slowly on top of the stove for 1–1¼ hours or until they're tender.

Toward the end of the cooking time, preheat the broiler to its highest setting. Line the broiler pan with foil and brush it with melted butter. Then brush each piece of apple with melted butter and dip it in sugar to coat it well all over. Place these on the foil and broil them about 2 inches away from the element for 6 minutes or until the sugar caramelizes, then turn them over and caramelize on the other side. When they're done they will keep warm without coming to any harm.

When the pheasants are cooked, remove them and the shallots to a warmed serving plate and keep warm. Discard the herbs, then boil the liquid in the casserole briskly without a lid until it has reduced slightly. Then whisk in the flour-and-butter paste with a balloon whisk, which will slightly thicken it when it comes back to the boil. Carve the pheasant and serve with the shallots and sauce poured over and garnished with the caramelized apples.

VENISON SAUSAGES BRAISED IN RED WINE (SEE PAGE 87)

Terrine of Venison
with Juniper and Pistachio Nuts

Serves 10–12

This is just about the easiest terrine in the world to make because you can buy the venison and the pork ready ground. The result is a lovely, rough country pâté. Serve it with thick slices of toasted country bread, and an excellent accompaniment would be the Confit of Cranberries on page 43.

1 pound ground venison (available in
   large supermarkets)
1 pound ground pork
8 ounces rindless smoked bacon
30 juniper berries
1 tablespoon mixed peppercorns

1 cup shelled pistachio nuts
1 heaping teaspoon chopped fresh thyme
¼ teaspoon ground mace
4 teaspoons salt
¾ cup dry white wine
⅛ cup brandy

*You will also need a 2-pound loaf pan 7½ × 4¼ × 3½ inches deep, preferably nonstick,
or a terrine of 2 quarts capacity.*

Preheat the oven to 300°F.

First of all, place the venison and the pork in a large bowl, then place the bacon slices on a board stacked on top of one another and cut them into thin strips about ⅛ inch wide, then add these to the bowl. After that crush the juniper berries quite coarsely with a mortar and pestle, add these to the bowl then crush the peppercorns, also quite coarsely, and add these. To deal with the pistachio nuts all you need to do is chop them in half, then they can go in along with the thyme, mace, salt and then finally the wine and brandy.

Now you've got quite a lot of mixing to do, so either use your hands or take a large fork and thoroughly combine everything. Cover the bowl with a cloth and leave it all to marinate for about 2 hours, then pack it into the loaf pan or terrine and cover the surface with a double thickness of foil, pleat the corners and fold it under the rim. Now place the terrine in a roasting pan and put it on the middle rack of the oven, then pour in about 1 inch of boiling water from the kettle and let the terrine cook for 1¾ hours. After that, remove it from the oven, leaving the foil on, then after 30 minutes place two 1-pound weights or the equivalent in cans of tomatoes or something similar on top of the terrine. When the terrine is completely cooled, place it in the fridge with the weights still on top and leave it overnight to really firm up. Don't forget to take it out of the fridge about an hour before serving, and serve cut into slices.

Venison Sausages
Braised in Red Wine

Serves 2–3

ℬangers are bangers, but there are some bangers that are extremely special—and venison sausages are positively five-star, especially when you serve them braised slowly with herbs, shallots, mushrooms and red wine. Then all you need is a dreamy pile of light, creamy mashed potatoes to go with them. (See photograph on page 84.)

½ tablespoon olive oil
1 pound venison sausages
8 ounces bacon or pancetta, diced
1 large clove garlic
8 ounces shallots
½ tablespoon juniper berries
1 ¼ cups red wine
1 teaspoon chopped fresh thyme

2 bay leaves
Salt and freshly ground black pepper
6 ounces whole cremini mushrooms
1 heaping teaspoon flour
2 teaspoons ground mustard
¼ stick butter, softened
2 tablespoons red-currant jelly

First take a large flameproof casserole and heat the oil in it. Then, with the heat at medium, brown the sausages evenly all over, taking care not to split the skins by turning them over too soon. Next, using a slotted spoon, transfer them to a plate while you brown the diced bacon along with the garlic and shallots. Now crush the juniper berries very slightly without breaking them—just enough to release their flavor. Return the sausages to the casserole, pour in the wine and add the berries, thyme and bay leaves. Now season lightly, bring it all up to a gentle simmer, put a lid on the casserole, turn the heat as low as possible and let it all simmer gently for 30 minutes.

After that, add the mushrooms, stirring them in well, then leave everything to cook gently for a further 20 minutes—this time without the lid so the liquid reduces slightly. To finish off remove the sausages and vegetables to a warm serving dish, mix the flour and mustard with the softened butter until you have a smooth paste and whisk this, a little at a time, into the casserole. Let everything bubble for a few more minutes, then take the casserole off the heat, return the sausages to the casserole, whisk in the red-currant jelly—and it's ready to serve.

CHAPTER FIVE

The Winter Vegetarian

I FIND VEGETARIAN COOKING A CHALLENGE, AND I LOVE A CHALLENGE—IN particular finding ways to make meals without meat or fish more varied and interesting when it comes to entertaining. Vegetarian food has certainly become much more integrated into mainstream cooking in recent years, and, because it has become far more inventive, most people barely notice the absence of fish or meat. In fact I often see committed carnivores actually choosing something vegetarian from a menu.

For something really special, why not go for a soufflé? It is such a treat and if you follow a few very simple rules (like getting the right-sized dish) there's never any need to worry. For a family vegetarian meal I would personally go for the Vegetarian Moussaka with Ricotta Topping (page 102) or Crêpe Cannelloni with Spinach and Four Cheeses (opposite). For a supper party the Gorgonzola Cheese and Apple Strudel with Spiced Pickled Pears (page 106) has won high praise among my vegetarian friends.

The vegetarian recipes included in this chapter are by no means the only ones in the book as a whole. For instance have a look at the chapter on soups—Roasted Pumpkin Soup with Melting Cheese (page 14), Chickpea, Chili and Cilantro Soup (page 11), or Curried Parsnip and Apple Soup with Parsnip Crisps (page 16) are all ideal. For other inspiration look up Camembert Croquettes with Fresh Date and Apple Chutney (page 38), Apple and Cider Salad with Melted Camembert Dressing (page 40) or Warm Lentil Salad with Walnuts and Goat Cheese (page 33), to mention just a few.

Crêpe Cannelloni
with Spinach and Four Cheeses

Serves 4–6

Crêpes make brilliant cannelloni—better and lighter, I think, than pasta. Four-star Italian cheeses and spinach make this a wonderful vegetarian version. If you're entertaining you may prefer to serve it as a starter in individual heatproof baking dishes, in which case you should place two crêpes per person in each.

FOR THE SAUCE:
2½ cups milk
½ stick butter
⅓ cup flour
1 bay leaf
Salt and freshly ground black pepper
A good grating of fresh nutmeg
⅓ cup heavy cream

FOR THE FILLING:
1 pound fresh spinach
1 tablespoon butter
⅔ cup ricotta cheese

1¼ cups crumbled Gorgonzola
⅔ cup grated Parmesan (Parmigiano-Reggiano)
Fresh nutmeg
Freshly ground black pepper
1 bunch scallions, finely sliced, including the green parts

1 quantity of Basic Crêpes (see page 179)

FOR THE TOPPING:
1 cup grated mozzarella
½ cup grated Parmigiano-Reggiano

You will also need a well-buttered dish measuring 9 × 9 × 2 inches.

Preheat the oven to 400°F.

Begin by making the sauce, and to do this place the milk, butter, flour and bay leaf in a saucepan and bring everything up to simmering point, whisking all the time, until the sauce has thickened. Season it with salt, pepper and nutmeg. Then turn the heat down to its lowest and let it simmer very gently for 2 minutes, and remove it from the heat before stirring in the cream. Then remove the bay leaf.

Meanwhile, place the spinach in a large saucepan with the butter and cook it briefly for 1–2 minutes, tossing it around until it wilts and collapses down, then drain it in a colander and squeeze it hard to get rid of all the excess juice. Now place the spinach in a bowl, chop it roughly with a knife and then add the ricotta, Gorgonzola, Parmesan and a grating of the nutmeg. Mix everything together, seasoning with pepper, but no salt as the cheeses can be quite salty. Next add the scallions and 4–5 tablespoons of the sauce.

Next lay a crêpe out and place 2 tablespoons of the filling onto it, then roll it up, tucking in the edges. Repeat this with the remaining crêpes. Lay the filled crêpes side by side in individual gratin dishes or a baking dish and scatter the mozzarella all over them. Next pour over the sauce. Finally sprinkle the Parmesan all over the surface. Then bake the cannelloni on the highest rack of the oven for 25–30 minutes until the top is brown and the sauce is bubbling. If you make individual cannelloni in separate dishes, the cooking time will be about 20 minutes.

Broccoli Soufflé
with Three Cheeses

*Serves 4 as a light lunch together with a green salad,
or 6–8 as a starter*

*T*he secret of a well-risen soufflé lies precisely in the size of dish you use. If you want it to look amazing use a small dish with a collar tied around—this way you can pile the mixture up high, then when it's cooked remove the collar to reveal a spectacular height! Of course it all tastes the same, but it's good to have some fun when you're cooking, and this is great fun! One thing to remember when making soufflés is that you must have the bowls and whisks spanking clean, then wipe them with a little lemon juice and paper towels to ensure they're absolutely grease-free.

Melted butter for the dish and
   parchment collar
⅓ cup freshly grated Parmesan
   (Parmigiano-Reggiano)
1 pound broccoli, with the very thick
   stalks trimmed
Salt
3 large eggs plus 2 egg whites

¼ stick butter
⅓ cup flour
⅔ cup milk
Freshly ground black pepper
¼ teaspoon cayenne pepper
¼ whole nutmeg, grated
⅓ cup grated sharp Cheddar
⅓ cup grated Gruyère

You will also need parchment paper, string and a 3-cup capacity soufflé dish measuring 5 inches diameter and 3 inches high, such as Apilco (available from kitchenware stores).

Preheat the oven to 400°F. Place the oven rack in the lower third of the oven with no rack above.

First of all prepare the soufflé dish and its collar. To do this, cut a piece of parchment paper from the roll, 20 × 12 inches in length. Fold in half along its length so that it now measures 20 × 6 inches doubled. Now turn up a 1-inch fold all along the length to stabilize the base of the collar.

Next butter the dish really well and sprinkle the inside with some of the Parmesan, tipping the dish from side to side to give the base and sides a light coating. Empty out the excess, then tie the paper collar around the dish with the 1-inch folded bit at the bottom. The paper will overlap around the circumference by 3 inches and stand 2 inches above the rim of the dish. Fix the collar in place with string and tie with a bow so that when it comes out of the oven you can remove it quickly and easily. Now butter the inside of the paper and that's it—the dish is now ready to receive the soufflé.

To make the soufflé, place the broccoli in a steamer, sprinkle with salt and steam over simmering water until tender—approximately 8–10 minutes. While the broccoli is cooking, prepare the eggs. Have ready a large bowl containing the extra egg whites and two small bowls. Separate the eggs into the small bowls one at a time, transferring the whites from the small bowl into the larger bowl as you go. When the broccoli is tender, remove it and leave to cool until barely warm. Then pop it into the processor and process it almost to a purée.

Next place the butter, flour and milk in a small saucepan and whisk with a balloon whisk over a medium heat until you have a smooth, glossy paste. Season to taste with salt and pepper, then season with about the same amount again—this extra is really to season the large volume of eggs. Transfer to a mixing bowl and add the cayenne, nutmeg, Cheddar, Gruyère and half of the grated Parmesan. Add the 3 egg yolks plus the broccoli and mix everything together thoroughly.

Now the vital part—the beating of the egg whites. If you're using an electric mixer, switch it on to low and beat the whites for approximately 30 seconds or until they start foaming. Then increase the speed of the mixer to medium and then to high, moving the beaters around and around the bowl while it's beating, until you get a smooth glossy mixture that stands in stiff peaks when the beaters are removed from the bowl. It's better to underbeat than overbeat, so watch carefully.

Next, using a large metal spoon, stir 1 spoonful of the egg whites into the broccoli to lighten the mixture, then empty the broccoli mixture into the egg whites and fold, using cutting and turning movements, until everything is well amalgamated. Don't be tempted to do any mixing—it must be careful folding done as quickly as possible. Now pour the mixture into the prepared dish, sprinkle the top with the remaining Parmesan and place on a rack in the lower third of the oven (with no rack above) for 40–45 minutes. When it's done it should be nicely browned on top, well risen and beginning to crack. It should feel springy in the center but it's important not to overcook it, as it should be nice and moist, almost runny inside, because as you are taking it from the oven to the table, and even as you're serving it, it will go on cooking. Divide among warm serving plates and serve it absolutely immediately.

NOTE: *This soufflé can be made with other vegetable purées: Parsnips, Jerusalem artichokes or zucchini would make lovely alternatives.*

Warm Roquefort Cheesecake
with Pears in Balsamic Vinaigrette

Serves 8

This savory cheesecake includes a clever blend of three cheese flavors, as the smooth fromage blanc and farmer's cheese gently complement the sharpness of the Roquefort. And, while cheese and pears are always good partners, this particular combination is a marriage made in heaven.

FOR THE CRUST:
2 cups white breadcrumbs
⅔ cup finely grated Pecorino Romano
   (or Parmigiano-Reggiano)
¼ stick butter, melted
Freshly ground black pepper

FOR THE FILLING:
3 large eggs
1 cup farmer cheese
½ cup fromage blanc (8% fat)
Salt and freshly ground black pepper
1½ cups coarsely crumbled Roquefort

2 tablespoons snipped fresh chives
4 scallions, finely sliced

FOR THE PEARS IN BALSAMIC
VINAIGRETTE:
4 firm but ripe pears
1 large clove garlic
1 teaspoon sea salt
2 teaspoons ground mustard
Freshly ground black pepper
1 tablespoon balsamic vinegar
⅓ cup extra virgin olive oil

You will also need a springform cake pan 9 inches in diameter.

Preheat the oven to 375°F.

First of all make the crust of the cheesecake by mixing the breadcrumbs and Pecorino together, then pour in the butter, adding a good grinding of pepper. Press the crumb mixture firmly down over the bottom of the pan, then bake in the preheated oven for 15–20 minutes. (This time will vary slightly, so it does need careful watching—the aim is for the crust to be crisp and toasted. If it is undercooked it does not have the lovely crunchy texture so necessary to the finished cheesecake.) Then remove it from the oven and turn the heat down to 350°F.

Now make the filling. First beat together the eggs and farmer cheese in a bowl, then stir in the fromage blanc and seasoning. After that stir the Roquefort in, together with the chives. Pour the mixture into the pan and scatter the sliced scallions over the top, then place it on the high rack of the oven and bake for 30–40 minutes or until the center feels springy to the touch. Allow the cheesecake to cool and settle for about 20 minutes before serving cut into slices.

The pears in balsamic vinaigrette can be prepared up to 2 hours before serving. Thinly pare off the skins of the pears using a potato peeler and being careful to leave the stems intact. Now lay each pear on its side with the stem flat on a board, then take a very sharp knife and make an incision through the tip of the stem. Turn the pear the right way up and gently cut it in half, first sliding the knife through the stem and then through the pear.

Now remove the central core of each half, then, with the pear core side down, slice it thinly but leave the slices joined at the top. Press gently and the slices will fan out.

Make up the vinaigrette by crushing the clove of garlic and sea salt together with a mortar and pestle until it becomes a creamy paste. Now add the mustard and several grinds of black pepper. Work these into the garlic, then, using a small whisk, add the balsamic vinegar and then the oil—whisking all the time to amalgamate. Serve 1 pear half with each portion of the cheesecake, with a little of the vinaigrette spooned over.

Red Onion Tarte Tatin

*Serves 6 as a starter
or 4 as a main course*

This is simply the old favorite apple tarte tatin turned into a savory version. The red onions are mellowed and caramelized with balsamic vinegar, and look spectacularly good. And the cheese and thyme pastry provides the perfect background. Everyone in my family says this is ace.

2½ pounds red onions
¼ stick butter
1 teaspoon superfine sugar
6 small thyme sprigs
Salt and freshly ground black pepper
1½ tablespoons chopped fresh thyme
1 tablespoon balsamic vinegar

FOR THE PASTRY:
⅔ cup flour

⅓ cup plus 1 tablespoon whole wheat
  flour
½ stick butter, softened
⅓ cup grated Cheddar
1 teaspoon chopped fresh thyme leaves
About 2–3 tablespoons cold water

TO SERVE:
A few shavings of Parmesan
  (Parmigiano-Reggiano)

You will also need either a cast-iron ovenproof skillet with a base diameter of 9 inches or a good solid baking pan of the same size (see page 247).

Preheat the oven to 350°F and preheat a solid baking sheet as well.

Begin by preparing the onions, which should have their outer papery skins removed and then be cut in half lengthwise from stem to root. After that, place the skillet over medium heat and as soon as it's hot, add the butter and the sugar, then as soon as the butter begins to sizzle, quickly scatter the sprigs of thyme in, then arrange the onions on the bottom of the skillet, cut side down. As you do this you need to think "jigsaw puzzle," so that after the onion halves have been placed in the skillet to cover the surface, all of those left over need to be cut into wedges and fitted in between to fill the gaps. Bear in mind that what you see when you turn the tart out is the cut side of the onions.

When the onions have all been fitted in, give them a good seasoning of salt and freshly ground black pepper, then scatter over the chopped thyme and sprinkle in the vinegar.

Now turn the heat down under the skillet and let the onions cook very gently for about 10 minutes. After that cover the skillet with foil and place it on the baking sheet on the rack just above the center of the oven and leave it there for the onions to cook for 50–60 minutes.

While the onions are cooking, make the pastry. This, if you like, can be done by mixing all the ingredients except the water in a processor. When the mixture resembles fine crumbs, gradually add enough cold water to make a soft dough. Then pop the dough into the fridge in a plastic bag for 30 minutes to rest.

As soon as the onions have had their cooking time, test them with a skewer: They should be cooked through but still retain some texture. Then, protecting your hands well, remove the skillet from the oven back onto direct heat and increase the oven temperature to 400°F. Then turn on the heat under the skillet containing the onions to medium, as what you now need to do is reduce all the lovely buttery oniony juices—this will probably take about 10 minutes, but do watch them carefully so that they do not burn. By this time you'll be left with very little syrupy liquid in the bottom of the skillet.

While that's all happening, roll out the pastry to a circle about 10 inches in diameter, then—again being careful to protect your hands—turn the heat off under the skillet and fit the pastry over the onions, pushing down and tucking in the edges all around the inside of the skillet. Then return the tart to the oven on the same baking sheet but this time on the higher rack and give it another 25–30 minutes until the pastry is crisp and golden.

When the tart is cooked, remove it from the oven and allow it to cool for 20 minutes before turning it out. When turning it out it's important to have a completely flat plate or board. Then protecting your hands with a dishcloth, place the plate on top of the pan, then turn it upside down, give it a good shake, and presto—Red Onion Tarte Tatin! If for any reason some of the onions are still in the pan, fear not: All you need to do is lift them out with a spatula and replace them into their own space in the tart. I think it's nice to serve this tart just warm with a few shavings of Parmesan sprinkled over.

NEXT PAGE: ITALIAN STUFFED EGGPLANT (SEE PAGE 98)

Italian Stuffed Eggplant

Serves 2 as a light supper dish or 4 as a starter

A part from tasting superb, this is particularly pretty to look at. I like to serve it as a first course, but with a salad and some good bread it would make a lovely supper dish for two people. Vegetarians can replace the anchovies with an extra teaspoon of capers. (See photograph on pages 96–97.)

1 medium to large eggplant, approximately 12–14 ounces
2–3 tablespoons olive oil
Salt and freshly ground black pepper
3 large ripe tomatoes
1 medium onion, finely chopped
1 large clove garlic, crushed
1 tablespoon torn fresh basil leaves

2 teaspoons sun-dried tomato paste
6 drained anchovy fillets, chopped
2 tablespoons drained small capers
5 ounces mozzarella
A scant ¼ cup fine fresh breadcrumbs
3 tablespoons freshly grated Parmesan (Parmigiano-Reggiano)
8 fresh basil leaves, lightly oiled

You will also need a large solid baking sheet 16 × 12 inches, lightly oiled, and a baking dish 16 × 12 inches, also oiled. Preheat the oven to 350°F.

First of all wipe the eggplant and trim off the stalk end, then use the very sharpest knife you have to cut it lengthwise into 8 thin slices about ¼ inch thick. When you get to the bulbous sides these slices should be chopped into small pieces and kept aside for the filling. Now arrange the slices of eggplant in rows on the baking sheet, then brush each slice lightly with olive oil and season with salt and pepper. Pop them into the oven on the high rack and let them precook for 15 minutes, by which time they will have softened enough for you to roll them up easily.

Next pour boiling water on the tomatoes and after 1 minute drain and slip the skins off. Then cut the tomatoes in half and, holding them in the palm of your hand, gently squeeze them until the seeds come out—it's best to do this over a plate or a bowl! Next using a sharp knife, chop the tomatoes into approximately ¼-inch dice. Now heat 1 tablespoon of the oil in a large solid skillet and fry the onion, chopped eggplant and garlic for about 5 minutes. Then add the chopped tomatoes, torn basil leaves and sun-dried tomato paste and continue to cook for about another 5 minutes. Give everything a good seasoning and add the chopped anchovies and the capers. Then remove the skillet from the heat and let the mixture cool slightly.

Now chop the mozzarella into very small dice. As soon as the eggplant slices are cool enough to handle, sprinkle each one with chopped mozzarella, placing it all along the center of each slice. On top of that put an equal amount of stuffing ingredients, leaving a border all around to allow for expansion. Roll up the slices and put them in the baking dish, making sure the overlapping ends are tucked underneath. Finally brush each one with oil, combine the fresh breadcrumbs and Parmesan, sprinkle the mixture over the eggplant, pop a basil leaf on top of each, then bake (same temperature) for about 20 minutes and serve immediately.

Roasted and Sun-Dried Tomato Risotto

Serves 2 as a supper dish or 3–4 as a light lunch

Oven-roasted tomatoes are the mainstay of this superb dish. Add to them some sun-dried tomatoes, Parmesan, a hint of saffron and some creamy, nutty rice and you have one of the nicest risottos imaginable.

FOR THE ROASTED TOMATOES:
1½ pounds tomatoes
Salt and freshly ground black pepper
1½ tablespoons extra virgin olive oil
1 large clove garlic, chopped
½ bunch basil leaves

FOR THE RISOTTO:
¼ stick butter
1 red medium onion, finely chopped
1¼ cups arborio or Italian canaroli rice
¼ teaspoon saffron threads

1¼ cups dry white wine
2 teaspoons sun-dried tomato paste
1½ cups boiling water
Salt and freshly ground black pepper
4 ounces sun-dried tomatoes, roughly
    chopped
⅔ cup freshly grated Parmesan (Parmi-
    giano-Reggiano) plus 1 ounce shaved
    into flakes with a potato peeler
1 tablespoon heavy cream

You will also need a solid shallow roasting pan 14 × 10 inches, and a 9-inch shallow ovenproof dish of about 3 pints capacity. Preheat the oven to 400°F.

First of all skin the tomatoes by pouring boiling water over them, then leave them for 1 minute exactly before draining them and slipping the skins off (if they're too hot, protect your hands with a cloth). Now slice each tomato in half and arrange the halves on the roasting tray, cut side up, then season with salt and pepper, sprinkle a few drops of olive oil on each one, followed by the chopped garlic, then finally top each one with half a basil leaf dipped in oil first to get a good coating.

Now pop them into the oven and roast the tomatoes for 50–60 minutes or until the edges of the tomatoes are slightly blackened. After that, remove them from the oven and then put the dish in the oven to preheat it, reducing the temperature to 350°F first. Now put the tomatoes and all their juices into a processor and blend. Next melt the butter in a large heavy saucepan and fry the onion for about 7 minutes until it is just tinged brown at the edges. After that add the rice and stir to coat all the grains with the buttery juices. Now crush the saffron threads to a powder with a mortar and pestle, then add this to the rice, together with the wine. Bring it up to boiling point, let it bubble for a minute, then add the tomato paste and boiling water. Give it all a good stir, season with salt and pepper and then add all the processed tomato mixture plus the sun-dried tomatoes. Stir again and bring it just up to simmering point, then transfer everything to the warm dish, return the dish to the oven and, using a timer, give it 35 minutes.

After that stir in the grated Parmesan and give it another 5–10 minutes—what you'll have to do here is to bite a grain of rice to check when it's ready. It should be tender but still retain some bite. Just before serving stir in the cream and top each portion with shavings of Parmesan and any leftover basil leaves.

Oven-Baked Wild Mushroom Risotto

Serves 6 as a starter

I've always loved real Italian risotto, a creamy mass with the rice grains "al dente"—but oh, the bother of all that stirring to make it. Then one day I was making a good old-fashioned rice pudding and I thought, why not try a risotto in the oven?

Why not indeed—it works like a dream and leaves you in peace to enjoy the company of your friends while it's cooking. I have since discovered, in fact, that in Liguria they do make a special kind of baked risotto called "arrosto," so my version turns out to be quite authentic after all.

½ ounce dried porcini (see page 233)
3 cups fresh cremini mushrooms
½ stick plus 1 tablespoon butter
1 medium onion, finely chopped
1 cup arborio or Italian canaroli rice
⅔ cup dry Madeira

1 teaspoon salt
Freshly ground black pepper
¼ cup freshly grated Parmesan
  (Parmigiano-Reggiano) plus ⅔ cup
  shaved into flakes with a potato peeler

You will also need a 9-inch shallow ovenproof dish of 2½ pints capacity, approximately 2 inches deep.

Preheat the oven to 300°F.

First of all you need to soak the dried mushrooms, and to do this you place them in a bowl and pour 2½ cups boiling water over them. Then just leave them to soak and soften for half an hour. Meanwhile chop the fresh mushrooms into about ½-inch chunks—not too small, as they shrink down quite a bit in the cooking.

Now melt the butter in a medium saucepan, add the onion and let it cook over a gentle heat for about 5 minutes, then add the fresh mushrooms, stir well and set aside.

When the porcini have had their half-hour soak, place a sieve over a bowl, line the sieve with a double sheet of absorbent paper towels and strain the mushrooms, reserving the liquid. Squeeze any excess liquid out of them, then chop them finely and transfer to the pan to join the other mushrooms and the onion. Keep the heat low and let the onion and mushrooms sweat gently and release their juices—which will take about 20 minutes. Meanwhile put the dish in the oven to warm.

Now add the rice and stir it around to get a good coating of butter, then add the Madeira, followed by the strained mushroom liquid. Add a teaspoon of salt and some freshly ground black pepper, bring it up to simmering point, then transfer everything from the pan to the warmed dish. Stir once then place it on the center rack of the oven without covering. Set a timer and give it 20 minutes exactly.

After that, gently stir in the grated Parmesan, turning the rice grains over. Now put the timer on again, and give it a further 15 minutes, then remove from the oven and put a clean cloth over it while you invite everyone to be seated. Like soufflés, risottos won't wait, so serve *presto pronto* on warmed plates and sprinkle with shavings of Parmesan.

OVEN-BAKED WILD MUSHROOM RISOTTO

Vegetarian Moussaka
with Ricotta Topping

Serves 4–6

*Y*es, it is possible to make an extremely good Greek-style moussaka without meat, and even nonvegetarians will admit it tastes every bit as good. Serve it with a large bowl of crunchy salad along with some warm pita bread.

2 eggplants, 8 ounces each
Salt
1¼ cups vegetable stock
⅓ cup Puy or other lentils
⅓ cup green lentils
⅓ cup olive oil
2 medium onions, finely chopped
1 large red bell pepper, seeded and
    chopped into ¼-inch dice
2 cloves garlic, crushed
One 14-ounce can chopped tomatoes,
    drained
1 cup red wine
¼ cup tomato paste or sun-dried
    tomato paste

1 teaspoon ground cinnamon
⅓ cup chopped fresh parsley
Freshly ground black pepper

FOR THE TOPPING:
1¼ cups whole milk
¼ cup flour
¼ stick butter
¼ whole nutmeg, grated
Salt and freshly ground black pepper
1 cup ricotta cheese
1 large egg, beaten
⅓ cup freshly grated Parmesan
    (Parmigiano-Reggiano)

You will also need a shallow dish approximately 9 × 9 × 2½ inches deep.

Preheat the oven to 350°F.

Begin by preparing the eggplants: To do this cut them into ½-inch dice, leaving the skins on. Place them by small handfuls in a colander, sprinkling with a little salt as you go, then put a small plate with a heavy weight on top—this will draw out any excess juices.

Meanwhile pour the stock into a saucepan together with the Puy lentils (but no salt), cover and simmer for 15 minutes before adding the green lentils. Cover again and cook for a further 15 minutes, by which time most of the liquid will have been absorbed and the lentils will be soft. While they're cooking heat half of the oil in a large solid skillet and fry the onions until they're soft and tinged brown at the edges (about 5 minutes), then add the chopped bell pepper and soften and brown that too for about another 4 minutes. Next add the garlic, cook for 1 minute more, then transfer everything to a plate.

Now transfer the eggplants to a clean towel to squeeze them dry, then add the remaining oil to the skillet, turn the heat up to high and toss the eggplants in it so they get evenly cooked. When they're starting to brown a little, add the tomatoes and the onion-and–bell pepper mixture to the pan. In a bowl mix the wine, tomato paste and cinnamon together, then pour it over the vegetables. Add the lentils and the chopped parsley, season well and let everything simmer gently while you make the topping.

All you do is place the milk, flour, butter and nutmeg in a saucepan and, using a balloon whisk, whisk until it comes to simmering point and becomes a smooth glossy sauce. Season with salt and pepper, remove it from the heat and let it cool a little before whisking in the ricotta cheese followed by the egg.

Finally transfer the vegetable-and-lentil mixture to the dish and spoon the cheese sauce over the top, using the back of a spoon to take it right up to the edges. Sprinkle with the Parmesan and transfer the dish to the preheated oven and bake on the middle rack for 1 hour. Then allow the moussaka to rest for 15 minutes before serving.

Mashed Black-Eyed Beancakes
with Ginger Onion Marmalade

Serves 4

Black-eyed peas are the lovely nutty beans that are popular in recipes from the deep south of America, and with the addition of other vegetables they make very good beancakes. Fried crisp and crunchy on the outside and served with this delectable Ginger Onion Marmalade, this makes a splendid vegetarian main course.

¾ cup dried black-eyed peas
⅔ cup green lentils
2½ cups water
1 bay leaf
2 fresh thyme sprigs
Salt and freshly ground black pepper
1 tablespoon olive oil
1 medium red onion, finely chopped
1 medium carrot, finely chopped
1 small red bell pepper, seeded and finely chopped

1 green chili, seeded and finely chopped
1 clove garlic, chopped
¼ teaspoon ground mace
1 teaspoon chopped fresh thyme
1 tablespoon sun-dried tomato paste
⅓ cup whole wheat flour
4–5 tablespoons olive oil for frying

To Garnish:
Watercress sprigs

First of all the black-eyed peas need soaking. This can be done by covering them with twice their volume of cold water and leaving them overnight or alternatively bringing them up to the boil, boiling for 10 minutes and then leaving to soak for 2 hours. The green lentils won't need soaking.

Once this is done, take a medium-sized saucepan, add the drained peas and the lentils, then pour in the water, add the bay leaf and sprigs of thyme, then bring everything up to a gentle simmer and let it cook for about 40–45 minutes, by which time all the water should have been absorbed and the peas and lentils will be completely soft. If there's any liquid still left, drain them in a colander. Remove the bay leaf and thyme sprigs. Now you need to mash the legumes to a pulp, and you can do this using a fork, potato masher or electric mixer. After that give them a really good seasoning with salt and freshly ground black pepper and put a clean towel over them to stop them becoming dry.

Now take a really large skillet, add the tablespoon of olive oil, then heat it over medium heat and add the onion, carrot, bell pepper, chili and garlic. Sauté them all together for about 6 minutes, moving them around the skillet to soften and turn golden brown at the edges.

After that mix all the vegetables into the mashed pea-and-lentil mixture, add the mace, chopped thyme and tomato paste, then dampen your hands and form the mixture into 12 round cakes measuring approximately 2½–3 inches in diameter. Then place them on a plate or a lightly oiled tray, cover with plastic wrap and keep them in the refrigerator until needed, but for 1 hour minimum.

When you're ready to serve the beancakes, coat them lightly with whole wheat flour seasoned with salt and freshly ground black pepper, then heat 2 tablespoons of the olive oil. When it is really hot reduce the heat to medium and fry the beancakes in two batches for 3 minutes on each side until they're crisp and golden, adding more oil if needed.

Drain them on paper towels and serve garnished with sprigs of watercress and the Ginger Onion Marmalade.

Ginger Onion Marmalade

This is not only a wonderful accompaniment to the beancakes but is great as a relish for all kinds of other dishes—meat, fish or vegetarian.

12 ounces onions	¼ cup white wine vinegar
2 tablespoons olive oil	¼ cup dark brown sugar
3 rosemary sprigs	1 tablespoon freshly grated gingerroot
1 cup dry white wine	Salt and freshly ground black pepper

First of all, peel and slice the onions into ¼-inch rings (slice any really large outside rings in half). Then take a solid medium-sized saucepan and heat the olive oil. When the oil is hot, add the onions and the rosemary, stir well, and toss the onions around till they're golden and tinged brown at the edges (about 10 minutes).

After that pour in the white wine and white wine vinegar, followed by the brown sugar and the ginger, then stir and bring everything up to simmering point. Add salt and pepper, then turn the heat down to low again and let everything simmer very gently for 1¼ hours or until all the liquid has almost disappeared. Then remove the rosemary, pour everything into a serving bowl and you can serve it warm—or I think it's quite nice cold with the hot beancakes.

Gorgonzola Cheese and Apple Strudel with Spiced Pickled Pears

Serves 6

Here is a recipe that provides something really stylish for vegetarian entertaining. Serve the strudel with the pickled pears. It's a brilliant combination of crisp pastry, melting cheese and the sharpness of the pears.

12 ounces young leeks weighed after
  trimming (this will be about 1½
  pounds bought weight)
8 ounces prepared weight of celery
  (reserve the leaves)
1 stick butter
1 small Rome apple
1 small dessert apple, such as Granny
  Smith
8 ounces mozzarella, cut in ½-inch cubes
12 scallions, white parts only, chopped

1 cup chopped walnuts
3 tablespoons chopped parsley, flat-leaf
  or curly
Salt and freshly ground black pepper
1 ounce white bread, crust removed
2 cloves garlic
10 sheets frozen phyllo pastry,
  18 × 10 inches, thawed
6 ounces Gorgonzola, cut in ½-inch
  cubes

You will also need a large flat baking sheet approximately 16 × 12 inches.   Preheat oven to 375°F.

First of all prepare the leeks by trimming and discarding the outer layers, then slice each one vertically almost in half and rinse them under cold running water, fanning them out to get rid of any grit and dust. Then dry them in a cloth and cut them into ½-inch pieces. Now rinse and chop the celery into slightly smaller pieces.

Then melt 3 tablespoons of the butter in a skillet 9 inches in diameter. Keeping the heat at medium, sauté the leeks and celery for about 7–8 minutes until just tinged brown; stir them and keep them on the move to stop them sticking at the edges. Then transfer them to a large bowl and while they are cooling you can deal with the other ingredients.

The apples need to be cored and chopped into ½-inch pieces, leaving the skins on, then as soon as the leeks and celery have cooled, add the apples, cubed mozzarella, scallions, walnuts and 1 tablespoon of the chopped parsley. Season everything well and stir to mix it all together.

Now you need to make a breadcrumb mixture, and to do this, place the bread, garlic, the rest of the parsley and0 the reserved celery leaves in a food processor. Switch it on and blend until everything is smooth. If you don't have a food processor, grate the bread, and chop everything else finely and mix together.

Next take a large clean cloth and dampen it under cold water, lay it out on a work surface, then carefully unwrap the phyllo pastry sheets and lay them on the damp cloth, folding it over. It is important to keep the pastry sheets in the cloth to prevent them drying out.

It is quite complicated to explain how to assemble a strudel, but to actually *do* it is very easy and only takes a few minutes.

Place a buttered baking sheet on a work surface. Because the phyllo sheets are too small to make a strudel for 6 people, we're going to have to "weld" them together. To do this, first of all melt the remaining butter in a small saucepan, then take 1 sheet of phyllo pastry (remembering to keep the rest covered), lay it on one end of the baking sheet and brush it with melted butter. Then place another sheet beside it overlapping it by about 2 inches, then brush that with melted butter. Place a third sheet next to the second overlapping it again by 2 inches.

Now sprinkle a quarter of the breadcrumb mixture all over the sheets and then place 2 more sheets of phyllo, this time horizontally, buttering the first one with melted butter and welding the other one with a 2-inch join. Brush that layer as before with melted butter and repeat the sprinkling of breadcrumbs. Then place the next 3 sheets as you did the first 3, again brushing with butter and sprinkling with crumbs. Then place the final 2 sheets horizontally and brush with butter.

After that place half the cheese and vegetable mixture all the way along the phyllo, sprinkle the cubes of Gorgonzola on top of that, then finish off with the rest of the mixture on top. Now just pat it together firmly with your hands. Take the edge of the pastry that is nearest to you, bring it up over the filling, then flip the whole thing over as if you were making a giant sausage roll. Neatly push in the vegetables before tucking the pastry ends underneath. Now brush the entire surface with the remaining butter, scatter the rest of the crumb mixture over the top and bake in the oven for 25–30 minutes or until it has turned a nice golden brown color.

To serve the strudel, cut off the ends (they are great for the bird feeder but not for your guests) and cut the strudel into slices, giving each person 1 pickled pear.

Spiced Pickled Pears

6 hard pears (Bosc or similar variety)	1 tablespoon mixed peppercorns
½ cup brown sugar	4 whole cloves
1 ½ cups cider vinegar	6 crushed juniper berries
1 tablespoon balsamic vinegar	

You will also need a flameproof casserole approximately 10 inches in diameter, large enough to hold the pears.   Preheat the oven to 375°F.

To pickle the pears, first peel them using a potato peeler, but be very careful to leave the stems intact as they look much prettier. Place all the rest of the ingredients in a flameproof casserole, then bring everything up to simmering point, stirring all the time to dissolve the sugar. Now carefully lower the pears into the hot liquid, laying them on their sides, cover with a lid and transfer the pears to the oven for 30 minutes.

After that remove the lid and carefully turn the pears over. Test with a skewer to see how they are cooking—they'll probably need another 30 minutes altogether, so cover with the lid and leave them in the oven till they feel tender when pierced with a skewer. Then remove them and allow them to cool in their liquid until needed. When serving, there's no need to reheat the pears as they taste much better cold.

C H A P T E R   S I X

The Top Ten Casseroles
and Braised Dishes

I REMEMBER GOING TO A VERY SMART, INTENSELY STYLISH RESTAURANT IN the eighties and the chef telling me, rather dismissively, that if he'd known I was coming he'd have made me a casserole. Oh, if only he had! Yet such are the swings of fashion that now my old seventies favorites are back in favor with young chefs. So let us not lament the lean years of nouvelle cuisine, but rather rejoice in this decade of diversity. Back in the charts are oxtails, Irish stews, mashed potatoes, beef, lamb and pork slowly braised in lashings of sauce, real comfort foods for cold days, evoking an aura of homeliness and contentment in the kitchen to dispel the trials of the day.

If casseroles are going to make a comeback in your life, you need to convince yourself that they're really *not* a lot of work. The preparation time is never that long, and while the meal is in the oven you are left completely free—a great deal easier than standing by a broiler or skillet. The other positive side is that all casseroles improve if they're made a day ahead, cooled, refrigerated and gently reheated when you need them. Just preheat the oven to 350°F and place the casserole covered in the oven for 40 minutes. So they're absolutely ideal for serving to friends: You can entertain in a much more relaxed way with no last-minute hurdles to overcome.

Still more good news is that they freeze well. If a casserole has been frozen, defrost it thoroughly, then remove the lid from the container and replace it with double foil, and reheat as above. In all cases make sure it has come to a gentle simmer before serving.

Pork Braised in Cider Vinegar Sauce

Serves 4

This recipe has an autumnal ring to it and is for me the first casserole of the winter months. Pork shoulder is an excellent cut for braising and this recipe is superb for serving to friends and family, because it just cooks away all by itself until you're ready to serve it. I also think it tastes even better the next day, so if you make it that far ahead, don't add the crème fraîche until it's reheated. The reheating will take about 25 minutes in a casserole over gentle direct heat. Note here, though, that it's important to use a good-quality cider vinegar.

1 tablespoon butter
2 tablespoons peanut oil
2 pounds pork shoulder, trimmed and cut
  into 1-inch cubes
12 shallots
2½ cups medium-sweet cider

⅔ cup cider vinegar
4 fresh thyme sprigs
2 bay leaves
Salt and freshly ground black pepper
⅓ cup crème fraîche

You will also need a wide, shallow flameproof casserole of 5 pints capacity.

Preheat the oven to 325°F.

First place the casserole over fairly high heat and add half the butter and 1 tablespoon of oil. Meanwhile, dry the pieces of meat with paper towels, then brown them a few at a time in the hot butter and oil, transferring them to a plate as they brown.

After that add the rest of the butter and oil, and when that's very hot add the shallots to the casserole and carefully brown these on all sides to a nice glossy caramel color. Now pour the cider and cider vinegar into the casserole, stir well, scraping the bottom and sides of the casserole then return the meat, add the thyme and the bay leaves and season well.

As soon as it's all come to simmering point, transfer the casserole without a lid to the oven for approximately 1 hour and 15 minutes or until the liquid is reduced and the meat is tender. Now remove the meat and shallots to a warm serving dish, discarding the herbs, then place the casserole back over direct heat. Bring it up to the boil and reduce the liquid to about half of its original volume. Finally whisk in the crème fraîche, taste to check the seasoning, then pour the sauce over the meat and serve. This is great served with Potato and Apple Rösti (page 154) and Spiced Sautéed Red Cabbage with Cranberries (page 155).

NOTE: *If you don't have a wide shallow casserole, use an ovenproof dish (same size), but preheat it first in the oven. Bring everything to a simmering point in a skillet before you pour it into the dish, then finish the sauce in a saucepan.*

Braised Lamb with Flageolet Beans

Serves 4

Though the lamb shoulder chop is quite an economical cut, it provides very sweet meat that responds perfectly to long slow cooking. The presoaked dried green flageolets absorb the flavors of the lamb, garlic and herbs, making this a comforting winter warmer.

1⅓ cups dried flageolet beans	½ tablespoon chopped fresh thyme leaves
2 pounds lamb shoulder chops, filleted	2½ cups lamb stock or water
2 tablespoons oil	Freshly ground black pepper
2 large onions, halved and cut into ½-inch rounds	4 small fresh thyme sprigs
2 cloves garlic, finely chopped	3 small bay leaves
¼ cup flour	8 ounces cherry tomatoes
	Salt

You will also need a flameproof casserole dish of approximately 4 pints capacity.

Preheat the oven to 275°F.

You start this recipe by soaking the beans. To do this, cover the beans with twice their volume of cold water, then soak them overnight. Alternatively, on the same day, boil them for 10 minutes, then leave them to soak for a minimum of 2 hours.

When you're ready to cook the lamb, preheat the oven, trim off any excess fat and then cut the lamb into cubes about ¾ inch thick. Now place the casserole over direct heat, add 1 tablespoon of oil, then as soon as it's smoking hot, brown the pieces of meat, a few at a time, wiping them first with paper towels so that they're absolutely dry when they hit the oil (don't add more than 6 pieces at a time). Then as soon as each piece is nicely browned on both sides, remove the cubes to a plate and carry on until all the meat is browned. Next add the other tablespoon of oil and, keeping the heat high, brown the onions around the edges, moving them around until they take on a nice dark caramel color—this will take about 5 minutes—then add the garlic, stir that into the onions and let it cook for another minute or so. Now sprinkle in the flour and give it all a good stir, allowing the flour to soak into the juices. Add the thyme leaves, then gradually add the stock, stirring all the while as you pour it in. Next return the meat to the casserole and season it well with freshly ground black pepper, but no salt at this stage. After that drain the beans, discarding their soaking water, and add them to the casserole as well. Finally add the thyme sprigs and bay leaves, and as soon as everything has come up to simmering point, place a tight-fitting lid on and transfer the casserole to the center rack of the oven. Give it 1½ hours, and toward the end of that time, pour boiling water over the tomatoes and then after 30 seconds drain off the water and slip the skins off. Add these to the casserole along with a good seasoning of salt, then replace the lid and carry on cooking for a further hour.

Before serving remove the bay leaves and sprigs of thyme and taste to check the seasoning.

A Bit of the Irish Stew with Crusted Dumplings

Serves 4–6

This is an updated version of my "Cookery Course" recipe, included here simply because Irish stew is one of the best casserole dishes in the entire world. If you top it with dumplings, then bake it in the oven so that they turn crusty and crunchy, you will have a heavenly banquet on your plate. Serve it as the Irish do, with simple boiled cabbage. (See photograph on pages 112–13.)

3 pounds lamb shoulder chops, filleted, and best end of neck cutlets mixed
2 tablespoons flour, seasoned
12 ounces onions, thickly sliced
8 ounces carrots, cut in chunks
2 medium leeks, washed and sliced
1 large potato (about 10 ounces), peeled and cut in chunks
Salt and freshly ground black pepper
2 tablespoons coarse pearl barley

FOR THE DUMPLINGS:
1⅓ cups self-rising flour
½ cup chopped fresh parsley
Salt and freshly ground black pepper
¾ cup shredded beef suet or grated chilled butter

TO GARNISH:
1 tablespoon chopped fresh parsley

You will also need a flameproof casserole of 3 quarts capacity.

Start off by drying the pieces of meat on paper towels, trim away any excess fat, cut the shoulder chops into 1½-inch cubes, then dip them along with the cutlets into the seasoned flour. Now arrange a layer of meat in the bottom of the casserole, followed by a layer of onions, carrots, leeks and potato and a good seasoning of salt and pepper. Then add some more meat and continue layering the ingredients until everything is in.

Next sprinkle in the pearl barley and pour in approximately 1 quart of hot water, then bring it all up to simmering point. Spoon off any scum that comes to the surface, cover with a tight-fitting lid and leave it to simmer over the lowest possible heat for 2 hours.

About 15 minutes before the end of the cooking time preheat the oven to 400°F, then make up the dumplings. Mix the flour and parsley with a seasoning of salt and pepper in a bowl, then mix in—but do not rub in—the suet. Now add just sufficient cold water to make a fairly stiff but elastic dough that leaves the bowl cleanly. Knead it lightly, then shape it into 12 dumplings.

When the stew is ready, remove the lid, place the dumplings all over the surface, then transfer the casserole to the highest rack of the oven (without a lid) and leave it there for 30 minutes or until the dumplings are golden brown and crusty. Serve the meat surrounding the vegetables and dumplings, with some of the liquid poured over and some in a gravy boat, and sprinkle with chopped parsley.

NEXT PAGE: A BIT OF THE IRISH STEW WITH CRUSTED DUMPLINGS

Pot-Roasted Beef in Red Wine
with Red Onion Marmalade

Serves 4–6

It has to be said that roasting meat does require a little attention, with basting and so on. But the great thing about a pot roast is that it feeds the same number of people, but leaves you in peace until you're ready to serve. Its other great virtue is that it enables you to use some of those very lean, delicious cuts of meat that are not suitable for roasting, such as brisket or round.

¼ stick butter
2½ pounds rolled brisket or round
  rump roast
2 bay leaves
1 small bunch thyme
2 cups red wine
Salt and freshly ground black pepper
1½ tablespoons flour

FOR THE RED ONION
MARMALADE:
¼ stick butter
12 ounces red onions, very finely chopped
1 teaspoon chopped fresh thyme
1 cup red wine
¼ cup red wine vinegar
Salt and freshly ground black pepper

You will also need a medium-sized flameproof casserole with a tight-fitting lid.

Preheat the oven to 275°F.

Take the casserole, melt half of the butter in it and when it begins to foam turn the heat up high. Dry the meat thoroughly with paper towels and then brown it on all sides in the hot butter, browning one flat side first, then turning it over on the other side, and moving it around to get the round edges browned as well.

Then remove the meat, wipe the casserole with some paper towels and return the meat to it, adding the bay leaves, thyme, the wine and some salt and pepper. Bring it all up to simmering point, put on a tight-fitting lid, using foil if necessary to seal it, then transfer it to the oven and leave it to cook without looking at it for 3 hours.

When the cooking time is up, remove the meat from the casserole, cover it with foil and leave it to relax for 10 minutes. Meanwhile remove the herbs, place the casserole over direct heat and boil briskly to reduce the liquid slightly. Mix the flour and remaining butter to a smooth paste, then add this mixture in small pieces to the hot liquid and whisk with a balloon whisk until it comes back to the boil and you have a smooth, slightly thickened sauce.

While the beef is cooking, make the Red Onion Marmalade. Melt the butter in a medium-sized saucepan, stir in the chopped onions and the thyme and let them soften for about 10 minutes. Then add the wine and wine vinegar, bring it all up to a gentle simmer and add a seasoning of salt and freshly ground black pepper. Turn the heat to its lowest setting and let the whole thing cook really slowly with the lid off for about 50 minutes to 1 hour or until all the liquid has evaporated. Remove it from the heat, but reheat gently before serving.

Meatballs in Goulash Sauce

Serves 4–6

This recipe never fails to please—ground beef and pork together with bell pepper and onion is a wonderful combination of flavors. The meatballs are very light and the sauce rich and creamy. A classic Hungarian accompaniment would be buttered noodles tossed with poppy seeds (see Note).

12 ounces lean ground beef
12 ounces ground pork
½ medium red bell pepper, seeded and
  finely chopped
1 small onion, very finely chopped
1 large clove garlic, crushed
⅓ cup fresh chopped parsley
1 cup breadcrumbs
1 large egg, beaten
Salt and freshly ground black pepper
2 tablespoons flour, seasoned
2 tablespoons olive oil

FOR THE SAUCE:

1 tablespoon olive oil
1 medium onion, chopped
½ medium red bell pepper, seeded and
  finely chopped
1 large clove garlic, crushed
2 tablespoons hot Hungarian paprika
1 pound ripe tomatoes, peeled and
  chopped, or 1 14-ounce can Italian
  chopped tomatoes
Salt and freshly ground black pepper
Approximately ½ cup crème fraîche
A little extra paprika

You will also need a large flameproof casserole of 2 quarts capacity with a tight-fitting lid.

Preheat the oven to 275°F.

First make the meatballs. In a large bowl place the ground meats, chopped bell pepper, onion, garlic, parsley and breadcrumbs. Mix well, then add the egg and a good seasoning of salt and freshly ground black pepper. Now combine everything as thoroughly as possible, using either your hands or a large fork. Then take pieces of the mixture, about a tablespoon at a time, squeeze and roll each one into a small round—you should get 24 altogether—then coat each one lightly with seasoned flour. Heat up the oil in the casserole, and when it's smoking hot, brown the meatballs a few at a time. Then transfer them to a plate.

Next make the sauce in the same pan. Heat the oil, add the onion and red bell pepper and cook for about 5 minutes, then add the garlic, cook for another minute, and stir in the paprika and any remaining bits of seasoned flour. Stir to soak up the juices, then add the tomatoes, season with salt and pepper, then bring it all up to simmering point, stirring all the time. Now add the meatballs to the sauce, bring back to simmering point, cover with a tight-fitting lid and transfer it to the middle rack of the oven for 1½ hours. Just before serving, lightly stir in the crème fraîche to give a marbled effect. Spoon the meatballs onto freshly cooked noodles and sprinkle a little extra paprika on as a garnish as they go to the table.

NOTE: *For the noodles use 3 ounces green tagliatelle per person, drained then tossed in 1 tablespoon butter and 1 teaspoon poppy seeds.*

Braised Steak in Madeira with Five Kinds of Mushrooms

Serves 4–6

This recipe is really a very moveable feast. For an everyday version you could replace the Madeira with cider or beer and use just one variety of mushroom.

½ ounce dried porcini mushrooms
2 pounds skirt or braising steak
   (1 thick slice)
2 medium onions
2 tablespoons olive oil
2 tablespoons flour
3 tablespoons butter
1¼ cups dry Madeira

1 bay leaf
A few fresh thyme sprigs
Salt and freshly ground black pepper
1½ cups button mushrooms
1½ cups portobello mushrooms
2 cups oyster mushrooms
2 cups shiitake mushrooms
1 large clove garlic, crushed

You will also need a large shallow flameproof casserole with a tight-fitting lid.

Preheat the oven to 250°F.

First of all soak the dried porcini by placing them in a bowl with 2 cups warm water for at least 30 minutes. Meanwhile, trim the beef of any hard gristle and membrane, and if it's a whole slice divide it into 4 pieces. Cut the onions in half lengthwise and then into ½-inch wedges. Now in the casserole heat half the olive oil and sauté the onions until nicely tinged brown at the edges, then remove them to a plate. Heat the remaining oil in the casserole, turning the heat up really high, then brown the pieces of meat, two at a time on both sides, and remove them as they're done to join the onions.

Next drain the porcini through a sieve lined with paper towels, reserving the liquid, and chop them roughly. Now stir the flour into the oil left in the casserole along with 1 tablespoon of butter, then slowly add the mushroom water, stirring well after each addition, and follow that with the Madeira, whisking well to blend everything. As soon as the liquid comes up to simmering point, add the onions and the browned beef to the casserole, along with the chopped porcini. Add the bay leaf and thyme, season with salt and pepper, then put a lid on and place the casserole in the oven for 1½ hours. After that chop the button and portobello mushrooms roughly (not too small). Add these to the casserole, sprinkling them on the steak and spooning the juices over, then replace the lid, return the casserole to the oven and let it cook slowly for another 1½ hours.

When you're ready to serve, slice the oyster and shiitake mushrooms into ½-inch strips, reserving a few small whole ones for garnish, then melt the remaining butter in a skillet, add the garlic and mushrooms and season with salt and pepper. Toss everything around in the pan for 2–3 minutes. Now remove the casserole from the oven, taste to check the seasoning, then serve the steaks with the sauce spooned over and garnished with the whole shiitake and oyster mushrooms.

BRAISED STEAK IN MADEIRA WITH FIVE KINDS OF MUSHROOMS

Braised Steak au Poivre in Red Wine

Serves 4

While the French classic steak au poivre, or peppered steak, is a wonderful idea, steak is expensive and in the winter the original recipe can be adapted to braising—which is far easier for entertaining and tastes every bit as good. I like to serve it with some crispy-skinned buttered-jacket potatoes.

½ tablespoon black peppercorns
2 tablespoons flour
2 pounds good-quality skirt or braising
    steak, cut into 2-inch pieces
3 tablespoons beef drippings or olive oil
2 large onions, finely chopped
2 large cloves garlic, crushed with 1 tea-
    spoon sea salt with a mortar and pestle

2 cups red wine
Salt
2 bay leaves
1 large thyme sprig
½ cup crème fraîche

You will also need a flameproof casserole with a tight-fitting lid.

Preheat the oven to 300°F.

Crush the peppercorns coarsely with a mortar and pestle, then mix them together with the flour on a plate. Now dip the pieces of meat into this mixture, pressing it well in on all sides. Next heat 2 tablespoons of the drippings or oil in the casserole, and when it is really hot and beginning to shimmer quickly brown the pieces of meat, about four at a time, on both sides, then transfer them to a plate.

After that add the remaining drippings or oil to the pan and brown the onions for 3–4 minutes, still keeping the heat high. Then add the crushed garlic and cook for another minute. Now add any remaining flour and pepper left on the plate to the pan, stirring well to soak up the juices, then add the wine a little at a time, continuing to stir to prevent any lumps forming, and scraping up any crusty residue from the bottom and edge of the pan. When it's at simmering point, add the meat to the sauce, season it with salt, then pop the bay leaves and thyme sprig in. Bring it back to a simmer then put a lid on the casserole and transfer it to the middle rack of the oven to cook for 2 hours or until the meat is tender.

When you're ready to serve, remove the herbs, add the crème fraîche, stir it well in, then taste to check for seasoning before serving.

Oxtail Braised in Guinness with Cannellini Beans

Serves 6

I am not surprised that oxtail has become rather fashionable in restaurants now, because any meat that is cooked near the bone has a special sweetness and succulence. But it's still a very economical dish to prepare at home, and the addition of cannellini beans in this recipe means that they too absorb all that lovely flavor. This version is a winner.

1⅓ cups dried cannellini beans	2 bay leaves
4 tablespoons olive oil	Freshly ground black pepper
3–3½ pounds oxtail	12 ounces portobello mushrooms
2 tablespoons flour, seasoned	2½ cups beef stock
2 large onions, halved and thickly sliced	2 cups Guinness
4 cloves garlic	12 ounces button mushrooms
2 good thyme sprigs	Salt

You will also need a flameproof casserole of 4 quarts capacity.   Preheat the oven to 300°F.

First the beans need to soak, and to do this either soak them in cold water overnight or put them in a large saucepan with 2 quarts of cold water and bring them up to the boil for 10 minutes, then turn the heat off and leave them to soak for a minimum of 2 hours.

To make the casserole, heat 2 tablespoons of the oil in a large skillet, then wipe the pieces of oxtail with paper towels and coat them lightly in seasoned flour and fry in hot oil on all sides until they are a nutty brown color. Then, using a slotted spoon, transfer the pieces of oxtail to a casserole. Now add the rest of the oil and as soon as that's hot, add the onions and fry these for about 5 minutes until brown at the edges before transferring them to join the oxtail in the casserole. Remove the skillet from the heat, then drain the beans in a colander. Add them to the casserole along with the garlic, thyme and bay leaves, and add a good seasoning of black pepper.

Next wipe the portobello mushrooms with some damp paper towels, halve them (or quarter them if they are very large), then add these to the casserole as well, tucking them in among the beans and oxtail. Now return the skillet to the heat. Add any remaining seasoned flour, stir it in to soak up the juices and gradually add the stock and the Guinness, whisking all the time until it reaches simmering point. Pour it over the oxtail and the rest of the ingredients, cover with a tight-fitting lid and place in the preheated oven for 2½ hours. Then add the button mushrooms, halved and wiped as above, put the lid back on and give the casserole a further hour in the oven. When you next remove it, you will see that some of the fat from the oxtail has bubbled up to the top—spoon this off by skimming a tablespoon across the surface. Then season everything well with salt before serving with a lightly cooked green vegetable.

Black Bean Chili
with Avocado Salsa

Serves 4–6

*T*he now-familiar chili con carne has suffered from its fair share of convenience shortcut versions, but when it's made properly with the right ingredients, it is still a wonderful concept. I think this version is even better than the original, using black beans and introducing the subtle flavoring of lime and cilantro—and adding a contrasting cold garnish at the end. (See photograph on pages 120–21.)

1⅓ cups dried black beans
1 bunch fresh cilantro (reserving leaves
   for the salsa)
2 tablespoons olive oil
2 medium onions, chopped
1 clove garlic, crushed
2 green chilies, seeded and chopped small
1 pound skirt or braising steak, cut into
   very small pieces
2 tablespoons flour
2 14-ounce cans chopped tomatoes
1 large red bell pepper
Salt

½ reserved cilantro leaves, roughly chopped
Juice of ½ lime

FOR THE SALSA:
2 large firm tomatoes
1 ripe firm avocado
½ small red onion, finely chopped
Salt and freshly ground black pepper
Juice of ½ lime
½ reserved chopped cilantro leaves
A few drops Tabasco sauce

TO SERVE:
1 cup crème fraîche

You will also need a flameproof casserole of 2 quarts capacity with a tight-fitting lid.

Either presoak the beans overnight or start this recipe 3 hours ahead of time and begin by placing the beans in a large saucepan, covering them with cold water and bringing them up to boiling point and boiling for 10 minutes. Then turn the heat off and let them soak for 3 hours. Toward the end of the soaking time preheat the oven to 300°F.

    Strip the leaves off the cilantro stalks into a bowl, cover with plastic wrap and place them in the fridge. Then chop the cilantro stalks very finely. After that take the casserole, heat half the oil in it and cook the onions, garlic, cilantro stalks and chilies gently for about 5 minutes. Then transfer them to a plate, spoon the rest of the oil into the casserole, turn the heat up high, add about a third of the beef and brown it well, keeping it on the move. Then remove it and brown the rest in 2 batches. Now return everything to the casserole and sprinkle in the flour, stir it in to soak up the juices, then add the drained beans, followed by the tomatoes. Stir well and bring it up to simmering point. Don't add any salt at this stage—just put the lid on and transfer the casserole to the oven to cook for an initial 1½ hours.

Toward the end of that time, seed and chop the bell pepper into smallish pieces. Then when the time is up, stir the bell pepper in to join the meat and beans. Put the lid back on and give it a further 30 minutes' cooking.

While the meat finishes cooking, make up the salsa. Skin the tomatoes by pouring boiling water over them, then leaving for exactly 1 minute before draining and slipping the skins off when they're cool enough to handle. Then cut each tomato in half and, holding each half over a saucer, squeeze gently to extract the seeds. Now chop the tomato flesh as finely as possible.

Next halve the avocado, remove the stone, cut each half into quarters and peel off the skin. Chop the avocado into minutely small dice, and do the same with the onion. Finally combine the tomato, avocado and onion together in a bowl, adding seasoning, the juice of half the lime, half the chopped cilantro leaves and a few drops of Tabasco.

Before serving the chili, add salt, tasting as you add. Then stir in the rest of the cilantro leaves and the juice of half the lime. I like to serve this chili with some plain brown basmati rice.

Beef in Designer Beer

Serves 4–6

In the sixties every other restaurant was a bistro and every other bistro served Carbonnade de Boeuf à la Flamande, a traditional Flemish recipe which translates as Beef in Beer. But like other once-hackneyed sixties recipes, I think it's been neglected and there's a whole new generation now who probably haven't yet tasted it. For them, here is the nineties version, the only difference being that we now have a vast range of beers with smart labels to choose from. Not sure which one to use? Do what I do and go for the prettiest label!

FOR THE CROUTONS:
1 tablespoon olive oil
1 clove garlic, crushed
6 slices French baguette, 1-inch thick,
  cut slightly diagonally
2 tablespoons whole grain mustard
1 cup grated Gruyère

1 tablespoon olive oil
2 pounds skirt or braising steak, cut into
  2-inch squares

12 ounces onions, quartered
2 cloves garlic, crushed
1 heaping tablespoon flour
2 cups designer beer (see above)
Salt and freshly ground black pepper
A few fresh thyme sprigs
2 bay leaves

You will also need a large, wide, flameproof casserole.

You can make the croutons well ahead of time, and to do this preheat the oven to 350°F. Then drizzle the olive oil onto a large solid baking sheet, add the crushed garlic, then using either your hands or a piece of paper towel, spread the oil and garlic all over the baking sheet. Now place the bread slices on top of the oil, then turn them over so that both sides have been lightly coated with the oil. Bake for 20–25 minutes till crisp and crunchy.

When you're ready to cook the beef, lower the oven temperature to 300°F. Take the flameproof casserole, place it over direct heat, then heat the oil until sizzling hot and fry the meat 3 or 4 pieces at a time until they turn a dark mahogany color on all sides. Make sure you don't overcrowd the pan or they will create steam and never become brown. As you brown the meat remove it to a plate, then when all the meat is ready add the onions to the pan, keeping the heat still high, and toss them around until they become darkly tinged at the edges—this will take about 5 minutes. After that add the crushed garlic, let that cook for about 30 seconds or so, then turn the heat down, return the meat to the casserole and sprinkle in the flour. Then, using a wooden spoon, stir until all the flour has been absorbed into the juices. It will look rather stodgy and unpromising at this stage but not to worry. The long slow cooking will transform its appearance.

Now gradually stir in the beer and when it's all in, let the whole thing gently come up to simmering point, and while that's happening add salt, freshly ground black pepper and the thyme sprigs and bay leaves. Then just as it begins to bubble put the lid on, transfer it to the center rack of the oven and leave it there for 2½ hours. Don't be tempted to taste it now or halfway through the cooking, as it does take 2½ hours for the beer to mellow and become a luscious sauce.

Just before you want to serve the beef, preheat the broiler. Spread the croutons with the mustard and sprinkle them with the grated Gruyère, then arrange them on top of the meat and pop the casserole under the broiler until the cheese is bubbling. Then serve immediately.

Autumn and Winter Entertaining

Here are a few menu suggestions for warm occasions during the cold seasons.

An Autumn Supper for Six People

First Course

APPLE AND CIDER SALAD WITH MELTED CAMEMBERT DRESSING

Main Course

PORK BRAISED IN CIDER VINEGAR SAUCE
(*recipe* × 1½)
SPICED SAUTÉED RED CABBAGE WITH
CRANBERRIES (*recipe* × 1½)
POTATO AND APPLE RÖSTI
(*recipe* × 1½)

Dessert

FALLEN CHOCOLATE SOUFFLÉ WITH
ARMAGNAC PRUNES AND CRÈME
FRAÎCHE SAUCE

A Sixties Supper for Six People

First Course

PRAWN COCKTAIL 2000

Main Course

BEEF IN DESIGNER BEER (*recipe* × 1½)
ROASTED ROOTS WITH HERBS
(*recipe* × 1½)

Dessert

CLASSIC CRÊPES SUZETTE

A Halloween Supper Party for Eight

First Course

ROASTED PUMPKIN SOUP WITH MELTING
CHEESE (*recipe* × 1½)

Main Course

BRAISED LAMB WITH FLAGEOLET BEANS
(*recipe* × 2)
MASHED POTATOES WITH GARLIC-
INFUSED OLIVE OIL (*recipe* × 2)

Dessert

FOUR-NUT CHOCOLATE BROWNIES

*Three Vegetarian Supper
Parties for Four*

ITALIAN STUFFED EGGPLANT

WARM ROQUEFORT CHEESECAKE WITH
PEARS IN BALSAMIC VINAIGRETTE

GREEN SALAD

PEARS BAKED IN MARSALA WINE

CURRIED PARSNIP AND APPLE SOUP
WITH PARSNIP CRISPS

MASHED BLACK-EYED BEANCAKES WITH
GINGER ONION MARMALADE

OVEN-ROASTED CAULIFLOWER
AND BROCCOLI WITH GARLIC
AND CORIANDER

BANOFFEE CHEESECAKE WITH TOFFEE
PECAN SAUCE

OVEN-BAKED WILD MUSHROOM
RISOTTO

RED ONION TARTE TATIN

GREEN SALAD

LEMON RICOTTA CHEESECAKE WITH
A CONFIT OF LEMONS

*A Quick and Easy Supper
for Four*

First Course

PAN-ROASTED ITALIAN ONIONS WITH
SAN DANIELE HAM AND SHAVED
PECORINO

Main Course

PEPPER-CRUSTED MONKFISH WITH
RED BELL PEPPER RELISH

PESTO MASH

Dessert

TIRAMISU

A Buffet for 18 People

BLINIS WITH SMOKED SALMON, CRÈME
FRAÎCHE AND DILL

BAKED EGGS IN WILD MUSHROOM
TARTLETS (*recipe* × 2)

FETA, OLIVE AND SUN-DRIED TOMATO
SCONES (*recipe* × 2)

RILLETTES OF DUCK WITH CONFIT OF
CRANBERRIES (*recipe* × 2)

SEARED SPICED SALMON STEAKS WITH
BLACK BEAN SALSA (*recipe* × 2)

BLACK BEAN CHILI WITH AVOCADO
SALSA (*recipe* × 2)

RICE

GORGONZOLA CHEESE AND APPLE
STRUDEL WITH SPICED PICKLED
PEARS

GREEN SALAD

Desserts

A RETURN TO THE BLACK FOREST

LEMON RICOTTA CHEESECAKE WITH
A CONFIT OF LEMONS (*recipe* × 2)

MASCARPONE CREAMS AND
CARAMEL SAUCE WITH CARAMELIZED
HAZELNUTS

CHAPTER SEVEN

A Sunday Lunch Revival and Other Meat Dishes

"They live well, eat and drink well, clothe warm and lodge soft . . . in a word the people of England eat the fat, drink the sweet, live better and fare better than the working people of any other nation in Europe. They spend more on back and belly than any other country."

SO WROTE DANIEL DEFOE IN 1726. EVEN AT THE END OF THE CENTURY cartoonists were depicting the gulf between Europeans on a meager diet and fat, jolly Englishmen consuming huge roasts and vast puddings. The truth is that two centuries later we may not be seen to be eating better than other European countries, but one thing that hasn't changed that much is that in Britain we are geologically geared up to rearing very good meat—the hill country of Wales and Scotland, the Lake District and the Peak District and the pastures of the West Country, where cereals won't grow.

What all this is leading up to is that because we have this special gift and because only 4.3 percent of the population are vegetarians (from which it follows that 95.7 percent still enjoy meat), we should celebrate it by keeping up the great British tradition of Sunday lunches. They may not be as vast as they were in the eighteenth century, thank goodness, but they remain an opportunity to enjoy a large roast, which can feed quite a number of people and still leave some for the next day. Cooked skillfully and lovingly, a roast is something that is unmatched anywhere in the world. I hope in the following pages you will join me in the great revival.

*ROAST HAM WITH BLACKENED CRACKLINGS
WITH CITRUS, RUM AND RAISIN SAUCE (SEE PAGE 130)*

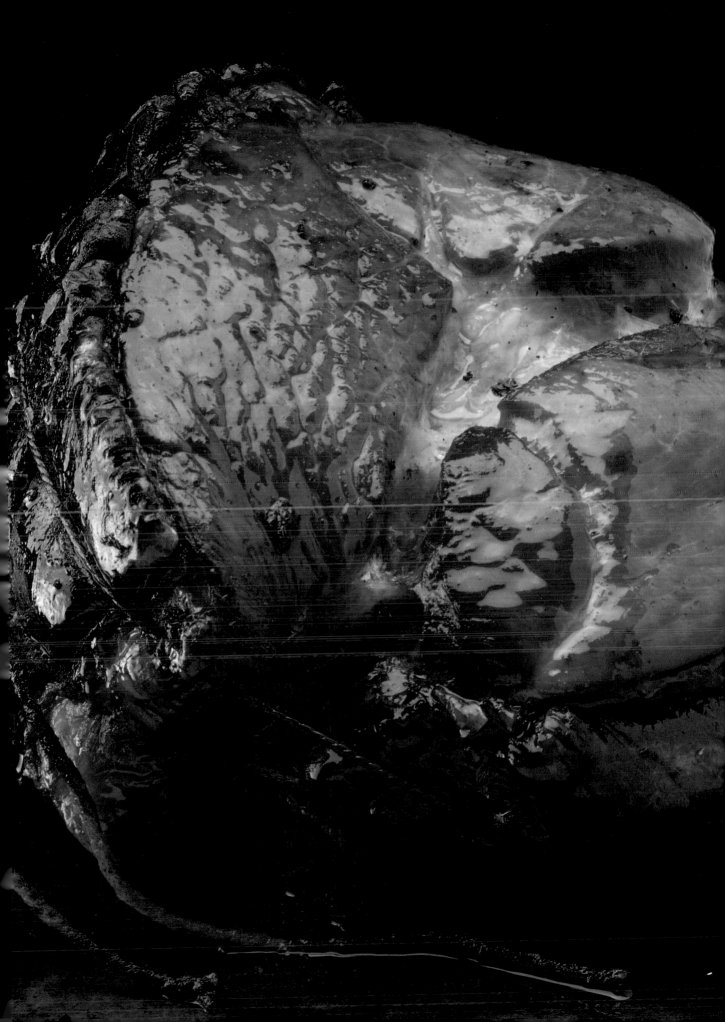

Roast Ham with Blackened Cracklings with Citrus, Rum and Raisin Sauce

Serves 6

H am is now much easier to cook than it used to be. Modern curing methods have eliminated the need for presoaking, which makes it perfect for roasting. If you leave the skin on, score it and paint it with dark molasses, it turns into superb cracklings during the cooking. It's then a very easy roast to carve, and serving it with Citrus, Rum and Raisin Sauce is a heavenly combination. If possible, always make this sweet-sharp sauce the day before you need it, so the raisins have plenty of time to absorb all the flavors and become nice and plump. (See photograph on page 129.)

5 pounds prime ham, smoked or
    unsmoked
1 tablespoon dark molasses
Sea salt crystals

FOR THE SAUCE:
1 large juicy orange

1 lime
⅓ cup dark rum
⅔ cup raisins
½ cup dark brown sugar
2 teaspoons cornstarch

You will also need a solid shallow roasting pan.

As soon as you buy the ham remove all the wrapping and dry the skin really well with paper towels. After that, using a very sharp knife, score the skin in a crisscross pattern making little ½-inch diamonds. This is quite easy to do if you insert the tip of the knife only, then holding the skin taut with one hand drag the tip of the knife down in long movements. When you've done this place the ham on a plate and store uncovered on the bottom of the fridge, if possible for 2 or 3 days before you need it. This means the skin will go on drying, which makes better cracklings.

You can make the sauce well in advance. All you do is remove the outer zest from the orange using a potato peeler so that you don't get any of the pith. Then pile the little strips on top of one another, and using a very sharp knife cut them into really thin needle-sized strips. If you've got the orange peel piled up and your knife is sharp this is a lot easier than it sounds. Next remove the zest from the lime, this time using a fine grater, and squeeze the juice from the lime and orange.

Place all the sauce ingredients except the cornstarch into a saucepan. Whisk the cornstarch into the mixture and place the pan over a gentle heat, whisking all the time until it starts to simmer. As soon as this happens the sauce will change from opaque to clear; then remove it from the heat, and as soon as it is cool enough pour it into a serving dish, cover with plastic wrap, and chill until needed.

To cook the ham preheat the oven to 475°F. If the molasses is very cold, warm it slightly, then using a pastry brush or a wedge of paper towel lightly coat all the little diamonds of skin. After that sprinkle the skin with salt crystals, pressing them well in.

Now place the ham in a roasting pan skin side up (if it won't stand up straight use a couple of wedges of foil to keep it in position). Now place the roasting pan in the oven and after 25 minutes turn the heat down to 350°F. Then continue to let the ham cook for 1¾–2 hours—it should feel tender all the way through when tested with a skewer. After it comes out of the oven give it at least 30 minutes' resting time, covered with foil, in a warm place. Remove the sauce from the fridge and serve the ham carved in slices, giving each person some cracklings and spooning some sauce over.

Pork Stroganoff with Three Mustards

Serves 2

This is what I'd call a five-star supper dish for two people, with the added bonus that it only takes about 20 minutes to prepare from start to finish. Serve it with plain boiled basmati rice and a salad of tossed green leaves.

12 ounces pork tenderloin
1½ cups small portobello mushrooms
1 teaspoon ground mustard
1 heaping teaspoon whole grain mustard
1 heaping teaspoon Dijon mustard
1 cup crème fraîche

1 tablespoon butter
½ tablespoon peanut oil
1 small onion, halved and thinly sliced
Salt and freshly ground black pepper
⅓ cup dry white wine

First of all prepare the pork by trimming it and cutting it into little strips 3 inches long and ¼ inch wide. Now prepare the mushrooms by slicing them through the stalk into thin slices. Then in a small bowl mix together the 3 mustards with the crème fraîche.

When you're ready to cook the pork, take a 9-inch solid skillet, then heat the butter and oil together over a medium heat, add the onion slices and fry them gently for about 2–3 minutes until they are soft. Then, using a slotted spoon, remove the onion to a plate, turn the heat up to its highest setting and when it's smoking hot add the strips of pork and fry them quickly, keeping them on the move all the time so they cook evenly without burning. After that add the mushrooms and toss these around to cook very briefly until their juices start to run. Next return the onion slices to the pan and stir them in. Season well with salt and pepper, then add the wine and let it bubble and reduce slightly before adding the crème fraîche mixture. Now stir everything together and let the sauce bubble and reduce to half its original volume. Then serve the stroganoff immediately spooned over plain basmati rice.

Autumn Lamb
Braised in Beaujolais

Serves 6–8

This is certainly one of the best ways to cook lamb in the autumn or winter months—slowly braising it under a tent of foil keeps it beautifully moist and really seems to develop its full flavor. Adding the root vegetables to cook in the braising juices is also very convenient and makes this an easy main course for entertaining. (See photograph on pages 136–137.)

4 tablespoons olive oil
8 small carrots (about 8 ounces)
2 turnips (about 8 ounces)
8 small red-skinned potatoes (about
*   1½ pounds)*
4 small parsnips (about 1 pound)
8 shallots or small onions (about
*   8 ounces)*
3 large cloves garlic, unpeeled
1 leg of lamb, 5–5½ pounds
Rock salt and freshly ground black
*   pepper*

1 bottle (750 ml) Beaujolais
1 teaspoon each chopped fresh thyme
*   and rosemary leaves*
A few fresh thyme sprigs
1 rosemary sprig
1 bay leaf
1 heaping teaspoon red-currant jelly

To Garnish:
2 tablespoons chopped fresh parsley or
*   1 tablespoon chopped fresh thyme*
*   leaves*

You will also need a roasting pan approximately 14½ × 10½ inches and 2 inches deep,
and a large shallow roasting pan.

Preheat the oven to 450°F.

First pour 3 tablespoons of the olive oil into the shallow roasting pan and put it into the oven as it preheats. Then prepare all the vegetables as follows: Scrub the carrots, turnips and potatoes; trim the carrots and turnips, leaving the carrots whole but chopping the turnips (with skins left on) into quarters, and cut the potatoes lengthwise into 4 pieces (unpeeled). Now peel the parsnips and cut them into halves; and finally peel the shallots but leave them whole.

Now dry the vegetables thoroughly with a clean cloth. When the oven is up to temperature, carefully remove the shallow roasting pan, using oven mitts to protect your hands. Place this over a medium heat on the stovetop and spoon the prepared vegetables and the unpeeled garlic into the oil. Turn them over to make sure they are well coated and return the pan to the top rack of the oven for 25–30 minutes, turning them over at half time so that they roast evenly.

While they are in the oven, prepare the lamb by placing it in the roasting pan and rubbing it all over with the remaining tablespoon of olive oil, some crushed rock salt and coarsely ground black pepper.

When the vegetables are nicely tinged brown at the edges, remove them from the oven and set aside. Place the roasting pan with the lamb in the oven on the highest rack that will take it, and let it start to roast for 30 minutes or until it has turned a good golden color.

Take the lamb out of the oven, then reduce the temperature to 325°F and spoon off any fat to use later. Place the roasting pan over medium heat on top of the stove, pour in the Beaujolais and baste the meat with it. Then sprinkle with the chopped thyme and rosemary.

As soon as the wine begins to bubble, turn off the heat and cover the whole pan with a tent of foil (without it touching the meat). Fold the foil tight under the rim of the pan and place it in the oven—on the center rack this time—and let it continue cooking for 1½ hours.

When the time is up, remove the roasting pan from the oven and once again transfer it to direct heat. Carefully remove the foil and baste the meat well with the wine. Spoon the browned vegetables all around in the wine, season them with salt and freshly ground black pepper and pop in the sprigs of thyme and rosemary and the bay leaf. When it has come back to simmering point, replace the foil and cook for a further 1½ hours.

After that, remove the meat and vegetables to warmed serving dishes, discarding the sprigs of herbs, then cover to keep warm. Place the roasting pan over direct heat once more and let the sauce reduce. Squeeze the garlic pulp out of the skins into the sauce and whisk this in along with the red-currant jelly.

Taste and season the sauce with salt and freshly ground black pepper, then pour it into a warm serving pitcher. Sprinkle the lamb and vegetables with the parsley or thyme and serve.

Classic Roast Pork with Cracklings and Roasted Stuffed Apples with Thyme and Parsley

Serves 8

This recipe is for pork loin roast, which provides maximum cracklings, but the butcher must chine it for you—that is, loosen the bone, yet leave it attached so that it can eventually be cut away to make carving easier.

How to get crisp, crunchy cracklings is not a problem if you follow a few simple guidelines. Buy the pork a couple of days before you need to cook it, remove any plastic wrap, put it on a plate immediately and dry it as thoroughly as possible with absorbent paper towels. After that, leave it uncovered in the lowest part of the refrigerator so that the skin can become as dry as possible before you start cooking.

5 pounds pork loin roast, chined
1 small onion
Sea salt and freshly ground black pepper
1 tablespoon flour

1 ¼ cups dry cider
1 ¼ cups vegetable stock (or potato water)

You will also need a solid roasting pan, approximately 12 × 10 inches.

Preheat the oven to 475°F.

While the oven is preheating, score the skin of the pork. It will be scored already, but it's always best to add a few more lines. To do this you can use the point of a very sharp paring knife, or you can even buy a special scalpel from a kitchenware store! What you need to do is score the skin all over into thin strips, bringing the blade of the knife about halfway through the fat beneath the skin.

Now place the pork in a pan, skin side up, halve the onion and wedge the 2 pieces in slightly underneath the meat. Now take about 1 tablespoon of crushed salt crystals and sprinkle it evenly over the skin, pressing it in as much as you can. Then place the pork on a high rack in the oven and roast the meat for 25 minutes. After that turn the heat down to 375°F and calculate the cooking time, allowing 35 minutes to the pound. In this case it would be 2½ hours.

There's no need to baste pork as there is enough fat to keep the meat moist. The way to tell if the meat is cooked is to insert a skewer in the thickest part, and the juices that run out should be absolutely clear without any trace of pinkness. When the pork is cooked remove it from the oven and give it at least 30 minutes' resting time before carving. While that is happening, tilt the pan and spoon all the fat off, leaving only the juices. The onion will probably be black and charred, which gives the gravy a lovely rich color. Leave the onion in, then place the roasting pan over direct heat, turned to low, sprinkle in the flour and quickly work it into the juices with a wooden spoon.

Now turn the heat up to medium and gradually add the cider and the stock, this time using a balloon whisk until it comes up to simmering point and you have a smooth rich gravy. Taste and season with salt and pepper, then discard the onion and pour the gravy into a warmed gravy boat.

Serve the pork carved in slices, giving everyone some cracklings and one roasted stuffed apple.

Roasted Stuffed Apples with Thyme and Parsley

1 pound good-quality pork sausage meat
1 tablespoon chopped fresh parsley
2 teaspoons chopped fresh thyme
Salt and freshly ground black pepper

8 small dessert apples (such as Granny Smith)
A little melted butter
8 small thyme sprigs

About half an hour before the end of the cooking time of the pork roast, prepare the apples. First of all in a small bowl mix the sausage meat, chopped parsley and thyme, and add a good seasoning of salt and pepper. Using a potato peeler or an apple corer, remove the core from the apples, then cut out a little more apple with a sharp knife to make the cavity slightly larger. Now divide the sausage meat mixture into eighths. Then roll each portion into a sausage shape and fit that into the cavity of each apple. There will be some at the top that won't go in. So just pat that into a neat round shape. Now make a small incision around the central circumference of the apple. Brush each one with melted butter and insert a little sprig of thyme on top. Place the apples on a shallow baking sheet. Then when the pork comes out of the oven, pop the apples in to roast for about 25 minutes.

NOTE: *If you're using the oven for roast potatoes and turning the heat up when the pork is cooked, the apples will cook quite comfortably on a lower rack at the higher temperature.*

NEXT PAGE: AUTUMN LAMB BRAISED IN BEAUJOLAIS (SEE PAGE 132)

Steak and Kidney Pudding

Serves 6

I’ve subtitled this recipe "Kate and Sidney make a comeback," after the Cockney slang version of this world-famous recipe. It's certainly time for a revival because it has been shamefully neglected and because it really is the ultimate in comfort food. Homemade is a far superior thing to any factory version and, believe it or not, it's dead simple to make. Once it's on the heat you can forget all about it till suppertime—except for the amazingly appetizing wafts coming out of the kitchen.

FOR THE SUET CRUST PASTRY:
2½ cups self-rising flour
Salt and freshly ground black pepper
6 ounces (1½ cups) shredded beef suet or grated chilled butter

FOR THE FILLING:
1¼ pounds chuck steak

8 ounces ox kidney after trimming, so buy 10 ounces
2 tablespoons flour, well-seasoned
1 medium onion, sliced
Cold water
1 teaspoon Worcestershire sauce
Salt and freshly ground black pepper

You will also need a well-buttered pudding basin of 3 pints capacity and a steamer.

To make the pastry, first sift the flour and salt into a large mixing bowl. Add some freshly ground black pepper, then add the suet and mix it into the flour using the blade of a knife. When it's evenly blended, add a few drops of cold water and start to mix with the knife, using curving movements and turning the mixture around. The aim is to bring it together as a dough, so keep adding drops of water until it begins to get really sticky. Now abandon the knife, go in with your hands and bring it all together until you have a nice smooth elastic dough that leaves the bowl clean. It's worth noting that suet pastry always needs more water than other types, so if it is still a bit dry just go on adding a few drops at a time. After that, take a quarter of the dough for the top, then roll the rest out fairly thickly. What you need is a round approximately 13 inches in diameter. Now line the basin with the pastry, pressing it well all around. To make the filling, chop the steak and kidney into fairly small cubes, toss them in the seasoned flour, then add them to the pastry-lined basin with the slices of onion. Add enough cold water to reach almost the top of the meat and sprinkle in the Worcestershire sauce and a seasoning of salt and pepper.

Roll out the pastry top, dampen its edges and put it in position on the pudding. Seal well and cover with a double sheet of foil, pleated in the center to allow room for expansion while cooking. Now secure it with string, making a little handle so that you can lift it out of the hot steamer. Then place it in a steamer over boiling water. Steam for 5 hours, topping off the boiling water halfway through. You can either serve the pudding by spooning portions straight out of the bowl, or slide a palette knife around the edge and turn the whole thing out onto a serving plate (which is more fun!).

Steak and Kidney Gravy

*A*lthough steak and kidney pudding has a lovely juicy filling, it's always nice to have a little extra gravy spooned around—and because there are always some meat trimmings left over, this is a good way to use them.

*Meat trimmings from the steak
    and kidney*
1 medium onion, halved
2½ cups water

Salt and freshly ground black pepper
1 teaspoon beef drippings
1 tablespoon flour
A few drops Worcestershire sauce

Simply place the meat trimmings in a saucepan with half the onion, cover with the water, add some seasoning and simmer for approximately 1 hour. Then strain the stock and in the same pan fry the remaining onion, chopped small, in the beef drippings until soft and blackened at the edges. Then stir in the flour and gradually add the stock little by little to make a smooth gravy. Taste to check the seasoning and add a few drops of Worcestershire sauce.

NEXT PAGE: SUNDAY LUNCH WITH
ROAST RIBS OF TRADITIONAL BEEF
AND ALL THE TRIMMINGS (SEE PAGE 142)

Roast Ribs of Traditional Beef
with Yorkshire Pudding and Horseradish,
Crème Fraîche and Mustard Sauce

Serves 6–8

I still think the roast beef of old England served with meaty gravy, crisp Yorkshire pudding and crunchy roast potatoes is not only one of the world's greatest meals, it is something the British do better than anyone else. The whole thing can be a bit daunting, so if you've never done it before, for the Sunday lunch novice there is a very easy-to-follow guide on page 146. (See photograph on pages 140–41.)

3-rib roast, wing end or sirloin
  of beef on the bone (approximately
  6 pounds)
½ tablespoon ground mustard
½ tablespoon flour
Salt and freshly ground black pepper
1 small onion, halved

FOR THE GRAVY:
¼ cup flour (about 1 heaping tablespoon)

Approximately 4 cups hot vegetable
  stock or water from the potatoes
Salt and freshly ground black pepper

FOR THE HORSERADISH, CRÈME
FRAÎCHE AND MUSTARD SAUCE:
4 tablespoons hot horseradish
1 heaping tablespoon crème fraîche
2 teaspoons whole grain mustard
Salt and freshly ground black pepper

You will also need a solid roasting pan.   Preheat the oven to 475°F.

If you dust the fat surface of the beef with the mustard and flour—just rub them in gently—then season with salt and pepper, it becomes extra crusty during cooking. So do that first, then place the meat in a roasting pan and tuck the 2 pieces of onion in close to the meat. The onion will caramelize as the beef cooks and give a lovely flavor to the gravy.

Now place the meat just above the center in the oven and give it 20 minutes' cooking at the initial temperature; after that turn the heat down to 375°F and cook it for 15 minutes to the pound for rare, adding another 15 minutes for medium-rare and another 30 minutes for well done. While the beef is cooking lift it out of the oven from time to time, tilt the pan and baste the meat really well with its own juices—this ensures that the flavor that is concentrated in the fat keeps permeating the meat, and at the same time the fat keeps everything moist and succulent. While you're basting close the oven door in order not to lose heat. When the beef is cooked, remove it from the oven, transfer it to a board and allow it to stand in a warm place for up to an hour, loosely covered with foil, before carving—to let all the precious juices that have bubbled up to the surface seep back into the flesh. Also, as the meat relaxes it will be easier to carve. Meanwhile, make the gravy.

After removing the meat from the roasting pan, tilt to see how much fat remains—you need about 2 tablespoons for this amount of gravy (the rest should be spooned into a dish and used for the Yorkshire Pudding, see opposite). Place the roasting pan over medium heat and sprinkle the flour into the fatty juices. Then, using a wire whisk, blend in the flour using a circular movement.

When you have a smooth paste, slowly add the hot vegetable stock, whisking all the time, and scraping the bottom of the pan to incorporate all the residue from the roast. When the gravy is bubbling, taste to see if it needs a little more seasoning, then let it carry on bubbling. Reduce it slightly to concentrate the flavor.

You can now pour the gravy into the gravy boat and keep it warm if lunch is imminent or, if not, leave it in the roasting pan and reheat gently just before serving.

To make the horseradish sauce, simply mix all the ingredients together in the bowl you're going to serve it in.

Traditional Yorkshire Pudding

Serves 6–8

1⅓ cups flour	¾ cup milk
2 large eggs	½ cup water
Salt and freshly ground black pepper	2 tablespoons beef drippings

You will also need a solid roasting pan measuring 11 × 9 inches. Preheat the oven to 425°F.

Begin by placing a sieve over a large mixing bowl, then sift the flour in, holding the sieve up high to give the flour a good airing as it goes down into the bowl. Now, with the back of a tablespoon, make a well in the center of the flour and break the eggs into it. Add the salt and pepper.

Now measure the milk and water into a measuring cup. Then begin to beat the eggs with an electric mixer, and as you beat them the flour around the edges will be slowly incorporated. When the mixture becomes stiff, simply add the milk-and-water mixture gradually, keeping the mixer going. Stop and scrape the sides of the bowl with a spatula so that any lumps can be pushed down into the batter, then beat again till all is smooth. Now the batter is ready for use and although it's been rumored that batter left to stand is better, I have found no foundation for this—so just make it whenever is convenient.

To cook the Yorkshire pudding, remove the meat from the oven (or if it's not ready place it on a lower rack) and turn the oven up to the above temperature. Spoon 2 tablespoons of beef drippings into the roasting pan and allow it to preheat in the oven. When the oven is up to temperature remove the pan using an oven mitt, and place it over direct heat (turned to medium). Then, when the drippings begin to shimmer and smoke a little, pour in the batter. Tip it evenly all around and then place the pan on a high rack in the oven and cook the Yorkshire pudding for 40 minutes or until golden brown and crisp. Serve it cut into squares *presto pronto*.

NOTE: *I remember when I was about five years old my Yorkshire grandmother giving me slices of hot Yorkshire pudding with light molasses spooned over as a dessert—try it sometime, it's really good.*

An Authentic Ragù Bolognese

Makes eight 8-ounce portions, each serving 2 people

In Britain it's really sad that so often stewed ground beef with the addition of herbs and tomato purée gets presented as bolognese sauce—even, dare I say it, in lesser Italian restaurants. Yet properly made, an authentic ragù bolognese bears absolutely no resemblance to this travesty. The real thing is a very slowly cooked, thick, concentrated, dark mahogany-colored sauce, and because of this, very little is needed to coat pasta and give it that evocative flavor of Italy. Making ragù is not at all difficult, and if you give a little of your time to make it in bulk, then freeze it for the future, you'll always have the basis of a delightful meal when there's no time to cook.

6 tablespoons extra virgin olive oil
2 medium onions, finely chopped
4 large cloves garlic, chopped
5 ounces pancetta or bacon
1 pound lean ground beef
1 pound ground pork
8 ounces chicken livers

Two 14-ounce cans Italian chopped tomatoes
14 ounces double-concentrate tomato paste
1 ¾ cups red wine
Salt and freshly ground black pepper
½ whole nutmeg, grated
1 bunch (or 1 ounce) fresh basil

You will also need a large flameproof casserole of 5 quarts capacity. Preheat the oven to 275°F.

First take a large skillet, the largest you have, heat 3 tablespoons of the oil and gently fry the onions and garlic over medium heat for about 10 minutes, stirring from time to time. While the onions are softening, chop the pancetta: The best way to do this after opening the package is to roll the contents into a sausage shape, then using a sharp knife slice it lengthwise into 4, then slice the lengths across as finely as possible. After 10 minutes, add this to the skillet to join the onions and garlic and continue cooking them all for another 5 minutes. Now transfer this mixture to the casserole. Add another tablespoon of oil to the skillet, turn the heat up to its highest, then add the ground beef and brown it, breaking it up and moving it around in the pan. When the beef is browned, add it to the casserole. Heat another tablespoon of oil and do exactly the same with the ground pork. While the pork is browning, trim the chicken livers, rinse them under cold running water, dry them thoroughly with paper towels and chop them minutely small. When the pork is browned, transfer that to the casserole, then heat the remaining tablespoon of oil and brown the pieces of chicken livers. Add these to the casserole.

Now you've finished with the skillet, so get rid of that and place the casserole over direct heat, give everything a good stir together, then add the tomatoes, the tomato paste, the red wine, a really good seasoning of salt and pepper and the nutmeg.

Allow this to come up to simmering point. Then strip the leaves from half the basil, chop them very finely and add them to the pot. As soon as everything is simmering, place the casserole on the center rack of the oven and leave it to cook slowly, without a lid, for 4 hours. It's a good idea to have a look after 3 hours to make sure all is well, but what you should end up with is a thick, concentrated sauce with only a trace of liquid left in it, then remove it from the oven, taste to check the seasoning, strip the leaves off the remaining basil, chop them small and stir them in.

Then when the sauce is completely cooled, divide it, using scales, by spooning 8 ounces into plastic freezer bags. Seal them, leaving a little bit of air at the top to allow room for expansion. Each 8-ounce package, thoroughly defrosted and reheated, will provide enough ragù for 8 ounces of pasta, which will serve 2 people.

N O T E : *If you don't have a 3-quart capacity ovenproof casserole you can use a large baking dish preheated in the oven, but make sure everything comes up to simmering point in a large saucepan first.*

Crêpe Cannelloni with Ragù

Serves 4

In Umbria in Italy they make crêpes for their cannelloni. Stuffed with ragù bolognese and topped with béchamel and mozzarella, it's a truly inspired version.

1 quantity crêpes (see page 179)
2 8-ounce portions ragù bolognese
  (see opposite)

Freshly grated nutmeg
Salt and freshly ground black pepper
¾ cup grated mozzarella

F O R   T H E   B É C H A M E L   S A U C E :
3 tablespoons butter
¼ cup flour
Scant 2 cups cold milk

F O R   T H E   T O P P I N G :
½ cup freshly grated Parmesan
  (Parmigiano-Reggiano)
½ tablespoon olive oil

You will also need an ovenproof baking dish 10 × 8 inches, 2 inches deep or the equivalent, well buttered.
Preheat the oven to 400°F.

Both the crêpes and the ragù can be made well ahead and chilled or frozen. Make the béchamel sauce by the all-in-one method, that is by adding everything (except the mozzarella) to a saucepan and whisking over medium heat till smooth and thickened. Then continue to cook gently for 5 minutes, whisking now and then to prevent it sticking. Now lay the crêpes out and place an equal quantity (about a heaping tablespoon) of cold ragù on each one and roll up, folding in the edges. Next lay the crêpes in the ovenproof dish side by side with the ends tucked up underneath, then sprinkle over the grated mozzarella. Pour the sauce over the top to give an even covering. Finally sprinkle over the grated Parmesan and oil and place the dish on a high rack in the oven for 30 minutes or until the surface is golden and the sauce bubbling.

N O T E : *You may assemble all this well in advance, but make sure everything is cold before you cover and chill it until needed. These can also be cooked, 3 crêpes per person, in individual ovenproof dishes—in which case cut the cooking time to 20 minutes.*

Timings for
One O'Clock Lunches for Eight

Sunday traditional lunches for eight guests with no last-minute panics. Impossible?
Not if you follow these straightforward timings.

Roast Ribs of Traditional Beef	Perfect Roast Potatoes	Compote of Glazed Shallots	Traditional Yorkshire Pudding
See Pages 142–43	*See Page 149*	*See Page 160*	*See Page 143*

Roast Ribs of Traditional Beef

See Pages 142–43

6-POUND RIB ROAST (OR SIRLOIN)

Timings below are for beef cooked to medium.

9:30 AM Place the beef in the oven, lower the oven temperature after 30 minutes, baste 3 times during roasting.

12 noon Remove the meat from the oven, cover loosely with foil and keep warm. Increase the oven temperature for the roast potatoes.

Cooking time: 2½ hours. Adjust cooking times.

Rare: 2 hours.

Medium rare: 2¼ hours.

Well done: 2¾ hours.

Perfect Roast Potatoes

See Page 149

12:10 PM Place the prepared potatoes in the oven on a high rack for 40–50 minutes.

Compote of Glazed Shallots

See Page 160

11:45 AM Place the prepared shallots over a gentle heat for 1¼ hour.

Traditional Yorkshire Pudding

See Page 143

12:20 PM Place the Yorkshire pudding on the middle rack for 40 minutes.

Gravy

Make at 12:45 PM.

Traditional Roast Stuffed Chicken

See Pages 76–77

TWO 4-POUND CHICKENS

10:45 AM Place them in the oven, baste every 30 minutes.

12 noon Raise the oven temperature to 425°F.

12:30 PM Remove the chickens from the oven. Keep them warm.

Cooking time: 1¾ hours

Perfect Roast Potatoes

See Page 149

12:10 PM Place the prepared potatoes on rack above the chickens for 40–50 minutes.

Sautéed Caramelized Fennel

See Page 158

(1½ Times Recipe)

12 noon Steam the fennel.

12:10 PM Place the fennel over direct heat for 40–50 minutes.

Steamed Broccoli

Cooking time: 8 minutes

Giblet Gravy

Make at 12:45 PM.

Roast Ham with Blackened Cracklings

✳

See Pages 130–31

5-POUND HAM

9:45 AM Place the ham in the oven, reducing the oven temperature after 25 minutes.

12 noon Raise the oven temperature to 425°F.

12:10 PM Remove the ham from the oven, keeping it warm and loosely covered with foil.

Cooking time: 2½ hours

Perfect Roast Potatoes

✳

See Page 149

12:10 PM Place the prepared potatoes in the oven on a high rack for 40–50 minutes.

Spiced Sautéed Red Cabbage

✳

See Page 155

(You will need 1½ times the recipe.)

Precook the cabbage at a convenient time during the morning.

12:50 PM Reheat gently for 8–10 minutes.

Citrus, Rum and Raisin Sauce

✳

See Page 130

Make at a convenient time in the morning. Chill until needed.

Classic Roast Pork with Cracklings

✳

See Pages 134–35

5-POUND LOIN OF PORK (CHINED)

9:45 AM Place the pork in the oven.

12 noon Raise the oven temperature to 425°F.

12:15 PM Remove the pork from the oven and keep warm.

Cooking time: 2½ hours

Perfect Roast Potatoes

✳

See Page 149

12:10 PM Place the prepared potatoes in the oven on a high rack for 40–50 minutes.

12:40 PM Place the stuffed apples on a low rack for 20 minutes. (They will cook at this slightly higher temperature quite comfortably if you are using the oven for roasted potatoes.)

Compote of Glazed Shallots

✳

See Page 160

11:45 AM Place the prepared shallots over a gentle heat for 1¼ hour.

Brussels Sprouts

✳

CHOOSE SMALL, TIGHT BRUSSELS SPROUTS, TRIMMED

Make a crosslike incision at the stalk end. Steam or boil for 5–8 minutes, then drain (reserve liquid for gravy). Toss in a little hot melted butter.

12:50 PM Make the gravy.

Autumn Lamb Braised in Beaujolais

✳

See Pages 132–33

5–5½-POUND LEG OF LAMB

8:45 AM Place the vegetables in the oven to brown 30 minutes; turn them over halfway.

9:15 AM Place the lamb in the oven; lower the temperature after 30 minutes.

11:15 AM Add the browned vegetables to the lamb.

12:45 PM Remove the lamb and vegetables, keep warm, finish the sauce.

Cooking time: 3½ hours

CHAPTER EIGHT

Winter Vegetable Selection

WHILE I WELCOME THE NEW VARIETIES OF SALAD INGREDIENTS FROM AROUND the world that can enliven our winter salads, I have to admit I'm not such a great fan of imported vegetables. I enjoy summer vegetables in the summer and early autumn and after that I'm quite happy to forget about them and look forward to whatever winter has to offer: onions, young leeks, shallots, tiny button Brussels sprouts, crisp squeaky cabbages, fragrant celery. And I love all the roots—celeriac, carrots, rutabagas, turnips, Jerusalem artichokes and, best of all, parsnips.

First and foremost I think we need to enjoy all these wonderful vegetables simply as they are, especially when they are accompanying dishes with lots of strong, rich flavors. Let us not underestimate simple boiled cabbage, or leeks cooked just in their own juices with a knob of butter, or a dish of carrots steamed then chopped small with a seasoning of black pepper—one of my particular favorites. However, the winter vegetable season does seem to go on for a long time and the limited varieties may get a bit repetitive, so it's also a good time to experiment with new ideas for cooking them, and I hope that's what you'll find on the following pages.

Because of the enormous popularity of oven-roasting vegetables in the *Summer Collection,* and seeing how liberating it is when you have to attend to other parts of the meal, I have included here new ideas for oven-roasting winter vegetables along the same lines. This chapter also celebrates the recent revival of mashed potatoes, which offers all kinds of variations and, when made carefully, is one of the real joys of winter.

Perfect Roast Potatoes

T he amounts here are not vital because it depends on who's greedy and who's on a diet and so on, but I find that eight ounces per person is enough—yielding three each and a few extras for inevitable second helpings! I like Désirée best of all, but in the U.S., Russet, Burbank or Idaho would be a good choice.

4 ounces drippings or lard   *Salt*
4 pounds potatoes

You will also need a shallow solid roasting pan 16 × 12 inches.

Preheat the oven to 425°F.

First place the roasting pan with the drippings in it on the highest rack of the oven while it preheats. Thinly peel the potatoes using a potato peeler, then cut them into fairly even-sized pieces, leaving the small ones whole. Then place them in a saucepan, pour over boiling water from a kettle, just to cover, then add salt and simmer for about 10 minutes. After that lift one out with a skewer and see if the outer edge is fluffy. You can test this by running the point of the skewer along the surface—if it stays smooth, give it a few more minutes.

Then drain off the water, reserving some for the gravy. Place the lid back on the saucepan and, holding the lid on firmly with your hand protected by a cloth or oven mitt, shake the saucepan vigorously up and down. This shaking roughens up the cooked edges of the potatoes and makes them floury and fluffy—this is the secret of the crunchy edges.

Now, still using the oven mitt to protect your hand, remove the hot roasting pan containing its sizzling drippings and transfer to direct heat (medium). Then use a long-handled spoon and quickly lower the potatoes into the hot drippings. When they are all in, tilt the pan and baste each one so it's completely coated with drippings. Now place them back on the highest rack of the oven and leave them unattended for 40–50 minutes or until they are golden brown. There's no need to turn them over at half-time—they will brown evenly by themselves. Sprinkle them with a little salt before serving immediately; they lose their crunch if you keep them waiting. If they're ready before you are, turn the oven off and leave them inside.

Fluffy Mashed Potatoes

Serves 4

Is there anyone anywhere who does not love a fluffy cloud of creamy mashed potatoes—especially if they are carefully and properly made? Grand chefs sometimes make a great deal of complicated techniques, but if you have an electric mixer it really couldn't be easier.

2 pounds potatoes (Idaho, Russet or
    Burbank)
Salt and freshly ground black pepper

½ stick butter
⅓ cup milk
½ cup crème fraîche

Use a potato peeler to pare off the skins as thinly as possible and then cut the potatoes into even-sized chunks, not too small. If they are large, quarter them, and if they are small, halve them. Put the potato chunks in a large saucepan, then pour boiling water over them, add ½ tablespoon of salt, put on a lid and simmer gently until they are absolutely tender—they should take approximately 25 minutes. The way to tell whether they are ready is to pierce them with a skewer in the thickest part; the potato should not be hard in the center. And you need to be careful here, because if they are slightly underdone you do get lumps!

When the potatoes are cooked, drain them. Cover them with a clean cloth to absorb some of the steam for about 5 minutes, then add the butter, milk and crème fraîche. When you first go in with the mixer use a slow speed to break the potatoes up, then increase it to high and whip them up to a smooth, creamy, fluffy mass. Taste and season with pepper and more salt if they need it.

Mashed Potatoes with Garlic-Infused Olive Oil

Serves 4

Dipping bread directly into fine olive oil brings out the full flavor. The same happens with potatoes—a sublime combination.

3 large cloves garlic, halved lengthwise
⅔ cup best-quality extra virgin
    olive oil

2 pounds potatoes (Idaho, Russet or
    Burbank)
Salt and freshly ground black pepper

First place the garlic and olive oil in a small saucepan over the gentlest heat possible—a heat diffuser is good for this—and leave for 1 hour for the garlic to infuse and become really soft. Prepare and cook the potatoes as above, then, using an electric mixer on a low speed, begin to break them up using half the garlic and oil. As soon as all that is incorporated, add the rest of the garlic and oil and whisk until smooth, seasoning well with salt and freshly ground black pepper.

Pesto Mash

Serves 2–3

*N*ot East meets West this time, but Italy meets Britain. Take a classic Italian sauce, add it to some mash (without the sausage) and what you have is a wonderful accompaniment to fish. It's best made with fresh pesto, available from the refrigerated section in supermarkets (rather than the bottled version, which is not as good).

1 pound potatoes (Idaho, Russet or Burbank)

½ cup fresh pesto
Salt and freshly ground black pepper

Prepare and cook the potatoes as in the basic recipe opposite, then add the pesto and a seasoning of salt and pepper. Using an electric mixer, start beating at a slow speed to break up the potatoes, then increase the speed to fast and whip them up to a smooth purée. Now return the saucepan to a low heat and use a wooden spoon to stir the potatoes until they become hot—about 1 minute. Check the seasoning and serve.

Colcannon Potatoes

Serves 4

*A*nother supremely good version of mashed potatoes, this is based on the Irish recipe for Colcannon potatoes, which were originally served in a fluffy pile with a sort of well in the center that was filled with melted butter. The idea was to dip each forkful into the butter before eating it! Perhaps our health consciousness would prohibit this today, but even without the butter it's extremely good.

1 ½ pounds potatoes (Idaho, Russet or Burbank)
¾ stick butter
8 ounces firm green cabbage, very finely sliced or shredded

12 scallions, trimmed and very finely sliced, including the green parts
A good grinding or two of nutmeg
⅓ cup half-and-half
Salt and freshly ground black pepper

Prepare and cook the potatoes as in the basic recipe opposite. Meanwhile melt ¼ stick butter in a large skillet and sauté the cabbage for about 3 minutes, keeping it on the move until it's tender and slightly golden at the edges. Then add the sliced scallions and continue to cook for another minute.

Next drain the potatoes, return them to the pan, cover with a clean cloth and leave them aside for 2 minutes to allow the cloth to absorb the excess steam. Now, using an electric mixer, add the nutmeg, half-and-half and remaining butter. Whisk the potatoes to a light fluffy mass before tasting and seasoning. Then stir in the contents of the skillet and serve with or without extra melted butter.

Potato and Apple Rösti

*T*his is extremely good served with pork dishes and really meaty pork sausages. I think it goes particularly well with the Pork Braised in Cider Vinegar Sauce on page 109. If you're cooking it for friends, it can all be made in advance and kept in the refrigerator until needed. And the best news of all is it gets cooked in the oven so there's no last-minute fuss and bother with frying.

2 medium round white potatoes (about 10 ounces)
2 tablespoons fresh lemon juice
2 medium Granny Smith apples

Salt and freshly ground black pepper
Freshly grated nutmeg
1 tablespoon flour
½ stick butter, melted

You will also need a solid ovenproof baking sheet 14 × 10 inches.

First of all place the scrubbed potatoes in a saucepan, add some salt and enough boiling water to just cover, then boil them for 8 minutes (it's important not to overboil them). Then drain off the water, and while they are cooling, you can deal with the apples.

First place the lemon juice into a shallow dish, then peel, core, quarter and grate the apples using the coarse side of a grater placed directly over the dish. When all the apple is grated, quickly toss it well in the lemon juice to prevent it turning brown.

Now peel the potatoes and grate them in the same way, but this time letting the shreds fall into a large bowl. Now transfer the apple to join the potato, squeezing it in your hand to leave any surplus juice behind. Give everything a good seasoning of salt and pepper and some nutmeg, and toss the two together to combine them as evenly as possible.

Now using your hands, shape the mixture into 8 small flat rounds about 2½ inches in diameter, squeezing firmly to form little cakes that have nice raggedy edges. As you make the little rösti cakes, place them on a plate, then put the flour on another small plate. Dust each cake lightly with flour, return it to the first plate, then cover them all with plastic wrap. They can now sit happily in the fridge for up to 6 hours.

When you're ready to cook the rösti, preheat the oven to 425°F. Brush the baking sheet with the melted butter, place the little rösti cakes on the sheet and brush the tops with melted butter. When the oven is up to heat, pop them on the high rack, give them 10 minutes using a timer, then using a spatula turn them over and give them another 10–15 minutes, by which time they will be crisp and golden on the outside, cooked through and ready to serve.

PREVIOUS PAGE: ROASTED ROOTS WITH HERBS (SEE PAGE 161)

Spiced Sautéed Red Cabbage
with Cranberries

Serves 4–6

I have always adored red cabbage cooked long and slow, but it's also extremely good cooked fast so that it retains some bite and crunchiness. Using cranberries rather than the usual apples gives this dish a jewel-like appearance, and their sharp flavor gives an edge to the spiciness.

1 pound red cabbage, cut into 4 sections
and cored
½ tablespoon peanut oil
1 medium onion, chopped
1 large clove garlic, finely chopped
⅓ teaspoon ground cloves

¾ teaspoon ground cinnamon
⅓ whole nutmeg, freshly grated
Salt and freshly ground black pepper
1 cup fresh cranberries
½ heaping tablespoon light brown sugar
1½ tablespoons red wine vinegar

You will also need a very large skillet or, even better, a wok.

First of all you need to shred the cabbage quite finely into ¼-inch shreds, discarding any tough stalky bits. Now heat the oil in the pan over a medium heat, stir in the onion, cook it for 2–3 minutes, then add the garlic and continue to cook for another 2–3 minutes. Then turn the heat up to its highest setting and add the cabbage. Using a wooden spoon, keep the cabbage constantly on the move so it comes into contact with the hot pan on all sides.

After about 3–4 minutes of cooking, still stirring, sprinkle in the spices and a seasoning of salt and pepper followed by the cranberries. Then turn the heat down and let it go on cooking for a further 5–10 minutes, stirring it once or twice during that time. Bite a piece to see if it's tender, then when it's ready turn the heat up again, sprinkle in the brown sugar and vinegar, give it all a few more good stirs and then it's ready to serve.

NOTE: *If you're careful not to overcook it in the beginning, you can prepare this in advance and just quickly heat it up for serving.*

Celery Baked in Vinaigrette
with Pancetta and Shallots

Serves 2

This is a great way to serve celery as a vegetable. I used parchment paper for this in the photograph opposite, as it looks very pretty if you take the whole parcel to the table—otherwise foil will do.

1 bunch celery
3 tablespoons light olive oil
6 shallots (split if the bulbs are dividing)
3 slices pancetta or smoked sliced bacon

1 or 2 thyme sprigs
1 rosemary sprig
4 sage leaves
Salt and freshly ground black pepper
½ tablespoon white wine vinegar

You will also need a double thickness of parchment paper, 15 × 24 inches when folded, and a large solid baking sheet. Preheat the oven to 475°F.

Begin by removing the tough outer ribs of the celery, then pare the outside of the root off, but leave it attached. Now cut across the celery about 3½ inches from the base. Stand the lower half upright and cut vertically through the center. Then cut each half into 4 to make 8 pieces, keeping them attached to the root. Save a couple of nice leaves (preferably attached to a small stem) and trim the top pieces of celery to a similar length to the base, cutting off any really tough and stringy edges. Now rinse all the pieces and dry them on paper towels.

Next heat 1 tablespoon of the oil in a skillet, then lightly brown the celery and shallots, keeping them on the move so they brown evenly. Now transfer them to a plate. Increase the heat under the pan, add the pancetta and fry the slices until they're really crisp—it will take 2–3 minutes and you'll need to keep turning them.

Next lay the parchment paper over the baking sheet and lightly brush a circle of oil 9 inches diameter on it. Arrange the celery in an attractive shape on the paper, putting the prettiest pieces on the top. Add the shallots, thyme, rosemary and sage leaves in among the celery, and season with salt and pepper.

Now combine the remaining olive oil and wine vinegar, sprinkle that over the vegetables, followed by the pancetta crumbled into pieces. Next fold the parchment paper over and seal, making pleats, all around—you may find a couple of metal (not plastic) paper clips useful here, as it's essential to keep the steam trapped inside. Place the parcel in the preheated oven for 20–25 minutes.

After that carefully unwrap the paper—you may need scissors—and serve the vegetables with the juices spooned over.

NOTE: *For 4 to 6 people, double the ingredients and make 2 parcels.*

CELERY BAKED IN VINAIGRETTE WITH PANCETTA AND SHALLOTS

Sautéed Caramelized Fennel

Serves 4–6

4 medium fennel bulbs
¼ stick butter
2 teaspoons granulated sugar

1 ¼ cups medium cider
¼ cup cider vinegar
Salt

You will need a wide saucepan with a lid, about 9–10 inches in diameter, into which the trimmed fennel will fit snugly.

To prepare the fennel bulbs, first cut off the leafy fronds and reserve them for a garnish. Now trim off the green shoot by cutting diagonally to make a V shape. Then slice off the root part at the other end, keeping the bulb intact, and remove any tough or brown outer layers, then slice across each bulb to cut it in half.

Then place the fennel on a steamer set in the saucepan with 1 inch of boiling water under it. Cover and steam for 10 minutes, then remove the fennel from the steamer, throw out the water, wipe the inside of the pan with paper towels and return it to the heat.

Next melt the butter and sugar in the saucepan, and when it starts to foam, stir it around the pan until the sugar dissolves, then add the fennel, cut side down. Keeping the heat fairly high, brown it for 5 minutes, then turn the pieces over and brown them on the other side for another 3 minutes.

Now combine the cider, cider vinegar and a little salt and pour this into the pan; then, keeping the cut side of the fennel facing upward, cover with a lid and simmer gently for 20 minutes. After that turn the fennel over again. Then continue to cook for a further 20–25 minutes (this time uncovered). Watch carefully during the last 10 minutes and test to see if it is cooked by inserting a skewer.

When the fennel is tender enough, raise the heat so that the remaining juices reduce to a glaze. Shake the pan carefully to give an even covering of the caramel glaze. Now transfer everything to a warm serving dish with the cut surfaces upward and scatter with the chopped fennel fronds as a garnish.

Oven-Roasted Cauliflower and Broccoli with Garlic and Coriander

Serves 4

These two particular vegetables can become a bit repetitive as winter wears on, so here's a deliciously different way to cook them—no water, just in the heat of the oven, which concentrates their flavors wonderfully.

8 ounces cauliflower

8 ounces broccoli

1 heaping teaspoon coriander seeds, coarsely crushed

2 cloves garlic

Salt and freshly ground black pepper

3 tablespoons olive oil

You will also need a large, solid, shallow baking sheet.

Preheat the oven to 400°F.

All you do is trim the cauliflower and broccoli into florets 1 inch in diameter, and place them in a mixing bowl, then sprinkle in the crushed coriander seeds. Crush the cloves of garlic together with ¾ teaspoon salt with a mortar and pestle until you have a paste. Whisk the oil into this, then pour the whole mixture over the broccoli and cauliflower. Use your hands to toss and mix everything together to get a nice coating of oil and coriander, then arrange the florets on the baking sheet and season with salt and pepper. Bake for 25–35 minutes or until tender when tested with a skewer, and serve immediately.

Compote of Glazed Shallots

Serves 8

This recipe is dead simple, yet it draws out all the sweet, fragrant flavor of the shallots and at the same time gives them a glazed pink, jewel-like appearance. These make an excellent partner to beef, or you can add a bit of sophistication to bangers and mash. Also, cider and cider vinegar can be used instead of wine to make it more economical.

1½ pound (approximately 24) small,
*   even-sized shallots, left whole (ones*
*   that split into twins count as 2)*
¼ cup red wine vinegar

2 cups dry red wine
Salt
1 heaping teaspoon sugar

Use a wide, shallow saucepan that will take the shallots in 1 layer, then simply place all the above ingredients except the sugar in it and bring everything up to simmering point. Then turn the heat down to its lowest setting and let the shallots simmer (just a few bubbles breaking the surface) for 1–1¼ hours. Turn the shallots over at halftime, and 10 minutes before the end of the cooking time sprinkle in the sugar. You should end up with tender shallots glistening with a lovely glaze. If your heat source is not low enough, you may need to use a diffuser. If it's more convenient, you can cook the shallots in advance and gently reheat them before serving.

Roasted Roots with Herbs

Serves 4

ecause oven-roasted vegetables in the *Summer Collection* were so very popular, I simply had to do a winter version. Here it is and once again it's a winner for entertaining, not least because all the vegetables get cooked together with little or no attention. (See photograph on pages 152–53.)

4 small carrots
4 small parsnips
½ rutabaga (about 5 ounces), cut into 1-inch wedges
1 small turnip, halved and then cut into ¾-inch slices
2 medium red onions, cut through the root into quarters

2 red potatoes (5 ounces each), cut into 6 wedges
1 large clove garlic, crushed
¼ cup olive oil
1 tablespoon chopped mixed fresh herbs (including thyme, rosemary and sage)
Salt and freshly ground black pepper

You will also need a solid baking sheet 16 × 12 inches.

Preheat the oven to its highest setting.

First scrub the carrots and parsnips, dry them well and place them in a large bowl with all the other prepared vegetables. Now add the crushed garlic, olive oil and mixed herbs, then using your hands, mix well to make sure they all have a good coating of the oil. You can leave them like this covered with plastic wrap for up to 2 hours until you are ready to cook them—in which case the oil will have nicely absorbed the flavor of the garlic and herbs.

Then arrange them on the baking sheet, sprinkle with salt and a good grinding of black pepper and cook in the preheated oven on the high rack for 35–40 minutes or until they are cooked through.

Roasted Rutabaga with Parmesan

Serves 4–6

This is another version of a parsnip recipe from my Christmas book. It has been said that even children will eat rutabaga when it tastes this good.

⅔ cup flour
½ cup freshly grated Parmesan
  (Parmigiano-Reggiano)
Salt and freshly ground black pepper
1½ pounds rutabagas, peeled and cut
  into large chiplike wedges approxi-
  mately 2 inches long

Peanut oil
¼ stick butter

You will also need a large solid baking sheet 14 × 10 inches.
Preheat the oven to 400°F.

Begin by combining the flour, Parmesan and a seasoning of salt and pepper in a mixing bowl. Now pop the rutabaga into a saucepan, cover with boiling water, add some salt, bring back to boiling point, then cover and simmer for 3 minutes.

Meanwhile have a kitchen tray ready. Drain the rutabaga and while it is still steaming drop the wedges, using kitchen tongs, a few at a time into the bowl to coat them with the flour and cheese. Do this quickly as the coating will stick only if they're still steamy. Then lay them out on the tray to cool, and refrigerate until you are ready to cook. For this you need to place the baking sheet in the oven while it's preheating, putting enough oil on the sheet to cover the bottom and adding the butter for flavor.

Then when the oven is up to heat remove the baking sheet, place it over direct heat turned to low, and arrange the prepared rutabaga wedges on it side by side. Baste the tops with the hot oil and butter then transfer them to the oven, using an oven mitt, to bake for 20 minutes. After that turn them over, remove any excess fat from the baking sheet and continue to bake them for a further 15–20 minutes or until they're crisp and golden.

Parsnips with a Mustard and Maple Glaze

Serves 4–6

People who normally don't like parsnips like this recipe. It's a very good combination of flavors, and if you get bored with plain roast parsnips at the end of winter, this is just what's needed.

3 pounds medium parsnips
Salt
¼ cup peanut oil
Freshly ground black pepper

FOR THE GLAZE:
4 tablespoons whole grain mustard
2 tablespoons pure maple syrup

You will also need a steamer rack and a good solid shallow baking sheet 14 × 10 inches.

Preheat the oven to 475°F.

First trim and peel the parsnips, then cut them in half through the center. Cut the top half into fourths and the bottom half into halves so that you have even-sized pieces. Cut out any woody stems from the center, then place the parsnips in the steamer, sprinkle with salt, cover with a lid and steam over simmering water for 6 minutes. Meanwhile put the baking sheet containing the oil on the top rack of the oven to preheat.

When the parsnips are ready, use an oven mitt to remove the baking sheet very carefully from the oven so as not to spill the oil, and place it over direct heat turned to low. Add the parsnips, rounded side up, to the sizzling oil. Then tilt the sheet and use a large spoon to baste the parsnips to make sure they are evenly coated with the oil. Give them a good grinding of pepper and return the sheet to the oven. Bake for 25 minutes, by which time the parsnips should be nicely browned and crispy.

Meanwhile make the glaze. Mix the mustard and maple syrup together in a bowl, then, using a brush, give the parsnip pieces a liberal coating of the glaze and return them to the oven for 8–10 minutes. Serve immediately.

CHAPTER NINE

Stars of the East

SINCE I WROTE THE *SUMMER COLLECTION* I HAVE BEEN PARTICULARLY fortunate in the course of my work for Sainsbury's *The Magazine* to have been able to visit the Far East. On one trip to Tokyo I discovered firsthand how the Japanese make what is undoubtedly the best soy sauce in the world. On another to Bangkok I attended daily classes at the Oriental Cookery School to learn the art of Thai cookery.

An important part of my job is to educate myself about new ingredients, then to share that knowledge and to try to help extend the boundaries. We certainly now live in a most exciting era of cooking. The world has become a smaller place with people zipping about from continent to continent at great speed, and ingredients are on the move too, enabling us to pop into supermarkets and literally shop around the world.

Even so, this can sometimes be frustrating when certain ingredients are not as widely available as we would like them to be. This is where you too can play your part. Be patient and *keep on* asking for ingredients. Between us we have to create a demand, and in doing this all our lives can be enriched by being able to share in new and different cuisines from around the world. You will find details of new ingredients used in this chapter on page 235 and possible sources on page 248. But don't forget, keep asking!

Chinese Crispy Beef Stir-Fry

Serves 2

The good thing about Chinese cooking is that it always manages to make a little meat go a long way. Rump steak is perfect for stir-frying, and for this recipe just 4 ounces per person is plenty.

4 ounces Asian rice noodles
Salt
1 stalk lemongrass
1 large clove garlic
1½-inch piece fresh gingerroot
6 scallions
1 medium leek
1 medium carrot

8 ounces rump steak
4 teaspoons cornstarch
1 teaspoon Chinese five-spice powder
3 tablespoons peanut oil
2 tablespoons soy sauce
3 tablespoons dry sherry
2 tablespoons water

You will also need a wok or a very large skillet.

The secret of a successful stir-fry is speed. So what you need to do is have everything prepared before you start. The first item on the list to prepare is the rice noodles. Place these in a large bowl with a little salt, then pour warm water over them and leave them to soak for exactly 15 minutes and no longer.

Now for the vegetables. First the lemongrass—remove the outer tougher leaves, trim off the woody tops, then slice the rest very finely. The garlic should be chopped finely. The piece of gingerroot needs to be peeled, cut into thin slices and then into tiny matchstick. Finely slice the white part of the scallions, then cut the tender green parts into 2-inch lengths and then into little strips. Now the leek: First halve the white part lengthwise and cut into similar matchstick-sized strips, then cut the green, tender part of the leek into diagonals to make diamond-shaped pieces. Cut the carrot lengthwise and then make this too into matchsticks.

Now for the meat. This is cut into 2-inch pieces and these are then cut lengthwise so that the meat, too, is now in thin strips. Next you need to take a small bowl and in it mix the cornstarch and the five-spice powder together. Mix the meat in this mixture until it is all well coated. Drain the noodles, shaking off any excess water, and then all is ready to cook.

Now place the wok over a high heat, without adding any oil at first. As soon as it's very hot, add 1 tablespoon of the oil, let it sizzle, then add the meat and toss it and stir-fry it in the hot oil for about 2 minutes. Then remove the meat to a plate. Add the remaining oil, let it sizzle and then add the lemongrass, garlic and ginger. Toss these around for about 30 seconds, then add the carrots, scallions and leek and toss these around also for 30 seconds. Next add the soy sauce, sherry and water. Then as soon as the liquid is very hot stir in the noodles, combining them with the vegetables. Finally return the meat to join all the vegetables, and toss everything together a couple of times and serve immediately in hot bowls.

Thai Green Curry with Chicken

Serves 4–6

This recipe is inspired by the Oriental Cookery School in Bangkok. You may have to hunt around for the ingredients, or you can get them by mail order (see page 248). The unique flavors of Thai cooking are so simple and—because you can use a good-quality cooked chicken from the supermarket—this recipe is actually incredibly easy. (See photograph on pages 168–69.)

FOR THE GREEN CURRY PASTE:
8 green Birdseye chilies (whole)
1 lemongrass stalk, thinly sliced and soaked for 30 minutes in 2 tablespoons lime juice
2 teaspoons kaffir lime peel, pared and thinly shredded (if not available, use regular lime)
7 thin slices Thai ginger (galangal)
1 heaping teaspoon chopped cilantro stalks
½ teaspoon ground roasted cumin
½ teaspoon ground roasted coriander
3 cloves garlic
5 Thai shallots (if not available, use regular shallots)

1 teaspoon shrimp paste (if not available, use 2 anchovies)

FOR THE CURRY:
2½ cups coconut milk
1½–2 tablespoons Thai fish sauce
1 teaspoon palm sugar or brown sugar
1 pound cooked chicken, shredded
1½ tablespoons fresh green peppercorns (or preserved in brine)
7 kaffir lime leaves (if available)
½ mild red chili, seeded and cut into hairlike shreds
1 ounce Thai basil leaves

You will also need a large flameproof casserole or a wok.

The curry paste can be made well ahead of time, and there's absolutely no work involved if you have a food processor or a blender because all you do is simply pop all the curry paste ingredients in and blend it to a paste (stopping once or twice to push the mixture back down from the sides onto the blades). In Thailand, of course, all these would be pounded by hand with a mortar and pestle, but food processors do cut out all the hard work.

What you need to end up with is a coarse paste, but don't worry if it doesn't look very green—that's because I have cut the chili content; in Thailand they use about 35! If you want yours to be green, then this is the answer! Your next task is to prepare all the rest of the ingredients.

To make the curry, first place the cans of coconut milk on a work surface, upside down. Then open them, and inside you will see the whole thing has separated into thick cream and thin watery milk. Divide these by pouring the milk into 1 bowl and the cream into another. Next place a wok, without any oil in it, over a very high heat, and then as soon as it becomes really hot, add three-quarters of the coconut cream. What you do now is literally fry it, stirring all the time so it doesn't catch. It will start to separate, the oil will begin to seep out and it will reduce. Ignore the curdled look—this is normal. You should note that when the cream begins to separate you can actually hear it give off a crackling noise. Next add the curry paste and three-quarters of the coconut milk, which should be added a little at a time, keeping the heat high and letting it reduce down slightly. Stay with it and keep stirring to prevent it sticking. Then add the fish sauce and palm sugar, stir these in and then add the chicken pieces and the peppercorns. Stir again and simmer everything for about 4–5 minutes, until the chicken is heated through. Then just before serving place the lime leaves one on top of the other, roll them up tightly and slice them into very fine shreds. Then add them along with the red chili and torn basil leaves. Serve with Thai fragrant rice.

N O T E : *You can, if you like, freeze the leftover coconut milk and cream for use later on.*

NEXT PAGE: THAI GREEN CURRY
WITH CHICKEN

Hung Shao Pork
with Stir-Fry Greens

Serves 2

It must have been about 20 years ago that I first met Ken Lo, the famous cookery writer and restaurateur, and asked him how to make this, which is one of my favorite Chinese dishes. He didn't just give me the recipe; he came around to the flat where we were living and cooked it, giving us a lesson on the principles of Chinese cookery at the same time. The great thing about this recipe, which is still a huge favorite, is that it transforms an inexpensive piece of pork roast into something exotic and unusual.

1 pound lean uncured side of pork, including the skin (buy it as a whole piece)
Salt
⅓ cup dark soy sauce
1 tablespoon water
½ tablespoon finely chopped fresh gingerroot
1 star anise
2-inch piece cinnamon stick, broken into shreds
1 teaspoon sugar
3 tablespoons dry sherry

FOR THE STIR-FRY VEGETABLES:
4 ounces broccoli
4 ounces Savoy cabbage
1 large leek
1-inch piece fresh gingerroot
1 large clove garlic
2 scallions
1 tablespoon dark soy sauce
2 tablespoons dry sherry
2 tablespoons water
2 tablespoons peanut oil

You will also need a medium-sized flameproof casserole, plus a wok or a large skillet.

First of all prepare the pork. What you need to do is cut it into 1-inch cubes, making quite sure that each piece still has the skin attached. You don't have to eat the skin, but its gelatinous properties are very important to the flavor of the finished dish. Now arrange the pieces of pork, skin side down, in the casserole and sprinkle them with a little salt and then with the soy sauce and the water. Next add the chopped ginger, sprinkling it all around, popping in the star anise and cinnamon as well. Now cover the casserole, turn on the heat and as soon as the juices start to simmer, turn the heat down to its lowest possible setting and cook the pork for 45 minutes. After that turn the pieces of pork over onto the other side, sprinkle in the sugar and the sherry, then cover again and continue to cook very slowly for a further 45 minutes, turning the meat over once or twice more during that time.

Toward the end of the cooking time, prepare the vegetables. To do this, first cut off the flowery heads of the broccoli, separating them and slicing them into small pieces. Then cut the stalky bits diagonally into very thin slices. The cabbage needs to be cored and sliced thinly and the leek cleaned, halved lengthwise and cut diagonally into slices. Peel the piece of ginger and slice this into little matchstick strips, and do the same with the garlic. Then chop the white part of the scallions into thin rounds and the tender, green part into matchstick pieces.

Now, in a measuring cup, mix together the soy sauce, sherry and water. Then about 3 minutes before the pork is ready, heat up a wok or a large skillet until it is very hot. Then add the oil and, when that's hot, add the ginger and garlic, tossing it about for 30 seconds. After that add the broccoli. Then add the cabbage, the leek and the green part of the scallions.

Stir-fry this for about 1 minute, then finally add the rest of the scallions and the soy sauce mixture. Then give it another few seconds, tossing and stirring, then serve the vegetables and the pork on a bed of plain boiled rice with any juices left in the wok poured over.

Marinated Cucumber and Sesame Salad

Serves 2

If you're serving Teriyaki Steak (see page 174), I think it's nice to have something cool and crunchy to go with it. This very simple salad makes a nice little side dish. I also like to serve it as a nibble before an Oriental meal.

2 tablespoons sesame seeds
½ cucumber
1½ tablespoons soy sauce
1 teaspoon mirin

1 teaspoon sake
1 teaspoon rice vinegar
½ teaspoon sugar

First of all begin by toasting the sesame seeds. Do this by using a small, solid skillet, preheat it over a medium heat, then add the sesame seeds and toast them, moving them around in the skillet to brown them evenly. As soon as they begin to splutter and pop and turn golden, they're ready. This will take about 1–2 minutes. Then remove them from the skillet to a plate. Next cut the cucumber in half lengthwise, then in quarters and then in eighths. Remove the seeds, chop into small, 1½-inch wedges, then place them in a bowl. After that measure the soy sauce, mirin, sake, rice vinegar and sugar into a screw-top jar, shake them together thoroughly, then pour them over the cucumber and leave to marinate for about 1 hour, giving them one good stir at halftime. Just before serving lightly crush the sesame seeds with a mortar and pestle and sprinkle them over the salad.

Singapore Stir-Fried Noodles

Serves 2

O nce again I have to thank Ken Lo for introducing me to this incredibly good recipe, which is a spectacular combination of flavors, textures and colors. If you can't get dried Chinese mushrooms or shrimp (see page 235) use more of the fresh ones and it will still be wonderful.

6 Chinese dried mushrooms
1 heaping tablespoon Chinese dried
 shrimp
4 ounces Asian rice noodles
2 tablespoons peanut oil
1 medium onion, chopped small
2 slices bacon, chopped small
1 large clove garlic, chopped
1 heaping teaspoon freshly grated
 gingerroot
½ tablespoon Madras curry powder

½ teaspoon salt
2 ounces cooked chicken or pork, finely
 shredded
2 ounces shelled prawns, cut into thirds
4 scallions, finely chopped, including
 green parts
1 ½ tablespoons soy sauce (Japanese is
 best)
2 tablespoons reserved mushroom-
 shrimp water
2 tablespoons dry sherry

You also need a wok or very large skillet.

First of all you need to soak the dried mushrooms and shrimp—to do this place them in a bowl and pour boiling water over them and leave them aside to soak for 30 minutes. Meanwhile you can get on with all the chopping of the other ingredients.

After the mushrooms and shrimp have soaked, drain off the water, reserving 2 tablespoons for later. Give the mushrooms a squeeze and chop them into fine shreds. Now place the noodles in a large bowl, cover them with warm water and leave them to soak for 15 minutes.

Next heat the oil in the wok and when it's very hot add the onion, mushrooms, soaked shrimp, chopped bacon, garlic and ginger. Stir them around in the hot oil, then reduce the heat and gently let all the ingredients cook together for about 15 minutes. This initial slow cooking allows all the delicious flavors and aromas to permeate the oil.

After 15 minutes add the curry powder and salt to the cooked ingredients, then drain the noodles in a colander—give them a really good shake to get rid of any excess water. Then turn the heat under the pan up to medium, add the chicken, then the fresh prawns, followed by the chopped scallions. Next add the drained noodles to the pan, then using either a large fork or some chopsticks toss the ingredients around so that everything is incorporated among the noodles. Finally combine the soy sauce, mushroom-shrimp water and sherry, sprinkle over the noodles, give everything a good stir and serve immediately on hot plates.

Teriyaki Steak

*T*eriyaki sauce must be one of the most popular Japanese sauces the world over. The following recipe is my own interpretation, as I find I like less sugar than the amount the more authentic recipes call for. You don't need the most expensive steak for this, either, because the marinade does a wonderful job of tenderizing and mellowing the meat.

2 tablespoons soy sauce (Japanese is best)
2 tablespoons sake
⅓ cup mirin
1 teaspoon sugar
2 teaspoons grated fresh gingerroot
1 large clove garlic, crushed
Two 6-ounce sirloin or flank steaks, 1 inch thick

1½ inches daikon radish, peeled
½ green chili, seeded
1 tablespoon peanut oil
Sansho pepper (if available)

FOR THE GARNISH:
2 cloves garlic
Watercress
Lemon wedges

Allow time for marinating the meat. This can be anything from overnight to a minimum of 1 hour before you cook the steaks. All you do is combine the soy sauce, sake, mirin, sugar, gingerroot and crushed garlic, then place the steaks in a small, shallow dish. Pour the marinade over, cover and leave them in a cool place, turning them once halfway through the marinating time.

Just before you want to cook the steaks, slice the remaining 2 whole cloves of garlic into rounds and set aside. Take the peeled daikon, grate it on the fine side of the grater, then squeeze it tightly in the palm of your hand to get rid of excess juices. Then take the green chili, grate it and mix it in with the daikon. Now form the mixture into two little cone-shaped mounds (these will be served as a garnish).

To cook the steaks, preheat the oil in a good solid skillet. Brown the garlic slices briefly, then remove them to a plate to keep warm. Now turn the heat to its highest setting and, when the skillet is very hot, scrape the marinade off the steaks, reserving it, and place them in the skillet. Now reduce the heat to medium and cook the steaks for 4 minutes each side if you like them medium rare, 3 minutes if very rare and 5 minutes for well done. Watch them carefully because the marinade tends to brown them more quickly. Two minutes before the end of your cooking time, pour in the marinade and reduce it by about a third. Now transfer the steaks to a carving board and, using a sharp knife, cut them into slightly diagonal ½-inch slices. Place these on warm serving plates, season with Sansho pepper, spoon the sauce over, sprinkle the browned garlic on top and garnish with watercress and lemon wedges. Serve with the little mounds of grated daikon and chili.

NOTE: *For information on Japanese ingredients, see page 235.*

Thai Prawn Curry with Pineapple

Serves 2

This lovely recipe from the Oriental Cookery School in Bangkok has been slightly adjusted to accommodate Western ingredients without, I think, losing its authenticity. It's incredibly easy and it really does taste exotic and unusual. If fresh prawns (or jumbo shrimp) are not available you can buy them from the frozen food section in large supermarkets.

1 pound uncooked prawns in their shells

FOR THE CURRY PASTE:
4 dried red chilies, soaked with the juice and zest of 1 lime for 30 minutes
1 tablespoon finely chopped lemongrass
1-inch cube fresh gingerroot
5 cloves garlic
7 Thai shallots (or normal shallots if not available)
1 teaspoon shrimp paste (if not available use 2 anchovies)

½ teaspoon salt
3 tablespoons Thai fish sauce

3½ cups coconut milk
1 pound fresh pineapple, cut into ¼-inch chunks

TO GARNISH:
2 kaffir lime leaves (if available)
2 medium red chilies, seeded and shredded into hairlike strips

You will also need a wok or a very large skillet.

If the prawns are frozen, defrost them by emptying them into a colander and leaving them for about an hour to defrost. Then cook the prawns (either fresh or frozen) in a skillet or wok placed over high heat. Add the prawns in their shells and dry-fry them in the hot pan for about 4–5 minutes, turning and tossing them around while you watch their beige and black stripes turn pink.

After that remove them from the heat and when they're cool enough to handle, peel off the shells, then make a slit all along their backs and remove any black thread. Now keep them covered and refrigerated until you need them.

To make the curry paste, all you do is put everything into a food processor or blender, then switch on to a high speed and blend until you have a rather coarse, rough-looking paste. Remove the paste and keep it covered in the fridge until you need it.

When you're ready to make the curry, empty the contents of the cans of coconut milk into a wok and stir while you bring it up to the boil, then boil until the fat begins to separate from the solids. This will take approximately 20 minutes, and if you listen carefully you'll hear a sizzle as the fat begins to come out and the whole thing is reduced. Ignore the curdled appearance. Now add the curry paste, give it 3 minutes' cooking time, enough for the flavors to develop, then add the prawns and the pineapple and let them heat through gently for another 2 minutes. During that time shred the lime leaves by placing one on top of the other, then roll them up tightly and cut into very thin shreds. Serve the curry with lime leaves and chili strips sprinkled over and some Thai fragrant rice as an accompaniment.

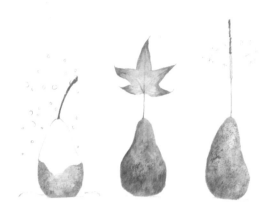

CHAPTER TEN

Autumn, Winter and Party Desserts

SOMETIMES I GET A BIT TIRED OF HEARING ABOUT CHOCOLATE TRUFFLE Torte! It was quite definitely the hit of my *Christmas* collection, and though I still love it myself I really felt that in this book I had to find a comparable chocolate dessert, simply so we can all enjoy a change. Well, the good news is I've found it—the best chocolate dessert to date and, yes, even better than the truffle torte. It is called Fallen Chocolate Soufflé (see page 186), and when we filmed it for the television series it got a ten out of ten vote from the entire crew. The secret with this recipe, as with all things chocolatey, is the quality of chocolate you use, so do read the note on page 233.

Because winter includes the Christmas party season I have been a bit indulgent on the chocolate front. Chocolate Mascarpone Cheesecake (see page 198) is a winner and so is A Return to the Black Forest (see page 222), my sixties revival of a chocolate roulade, filled with sour cherries, chocolate and cream. And can I also recommend what I think is the definitive recipe for Tiramisu (see page 193), that delightful combination of bitter chocolate, coffee, ladyfingers and mascarpone.

If you are watching your waistline you can skip this chapter, or alternatively, do what I do: Just cook one of them a week, on Sundays!

Grilled Autumn Fruits
with Sabayon Cider Sauce

Serves 4

This is a very pretty and colorful dessert for the autumn or winter. It can be made well in advance as the fruits are served at room temperature, with a sauce to go with them that can either be warm or cooled.

2 dessert apples (such as Granny Smith)
2 small ripe pears
10 ripe red plums
Juice of 1 lemon
1 large orange
¼ cup plus 1 tablespoon superfine sugar

FOR THE SAUCE:
3 large egg yolks
¼ cup plus 1 tablespoon superfine sugar
⅔ cup dry cider (the reserved juices from the fruits can be added to this)

You will also need a large broiler pan lined with foil and a shallow plate or dish to put the cooked fruits on.

First prepare the apples and pears. Leave the peel on the fruit but core them and cut the apples into eighths and the pears into quarters. Then halve the plums and remove the stones. Place them in a bowl and toss in the lemon juice.

The orange should be cut into double segments, so place it on a board and, using your sharpest knife, pare off all the skin and pith. Then, holding it in 1 hand over the same bowl to catch the juices, cut out the double segments by slicing the knife in at the line of pith that divides the segments (you need to cut out each wedge with as much of the pithy membrane left behind as possible). As you cut them out, add them to the rest of the fruit.

To cook the fruit, preheat the broiler to its highest setting about 20 minutes in advance and arrange the fruits in the broiler pan (if it's small you might have to cook them in 2 batches). Sprinkle the fruits with the ¼ cup sugar, then place them under the hot broiler about 4 inches from the heat. They will take about 15–20 minutes to become caramelized and tinged brown at the edges. Keep an eye on them and turn them over at halftime, sprinkling on the extra tablespoon of sugar. If a lot of juice comes out and creates too much steam, pour it from the corner of the pan into the bowl. The plums will probably cook quickest, so remove them first along with the rest of the fruits as they caramelize.

Then make the sauce. Place the egg yolks and sugar in a bowl and beat these with an electric handheld mixer until they start to thicken. Now set the bowl over a small saucepan of simmering water and add the cider and fruit juice a little at a time, continuing to beat as you're adding it. When all the liquid is in, carry on beating until the sauce thickens to a fluffy consistency. Draw the beaters across the surface: It is ready when there is no visible liquid left underneath. Pour the sauce into a pitcher and serve warm along with the fruit.

Spiced Lambrusco Jellies with
Brandy Cream and Frosted Black Grapes

Serves 6

It was in Parma in Italy that I first tasted the dry Lambrusco that is local to that region. Because it's fizzy it makes a lovely bubbly, spicy jelly which slips down coolly at the end of a filling meal. If you can't get hold of a dry Lambrusco, a sparkling red Burgundy from California would be fine.

FOR THE JELLY:
2½ cups water
Zest and juice of 1 orange
⅓ cup superfine sugar
1 cinnamon stick
6 cloves
1 blade mace
1-inch piece gingerroot, peeled and sliced
2 envelopes unflavored gelatin
2 cups dry red Lambrusco

FOR THE BRANDY CREAM:
⅔ cup heavy cream
1 tablespoon brandy
1 tablespoon orange juice
2 tablespoons superfine sugar
1 teaspoon finely grated orange zest

FOR THE FROSTED GRAPES:
6 small clusters of black grapes
   (3 in each cluster)
1 egg white, very lightly beaten
¼ cup superfine sugar

You will also need six 1-cup stemmed glasses.

To make the jelly, pour the water into a small saucepan and add the orange zest, sugar and spices. Then place it over a medium heat and bring to just below boiling point. At that stage remove from the heat and leave to infuse for about an hour to allow the spices to impart their flavors.

After that strain the spices out, discard them and bring the liquid to just below simmering point. Take the pan off the heat and sprinkle in the gelatin, whisking the mixture with a balloon whisk at the same time. Now leave it aside to melt the gelatin, stirring once or twice to ensure it has all dissolved into the liquid.

Next add the orange juice and strain the contents of the pan through a fine sieve lined with paper towels. Leave it to cool, then cover and chill in the refrigerator until just on the point of setting (about 1–1½ hours). After that add the wine and stir to blend well, then pour into the glasses. Chill the jellies, covered with plastic wrap, for about 4 hours, by which time they should have a lovely soft set.

While the jellies are setting make the brandy cream by simply combining the ingredients in a small bowl, cover with plastic wrap and leave in the fridge to chill. Remember to remove the jellies from the fridge 30 minutes before you need to serve them.

For the grapes all you do is dip each cluster in the beaten egg white, then coat generously with the superfine sugar. Leave them on a sheet of parchment paper to dry. Top each jelly with the brandy cream and decorate with frosted grapes.

Basic Crêpes with Sugar and Lemon

Makes 12–14 in a 7-inch pan

No winter cookbook would be complete without a crêpe recipe. Every year there are people making crêpes for the first time, and I admit it can be a hazardous affair if you don't know the ropes. So here is my tried and trusted crêpe recipe, and once you get into the swing, you can make loads extra for the freezer and try the recipes on pages 89 and 145.

⅔ cup plus 2 tablespoons flour, sifted
A pinch of salt
2 large eggs
1 cup milk mixed with ⅓ cup water
½ stick butter

To Serve:
Superfine sugar
Freshly squeezed lemon juice
Lemon wedges

You will also need a good solid 7-inch crêpe pan or skillet, some paper towels, parchment paper, a flexible metal spatula or palette knife, and a ladle.

First of all sift the flour and salt into a large mixing bowl with the sieve held high above the bowl so the flour gets an airing. Now make a well in the center of the flour and break the eggs into it. Then begin whisking the eggs—any sort of whisk or even a fork will do—incorporating any bits of flour from around the edge of the bowl as you do so.

Next gradually add small quantities of the milk-and-water mixture, still whisking (don't worry about any lumps as they will eventually disappear as you whisk). When all the liquid has been added, use a rubber spatula to scrape any elusive bits of flour from around the edge into the center, then whisk once more until the batter is smooth, with the consistency of light cream. Now melt the butter in the pan. Spoon 2 tablespoons of it into the batter and whisk it in, then pour the rest into a bowl and use it to lubricate the pan, using a wedge of paper towel to smear it around before you make each crêpe.

Now get the pan really hot, then turn the heat down to medium and, to start with, do a test crêpe to see if you're using the correct amount of batter. I find 2 tablespoons about right for a 7-inch pan. It's also helpful if you spoon the batter into a ladle so it can be poured into the hot pan in one go. As soon as the batter hits the hot pan, tip it around from side to side to get the bottom evenly coated with batter. It should take only half a minute or so to cook; you can lift the edge with a spatula to see if it's tinged gold as it should be. Flip the pancake over with a spatula—the other side will need only a few seconds—then simply slide it out of the pan onto a plate.

Stack the crêpes as you make them between sheets of parchment paper on a plate fitted over simmering water, to keep them warm while you make the rest.

To serve, sprinkle each crêpe with freshly squeezed lemon juice and superfine sugar, fold in half, then in half again to form a triangle, or else simply roll it up. Serve sprinkled with a little more sugar and lemon juice and lemon wedges.

Pears Baked in Marsala Wine

Serves 8

The rich, dark flavor of Marsala combined with fragrant pear juice is a quite stunning combination. When you shop for the pears, looks are important: A good pear shape and a long, intact stem are essential, and the fruit needs to be hard and not ripe—which is perhaps fortunate as ripe pears always seem difficult to find.

FOR THE PEARS:
8 large hard pears
2½ cups Marsala
¼ cup superfine sugar
2 whole cinnamon sticks

1 vanilla bean
1 tablespoon cornstarch

TO SERVE:
2½ cups crème fraîche

You will also need a large flameproof casserole with a tight-fitting lid.

Preheat the oven to 250°F.

Using a potato peeler thinly pare off the outer skin of the pears, but leave the stalks intact. Then slice off a thin little disc from each pear base so they can sit upright. Now lay the pears on their side in the casserole. Pour in the Marsala, then sprinkle over the sugar and add the cinnamon sticks and vanilla bean.

Now bring everything up to simmering point, then cover the casserole and bake the pears on a low rack in the oven for about 1½ hours. After that remove the casserole from the oven, turn the pears over onto their other side, then replace the lid and return them to the oven for a further 1½ hours.

When the pears are cooked, transfer them to a serving bowl to cool, leaving the liquid in the casserole. Then remove the cinnamon sticks and vanilla bean. Place the casserole over direct heat and then, in a cup, mix the cornstarch with a little cold water until you have a smooth paste. Add this to the casserole, whisking with a balloon whisk as you add it. Bring the syrup just up to simmering point, by which time it will have thickened slightly. Then remove from the heat and when the syrup is cool, spoon it over the pears, basting them well.

Now cover the pears with foil or plastic wrap and place them in the fridge to chill thoroughly. Serve the pears sitting upright in individual dishes with the sauce spooned over and the crème fraîche passed around separately.

NOTE: *This recipe can also be made, as in the photograph opposite, with red wine or strong dry cider—each version has its own particular charm.*

PEARS BAKED IN MARSALA WINE, RED WINE AND DRY CIDER

Iced Apple Soufflé with Caramelized Apple

Serves 6

I first tasted this amazingly good dessert at a meal cooked by a friend, Lesley Nathan, in the summer, when she made it with strawberries. This is her recipe, adapted for winter with apples, and every bit as wonderful.

4 Granny Smith apples
1½ cups extra strong vintage cider
Zest and juice of 1 large lemon
   (⅓ cup juice)
¾ cup superfine sugar
1 cup crème fraîche, very well chilled
4 large egg whites

FOR THE CARAMELIZED APPLE:
1 small (4-ounce) dessert apple, (such
   as a Granny Smith)
¼ stick butter
1½ tablespoons superfine sugar

You will also need 6 half-cup straight-sided ramekins, parchment paper for making collars and small rubber bands.

First wash the Granny Smith apples and, leaving the skins on, core and chop them roughly. After that place them in a saucepan with the cider, lemon zest, lemon juice and sugar. Now bring it all up to the boil and simmer gently until the apples are mushy, which will take about 15–20 minutes. Then remove them from the heat and allow them to cool slightly before passing them through a fine nylon sieve, pushing the purée through with a ladle. Now discard the skins left in the sieve and leave the apple purée to get completely cold.

Meanwhile prepare the ramekins. First make collars for each of them: Cut 6 pieces of parchment paper measuring 7 × 12 inches, fold each in half along its length to 3½ × 12 inches, then fold one of the long edges over 1 inch, giving you a thicker piece at the bottom to stabilize the collar. You will now have collars measuring 2½ × 12 inches, so wrap each collar around the ramekins, keeping the fold to the bottom and hold them in place with a rubber band.

When the purée is completely cold, remove the crème fraîche from the refrigerator, transfer it to a bowl and whip until it starts to thicken—but be careful not to let it get too stiff. Next put the egg whites in a large bowl and, using an electric mixer with squeaky-clean beaters, beat to the stiff-peak stage. Then fold a third of the egg whites into the apple purée along with the crème fraîche, and when everything is completely amalgamated, very gently fold in the remaining egg whites. Pour everything into a large pitcher and then into the collared ramekins. The mixture will come right up into the top of the collars. Now stand the ramekins on a tray and freeze for 4–6 hours, making sure they are standing level.

To make the caramelized apple slices, cut the apple into quarters and remove the core, then cut these into slices ⅛ inch thick. You will need 30 thin slices. Next take a large, solid skillet, 8–9 inches in diameter. Melt half the butter. When it starts to foam, sprinkle in half the sugar. Stir it around, keeping the heat high, add the apple slices and cook them

30–40 seconds on each side until golden brown and slightly crisp. You will need to do this in 2 batches. Lay the first batch on parchment paper, then add the remaining butter and sugar, if necessary, and cook the rest. These can be made up to 2 hours in advance.

Take the ramekins out of the freezer and transfer to the fridge 20 minutes before serving. Then just peel away the collars, having removed the rubber bands. Finally, arrange the apple slices in circles on top before serving.

Lime and Mango Ice Cream

Makes 1 quart

This is a beautiful ice cream, but it is most important that the mangoes are extremely ripe—almost bordering on overripe. The way to test this is to hold one and check that it feels heavy when held in the hand and also gives off a powerful and fragrant aroma through the skin. If you can only buy underripe mangoes, they should be placed in a brown paper bag and left to ripen in the dark at room temperature.

½ cup granulated sugar
⅔ cup water
5 large, extremely ripe mangoes

3–4 limes
1 cup crème fraîche

You will also need a shallow plastic container measuring 10 × 6 × 2 inches, with lid.

First thoroughly dissolve the sugar in the water over a low heat, then turn the heat up a little bit and simmer gently for 15 minutes, without allowing the liquid to evaporate. Then remove it from the heat and leave aside to cool slightly.

To prepare the mangoes, slice them in half along the length of the stone on either side of it (and have a plate underneath to catch all of the precious juice). Now use a spoon to scrape all the flesh away from the skin, then place this into a blender. Next, using a sharp paring knife, remove the skin from the flesh around the stone, then scrape all the flesh from this into the blender, leaving the stone and any fibrous threads behind.

Now blend the mangoes until you have a smooth purée. If you don't have a blender or processor, place a plastic sieve over a bowl and push the flesh of the fruit through. Either way should yield about 2½ cups of purée. Then squeeze the limes to produce ½ cup juice. Add the juice and sugar syrup to the purée and combine thoroughly.

Next spoon out the crème fraîche into another bowl and whip it lightly till it increases in volume and thickness. Now use a metal spoon to fold the fruit purée into the crème fraîche, and place the mixture in the plastic container and place it in the coldest part of the freezer for about 2 hours or until it is beginning to freeze around the edges. Then, using an electric mixer, beat the frozen edges into the middle, replace the lid and return it to the freezer for another 2–3 hours, then repeat the whole process. After that freeze again until it is quite frozen.

Before serving, place the container in the body of the fridge for about 1 hour. If you have an ice-cream maker, freeze-churn according to the manufacturer's instructions.

Banoffee Cheesecake with Toffee Pecan Sauce

Serves 6–8

The magic word *banoffee* is simply an amalgam of *banana* and *toffee*. But here I have incorporated these ingredients into a quite magical cheesecake.

FOR THE CRUST:
¾ cup pecans (use half for the crust and half for the sauce — see below)
4 ounces oatmeal cookies, crushed
3 tablespoons butter, melted

FOR THE FILLING:
3 medium-sized ripe bananas (8 ounces peeled)
1 tablespoon lemon juice
3 large eggs
1½ cups soft farmer cheese
1 cup fromage blanc (8% fat)

¾ cup superfine sugar

FOR THE SAUCE:
½ stick butter
⅓ cup brown sugar
¼ cup granulated sugar
½ cup light molasses
⅔ cup heavy cream
A few drops vanilla extract

FOR THE TOPPING:
2 tablespoons lemon juice
3 medium-sized ripe bananas

You will also need a springform cake pan, 8 inches in diameter, lightly buttered. Preheat the oven to 400°F.

Begin by toasting all the pecans. Place them on a baking sheet and bake in the oven for 7 minutes until lightly toasted or, if you watch them like a hawk, you can toast them under a broiler. Then chop them quite small.

Place the crushed cookies in a bowl. Add the melted butter and half the pecans, mix them well, then press all this into the bottom of the cake pan and prebake the crust in the oven for 15 minutes. Then lower the temperature to 300°F.

For the filling, first blend the bananas and lemon juice in a food processor until smooth, then simply add all the rest of the filling ingredients. Blend again then pour it all over the cookie crust and bake on the middle rack of the oven for 1 hour. Turn off the oven and leave the cheesecake inside to cool slowly until completely cooled; this slow cooling will stop the cheesecake cracking.

To make the sauce, place the butter, sugars and molasses in a saucepan and, over very low heat, allow everything to dissolve completely. Let it cook for about 5 minutes. Pour in the cream and vanilla extract and stir until everything is smooth, then add the rest of the chopped pecans. Remove it from the heat and allow it to cool completely before pouring it into a pitcher ready for serving.

When you are ready to assemble the cheesecake put the 2 tablespoons of lemon juice into a bowl. Slice the remaining bananas at an oblique angle into ¼-inch slices, and gently toss them around to get an even coating of juice. If you like you can spoon a small circle of sauce onto the center of the cheesecake, then layer the bananas in overlapping circles all around it. Serve the cheesecake cut into slices with the rest of the sauce passed around separately.

BANOFFEE CHEESECAKE WITH TOFFEE PECAN SAUCE

Fallen Chocolate Soufflé with Armagnac Prunes and Crème Fraîche Sauce

Serves 8–10

*Y*es, it's really true—this soufflé is supposed to puff like a normal one, but then it is removed from the oven and allowed slowly to subside into a lovely, dark, squidgey chocolate dessert. It is served slightly chilled with a prune and crème fraîche sauce. The only problem I can foresee with this recipe is that someone will write and tell me that their soufflé wouldn't sink! Let me preempt that by saying don't worry— I'm sure it will taste just as good. This also works superbly with prunes in Amaretto or port, so use whichever flavor you like best.

FOR THE PRUNES:
12 large California pitted prunes
⅔ cup water
⅔ cup Armagnac

FOR THE SOUFFLÉ:
7 ounces good-quality dark unsweetened chocolate (see note on page 233)
1 stick unsalted butter

1 tablespoon Armagnac
4 large eggs, separated
½ cup superfine sugar
A little sifted cocoa powder for dusting

FOR THE PRUNE AND CRÈME FRAÎCHE SAUCE:
The remainder of the soaked prunes
¾ cup crème fraîche

You will also need an 8-inch springform cake pan, greased and lined with parchment paper.

The prunes need to be soaked overnight, so simply place them in a saucepan with the water, bring them up to simmering point, remove from the heat, then pour the prunes and their cooking liquid into a bowl and stir in the Armagnac while they're still warm. Leave to cool, then cover the bowl with plastic wrap and chill in the refrigerator overnight.

To make the soufflé, preheat the oven to 325°F. Meanwhile, break the chocolate into squares and place them with the butter into a bowl fitted over a saucepan containing some barely simmering water (making sure the bowl does not touch the water). Leave the chocolate for a few moments to melt, then stir until you have a smooth, glossy mixture. Now remove the bowl from the heat, add the Armagnac and leave to cool.

Next take a large, roomy bowl and combine the egg yolks and superfine sugar in it. Then beat them together for about 5–6 minutes, using an electric mixer—when you lift up the beaters and the mixture drops off, making ribbonlike trails, it's ready.

Now count out 18 of the soaked prunes, cut each one in half and combine the halves with the beaten egg mixture along with the melted chocolate.

Next you'll need to wash the beaters thoroughly with hot soapy water to remove all the grease, and dry them well. In another bowl beat the egg whites till they form soft peaks. After that, fold them carefully into the chocolate mixture. Spoon this mixture into the prepared pan and bake the soufflé in the center of the oven for about 30 minutes or until the center feels springy to the touch. Allow the soufflé to cool in the pan (it's great fun watching it fall very slowly). When it's quite cool, remove it from the pan, peel off the paper, then cover and chill for several hours (or it can be made 2–3 days ahead if more convenient).

To make the sauce, simply purée the reserved prunes and their liquid, place the purée in a serving bowl and lightly stir in the crème fraîche to give a sort of marbled effect. Pass the sauce around separately to serve with the soufflé. Serve the soufflé dusted with cocoa powder and cut into *small* slices (it's very rich).

N O T E : *The prunes soaked in Armagnac and served with crème fraîche make an extremely good dessert in their own right. Also, the soufflé and sauce freeze very well for up to a month.*

Spiced Cranberry and Orange Jellies

Serves 4

I like to serve a jelly at a celebration dinner because it is so nice to have something cool, light and refreshing at the end of a meal that has included a lot of rich food. This jelly is incredibly simple to make, but don't be tempted to jazz it up—I've tried that and found this simple version to be best by far.

2½ cups cranberry juice cocktail
2 envelopes unflavored gelatin
Juice and zest of 2 oranges
½ teaspoon ground ginger
1 cinnamon stick, broken into pieces
⅓ cup superfine sugar

FOR THE FROSTED
CRANBERRIES:
Approximately 20 fresh cranberries
1 large egg white, beaten
1 tablespoon superfine sugar

↩ *You will also need four 1-cup stemmed glasses.*

First measure the cranberry juice into a bowl and sprinkle in the gelatin. Next use a potato peeler to pare off the outer zest of the oranges, and put the zest in a saucepan with the cranberry juice–gelatin mixture, orange juice, ginger, cinnamon, and sugar. Bring everything up to a gentle simmer, then remove from the heat and leave aside for approximately 2 hours, until the jelly is just on the point of setting.

Now strain the jelly through a nylon sieve into a pitcher, pour into the stemmed glasses, cover and chill in the fridge until needed.

For the frosted cranberries all you need to do is dip each berry into the beaten egg white and roll it in superfine sugar to give a generous coating. Then leave the berries spread out on parchment paper to become crisp.

Remove the jellies from the fridge half an hour before serving and pile about 5 frosted cranberries on top of each glass.

N O T E : *If you prefer, you can make the jelly in a 3-cup jelly mold.*

Lemon Ricotta Cheesecake
with a Confit of Lemons

Serves 6

This is a very light, fluffy lemony cheesecake which, if you serve it with a Confit of Lemons (see opposite), makes a delightfully refreshing end to a rich meal.

FOR THE CRUST:
4 ounces oatmeal cookies
¼ cup slivered almonds
½ stick butter, melted

3–4 lemons
1 envelope unflavored gelatin

2 large egg yolks
¼ cup plus 1 tablespoon superfine
  sugar
1½ cups ricotta cheese
1¼ cups heavy cream

You will also need a 7-inch or 8-inch springform cake pan.
Line the sides with baking parchment paper to come 1 inch above the rim.
Preheat the oven to 400°F.

First of all, prepare the crust by crushing the cookies. The best way to do this is to lay them flat inside a plastic bag, then roll them with a rolling pin to crush them coarsely. Then put them into a bowl along with the slivered almonds and stir the melted butter into them. After that, press this mixture evenly and firmly onto the bottom of the pan and then place in the oven to prebake for 15 minutes. After that remove it from the oven and allow it to cool completely.

Meanwhile remove the zest from the lemons using a fine grater (it can be grated onto a board and chopped even more finely if required). Then take the juice from the lemons and measure ⅔ cup. Next put 3 tablespoons of the lemon juice into a small bowl, sprinkle the gelatin over, then place the bowl in a small saucepan with 1 inch simmering water and leave it to dissolve for 10 minutes, or until it is absolutely clear and transparent.

Now put the egg yolks, sugar and ricotta cheese into a food processor or blender and blend it all on a high speed for about 1 minute. Then add the remaining lemon juice, the zest and the gelatin, which should be poured through a strainer. Blend everything again now until it's all absolutely smooth. Then take a large bowl and beat the cream until you get a floppy consistency, then pour this in to join the rest of the cheese mixture and blend again, this time for just a few seconds. Next pour everything over the cookie crust, cover with foil and chill in the refrigerator for a minimum of 3 hours.

To serve the cheesecake, carefully remove it from the pan onto a serving plate, decorate with a circle of lemon confit slices and serve the rest of the confit separately.

Confit of Lemons

Serves 6

2 large juicy lemons (unwaxed if
  possible)

1½ cups water
½ cup granulated sugar

*You will also need a nonaluminum saucepan approximately 8 inches in diameter and a circle of
parchment paper of the same diameter to keep the lemons under the surface of the liquid.*

Take one and a half of the lemons and slice them into thin rings about ⅛ inch thick, discarding the end pieces and seeds. Place these in a saucepan and add sufficient cold water to just cover them, bring to a simmer for 3 minutes, then drain through a sieve and discard the water. Now pour the 1½ cups water into the same pan, add the sugar, stir over a gentle heat until all the grains have dissolved, then add the lemon slices. Once the liquid has returned to a very gentle simmer, lay the circle of parchment paper on the surface of the liquid—this will help the lemon slices to cook evenly.

Now continue to cook them at the very gentlest simmer, without a lid, for 45 minutes, until the skins are tender. Check them at 30 minutes by inserting the tip of a knife just in case they are cooking a little faster. When they are tender remove them with a slotted spoon to a shallow dish. The liquid will be much reduced at this stage, but what we want is about ⅔ cup; if you have much more than this increase the heat a little and reduce further. Then squeeze the juice from the remaining half lemon, pour it into the syrup and pour this over the lemon slices. Cover and leave overnight if possible.

Mascarpone Creams and Caramel Sauce with Caramelized Hazelnuts

Serves 6

Rich, luscious mascarpone lightened by yogurt makes these little velvety creams cool and soothing after a rich main course. The contrast of the dark flavors of the caramel is an extra delight. People tend to get worried about caramel—so here are two things to remember. First, if it sets too hard, just place it over a gentle heat to soften again, and second, to clean the saucepan, place it over a gentle heat, filled with warm soapy water.

FOR THE CREAMS:
⅔ cup light cream
1 envelope unflavored gelatin
⅓ cup superfine sugar
1¼ cups mascarpone (Italian cream cheese)
1½ cups whole-milk plain yogurt
2 teaspoons vanilla extract

FOR THE CARAMELIZED SAUCE AND NUTS:
1 cup plus 2 tablespoons granulated sugar
2 tablespoons hot water
⅔ cup heavy cream
1 teaspoon vanilla extract
¼ cup (approximately 30) whole shelled hazelnuts, lightly toasted

You will also need six ¾-cup pudding cups or ramekins and some plastic wrap.

First prepare the little pots by lining them with plastic wrap, which will make them no problem to turn out later on. The easiest way to do this is as follows—using a piece of paper towel dabbed in a flavorless oil (such as peanut), lightly oil the inside of each pot, then take some pieces of plastic wrap approximately 10 inches in length and push them inside the pots, then, using a clean pastry brush, push it into the sides and base, making sure it overlaps at the rim.

After that you can make the creams. First measure 3 tablespoons of the light cream into a small dish and sprinkle the gelatin into this. Stir it around then leave it for about 10 minutes until it has soaked into the cream. Meanwhile heat the sugar and remaining cream very gently in a small saucepan until all the sugar crystals have dissolved (you can see this quite clearly if you coat the back of a wooden spoon). Now add the soaked gelatin to the pan, remove it from the heat and whisk until all the gelatin has melted. Then leave it aside to cool slightly.

Next spoon the mascarpone into a large bowl and whisk it down to soften it, then add the yogurt and vanilla. Whisk again, then when everything is smooth pour the cream and gelatin through a sieve into the bowl and mix once more. Now pour the mixture into the little pots, filling them to within ½ inch of the tops. Cover each pot with a little extra plastic wrap, place them on a tray and leave in the fridge until well chilled and set—at least 3 hours.

To make the caramel sauce, put the granulated sugar into a medium-sized skillet over a very gentle heat. When the sugar has dissolved, turn the heat up to high so the liquid begins to bubble and darken. Stir and simmer until the mixture becomes the color of dark honey. This will probably take 7–8 minutes, but watch it carefully as it only takes a few seconds to change from caramel to burnt sugar! Take the pan off the heat and add the hot water. This will make it bubble and splutter, but it *will* die down. Now spoon 2 tablespoons of caramel into a bowl. Add the cream and vanilla to the remaining caramel in the pan and then pour that into a serving pitcher for later. Dip the hazelnuts in the bowl containing the caramel a few at a time to get them coated, then spread them on a tray lined with parchment paper and leave them to harden.

To serve the creams: Remove them from the fridge about half an hour before serving, take the top layer of plastic wrap away, turn each pot out onto individual serving plates and gently pull the edges of the plastic wrap used to line the pot. Then spoon the sauce over and garnish with the nuts.

Tiramisu

Serves 6

There isn't a classic recipe for tiramisu as such, as there are many versions both in Italy and around the world, but the following one is I think the nicest I've come across. For lovers of strong coffee, dark chocolate and the rich creaminess of mascarpone, it is one of the nicest, easiest and most popular desserts of the party season.

3 large egg yolks
¼ cup superfine sugar
1¼ cups mascarpone (Italian cream cheese)
2 large egg whites
About 24 ladyfingers (or boudoir cookies)

⅔ cup very strong espresso coffee
3 tablespoons dark rum
2 ounces good-quality dark unsweetened chocolate (see note on page 233), chopped
A little sifted cocoa powder for dusting

You will also need six 1-cup stemmed glasses.

First put the egg yolks into a medium-sized bowl together with the sugar and beat with an electric mixer on high speed for about 3 minutes or until the mixture forms a light, pale mousse. In a separate large bowl stir the mascarpone with a wooden spoon to soften it, then gradually beat in the egg yolk mixture. After each addition beat well until the mixture is smooth before adding more. Now wash and dry the beaters of the mixer so they are perfectly clean, then in a third bowl beat the egg whites until they form soft peaks. Now lightly fold this into the mascarpone mixture and then put the bowl aside.

Next break the ladyfingers in half, then pour the coffee and rum into a shallow dish and then dip the ladyfingers briefly into it, turning them over—they will absorb the liquid very quickly. Now simply layer the desserts by putting 3 of the soaked ladyfinger halves into each glass, followed by a tablespoon of mascarpone mixture and a layer of chocolate. Repeat the whole process, putting 5 halves in next, followed by the mascarpone, finishing with a layer of chopped chocolate and a final dusting of cocoa powder. Cover the glasses with plastic wrap, then chill in the refrigerator for several hours and serve straight from the fridge—I think it tastes better very cold.

TIRAMISU

Apple Crêpes with Calvados

Serves 6

*C*alvados has all the concentrated flavor and aroma of an apple loft and it is a wonderful pantry cooking ingredient, but if you don't have any Calvados you can make this recipe using strong cider. Either way you end up with a mouthwatering combination of apples, crêpes and cinnamon—made even more special if served with some well-chilled cream laced with Calvados (or cider).

1 large Granny Smith apple
2 tablespoons Calvados
⅓ cup plus 1 tablespoon flour
¼ cup buckwheat flour
1 teaspoon ground cinnamon
2 large eggs
1 cup crème fraîche

½ stick butter, melted

To Serve:
Superfine sugar
Heavy cream, well chilled
2 tablespoons Calvados

You will also need a small, solid skillet.

Begin by peeling and coring the apple, then cut it into quarters and grate it on the coarse side of the grater into a bowl. Then toss the grated apple around in 2 tablespoons of Calvados and leave it aside for 10 minutes. Meanwhile sift the flour, buckwheat flour and cinnamon into a bowl. Then in a separate bowl, whisk the eggs and crème fraîche together, then gradually blend this into the flour mixture using an electric mixer until you have a smooth, lump-free batter. Then stir in the apple and Calvados.

Before you make the crêpes, put a large plate in a warm oven so that as you make them they can be kept warm, covered with some foil.

To make the crêpes, melt the butter in the skillet, then pour it into a cup. To make your first crêpe, heat the skillet over medium heat until it is really hot, then use 1 tablespoon of the batter to make each crêpe, cook until it becomes crisp at the edges and is a lovely golden color underneath, then, using a metal spatula, turn the crêpe over and cook the other side until crisp and golden (this should take about 45 seconds on each side). Remove the crêpe to a warm plate. Use a wedge of paper towel to lubricate the pan again with melted butter, then continue cooking the crêpes until the batter is all used up.

When you are ready to serve the crêpes, transfer them to warmed serving plates, giving each person three or four, lightly dusted with superfine sugar. Then combine the cream and Calvados, put a little on each serving and pass the rest around separately. For a special occasion you could flame these by leaving them piled on a large plate, dusting with superfine sugar, then warming 3 tablespoons of Calvados in a small pan, lighting it with a match and pouring the flaming Calvados over the pancakes. When the flame has died down serve each person 3 or 4 crêpes, with the cream served separately.

Classic Crêpes Suzette

Serves 6

T his is another qualifier for my sixties recipe revival. There was a time when this recipe was certainly overexposed, but now that it has become a forgotten rarity, we can all reappreciate its undoubted charm, which remains in spite of changes in fashion.

FOR THE CRÊPES:
1 quantity basic crêpes (see page 179), with the addition of the grated zest of 1 medium orange and 1 tablespoon superfine sugar mixed into the batter

FOR THE SAUCE:
⅔ cup orange juice (from 3–4 medium oranges)

Grated zest of 1 medium orange
Grated zest and juice of 1 small lemon
1 tablespoon superfine sugar
3 tablespoons Grand Marnier, Cointreau or brandy
½ stick unsalted butter

A little extra Grand Marnier for flaming

⌒ You will also need a heavy-bottomed 10-inch skillet.

These little crêpes should be thinner than the basic crêpes, so when you're making them as described on page 179 with the above additions to the batter, use only 1½ tablespoons of batter at a time in the crêpe pan. If they look a bit ragged in the pan, no matter because they are going to be folded anyway. You should end up with 15 or 16 crêpes.

For the sauce, mix all the ingredients—with the exception of the butter—in a bowl. At the same time warm the plates on which the crêpes are going to be served. Now melt the butter in the skillet, pour in the sauce and allow it to heat very gently. Then place the first crêpe in the skillet and give it time to warm through before folding it in half and then half again to make a triangular shape. Slide this onto the very edge of the skillet, tilt the skillet slightly so the sauce runs back into the center, then add the next crêpe. Continue like this until they're all reheated, folded and well soaked with the sauce.

You can flame them at this point if you like. Heat a ladle by holding it over a flame or by resting it on the edge of a hot plate, then, away from the heat, pour a little Grand Marnier into it, return it to the heat to warm the spirit, then light it. Carry the flaming ladle to the table over the pan and pour the flames over the crêpes before serving on the warmed plates.

Chocolate Mascarpone Cheesecake with Fruit and Nuts Served with Crème Fraîche

Serves 6–8

This is quite simply a chocolate cheesecake to die for. If you like chocolate, if you like dark chocolate with fruit and nuts and if you like luscious, velvet-textured mascarpone . . . need I say more? (See photograph on pages 196–97.)

FOR THE FILLING:
1 cup whole hazelnuts
3½ ounces good-quality dark unsweetened chocolate (see note on page 233)
1¼ cups mascarpone (Italian cream cheese)
1 cup fromage blanc (8% fat)
2 large eggs
3 tablespoons superfine sugar
½ cup raisins

FOR THE CRUST:
4 ounces oatmeal cookies

⅓ cup chopped toasted hazelnuts
¼ stick butter, melted

FOR THE CHOCOLATE CURLS TO DECORATE:
3½ ounces good-quality dark unsweetened chocolate

TO SERVE:
1 teaspoon cocoa powder
Crème fraîche or heavy cream

You will also need a 7-inch cake pan, preferably springform, with a depth of 3 inches; if shallower than this, line the sides with parchment paper.

Preheat the oven to 400°F.

Before embarking on a baked cheesecake remember that, to prevent cracking, it's best cooled slowly in a switched-off oven. So you also need to make it well ahead.

First of all arrange the whole hazelnuts on a baking sheet, then place them into the oven and toast to a golden brown; use a timer and have a look after 5 minutes, giving them 5 minutes extra if they need it. Then remove them from the hot sheet to cool.

Meanwhile, make the crust of the cheesecake by crushing the cookies with a rolling pin—not too finely, though, as it's nice to have a fairly uneven texture. Scoop all the crushed cookie crumbs into a bowl, then add the chopped nuts and melted butter and mix everything very thoroughly before pressing it very firmly into the bottom of the cake pan. Now place the pan in the oven and prebake the crust for 20 minutes. Then remove it and let it cool while you make the filling. Reduce the oven temperature to 300°F.

PREVIOUS PAGE: CHOCOLATE MASCARPONE CHEESECAKE WITH FRUIT AND NUTS SERVED WITH CRÈME FRAÎCHE

To make the filling, first place 2 inches of water in a saucepan, then put the saucepan on to heat. Meanwhile, break the chocolate into small squares and place in a bowl. As soon as the water is boiling remove the pan from the heat and place the bowl on top until everything melts. Don't be tempted to put the bowl on top of the saucepan while the water is still boiling—because of the high cocoa solid content this chocolate mustn't get overheated or it will separate. Now spoon the mascarpone and fromage blanc into a large bowl and beat them together until smooth, preferably with an electric mixer. Then add the eggs and sugar and give it another good beating before adding the melted chocolate—use a rubber spatula so that you get every last bit of chocolate from the bowl—and then lightly fold the chocolate into the egg mixture. Finally add the raisins and the whole toasted hazelnuts.

Now pour the mixture into the pan, smoothing it out with the back of a spoon, then place it on the center rack of the oven and bake for 1¼ hours. After that turn the oven off, but leave the cheesecake inside until it's completely cooled.

For the Chocolate Curls

Melt the chocolate as before, then pour it onto a flat, smooth surface. The underside of a large plate will do. It should form a circle of about 6 inches diameter and ¼ inch thick. Place the plate into the fridge to chill for 45 minutes. What you want is the chocolate to be set hard enough so that if you press the surface of the chocolate it doesn't leave an indentation.

Now take it from the fridge, and if you want curls like those in our photograph use a cheese slicer; otherwise a sharp knife will do if you hold the blade in both hands. Just pull it all along the chocolate toward you and it should curl up. What is very important to know here is that if it doesn't curl and you end up with a pile of chocolate shavings they'll look just as nice—either way, place them in a rigid plastic container and then put this in the fridge until you need them.

To serve the cheesecake, sprinkle the surface with chocolate curls, dust with a sprinkling of cocoa powder and serve in slices with crème fraîche or cream passed around separately.

CHAPTER ELEVEN

Proper Puddings

IN MY ATTEMPT TO REVIVE SUNDAY LUNCH I AM INCLUDING PROPER, OLD-fashioned British puddings here. Whatever your views on health and diet, Sunday *is* a feast day, and the joy of cooking and eating a proper pudding must increase our sense of well-being, and that surely has to be a healthy thing.

If you enjoyed the little Sticky Toffee Puddings in the *Christmas* book, I can promise you will love the little Sticky Gingerbread Puddings with Ginger Wine and Brandy Sauce in this chapter (see page 202), which can also be made well in advance and frozen. And if you really want to spoil your family and friends, do get the hang of making proper custard: It isn't difficult and with the addition of a little cornstarch to stabilize it, it will never curdle.

I doubt if anyone anywhere does not love bread and butter pudding, and I've included two here—one made with dark chunky marmalade on page 211 and the other a very sophisticated chocolate version on page 208. Both are to die for.

Steamed Treacle Sponge Pudding

Serves 6–8

If the winter weather is getting you down or you're feeling gray or sad, I'm certain a steamed treacle sponge will put you right in no time at all. It takes moments to prepare, will steam away happily all by itself without needing attention, and is the ultimate in comfort foods. Because treacle is not commonly available in the States, you will most likely want to make this using molasses.

3 tablespoons light molasses or treacle
1½ cups self-rising flour
1½ sticks butter, softened
3 large eggs
1 cup light brown sugar
1 tablespoon dark molasses or black
   treacle

To Serve:
3 tablespoons light molasses or treacle
Custard or crème fraîche

You will also need a well-buttered 1-quart pudding basin, and a double sheet of foil measuring 16 × 12 inches.

First of all butter the basin, then measure 3 tablespoons of light molasses into it (grease the spoon first). Now take a large mixing bowl, sift the flour into it and add the softened butter, eggs, brown sugar and dark molasses. Then use an electric mixer (or a large fork and a lot of elbow grease) and beat the mixture for about 2 minutes until it's thoroughly blended.

Now spoon the mixture into the basin, use the back of a spoon to level the top, then place the foil over, making a pleat in the center. Then pull it down the outside of the basin and tie the string around the rim, taking it over the top and tying it on the other side to make yourself a handle for lifting. Then trim off the excess foil all the way around. Now place the pudding in a steamer fitted over a saucepan of boiling water and steam the pudding for 2 hours, checking the water level halfway through.

To serve, loosen the pudding all around using a metal spatula, invert it onto a warmed plate and pour another 3 tablespoons of light molasses (warmed if you like) over the top before taking it to the table. Serve with custard or some well-chilled crème fraîche.

Sticky Gingerbread Puddings
with Ginger Wine and Brandy Sauce

Serves 8

For quite a long time now I've been trying to come up with an idea that matches the charm and popularity of the Sticky Toffee Puddings in the *Christmas* book. This is quite definitely it—it has the same degree of lightness and this time the fragrance and spiciness of preserved ginger, which takes the edge off the sweetness beautifully. (See photograph on pages 204–5.)

4 ounces preserved ginger in syrup
  (8 pieces)
1⅓ cups self-rising flour
⅓ teaspoon ground cinnamon
⅓ teaspoon ground cloves
¼ teaspoon ground ginger
2 large eggs
¼ stick butter, softened
⅔ cup dark brown sugar
1 tablespoon dark molasses
1 heaping teaspoon freshly grated
  gingerroot
¾ cup warm water

1 medium Rome apple (about 6 ounces),
  peeled, cored and chopped small

FOR THE GINGER WINE
AND BRANDY SAUCE:
1 cup dark brown sugar
1 stick unsalted butter
¼ cup ginger wine
2 tablespoons brandy
2 pieces preserved ginger, chopped
  small

TO SERVE:
Heavy cream, well chilled

You will also need eight ¾-cup pudding cups, well buttered, and a solid baking sheet.

Preheat the oven to 350°F.

First of all place the pieces of preserved ginger in a food processor and turn the motor on for about 7–10 seconds. Be careful not to process for too long—the ginger should be chopped small, but not puréed! After that sift the flour and spices into a mixing bowl. Then add the eggs, butter and brown sugar. The way to deal with the molasses is to grease the spoon first and, using a rubber spatula or another spoon, push it into the bowl to join the rest of the ingredients. Now add the freshly grated ginger. Then, using an electric mixer, beat everything together gradually, adding the water until you have a smooth mixture. Finally fold in the apple and preserved ginger.

Now divide the mixture among the buttered pudding cups, stand them on a baking sheet and bake in the center of the oven for 35 minutes or until they feel firm and springy to the touch. After that remove them from the oven and let them stand for about 5 minutes, then run a metal spatula around the edges of the cups and turn them out. Allow the puddings to cool completely and keep them wrapped in plastic wrap until you need them.

To make the sauce, all you do is gently melt together the brown sugar and butter until all the sugar has completely dissolved, then whisk in the ginger wine and brandy, add the chopped ginger, and the sauce is ready to serve.

To serve the puddings, preheat the broiler to its highest setting and arrange the puddings on a heatproof dish or tray. Spoon the sauce over, making sure that no little bits of ginger are actually on the top of the puddings, then place the whole thing under the broiler so that the tops of the puddings are about 5 inches from the source of heat. Now allow them to heat through—this will take about 6–8 minutes, by which time the tops will be slightly crunchy and the sauce will be hot and bubbly. Serve with chilled heavy cream.

NOTE: *If you want to make these puddings in advance, they freeze beautifully, and after defrosting should be reheated as above.*

NEXT PAGE: STICKY GINGERBREAD PUDDINGS
WITH GINGER WINE AND BRANDY SAUCE

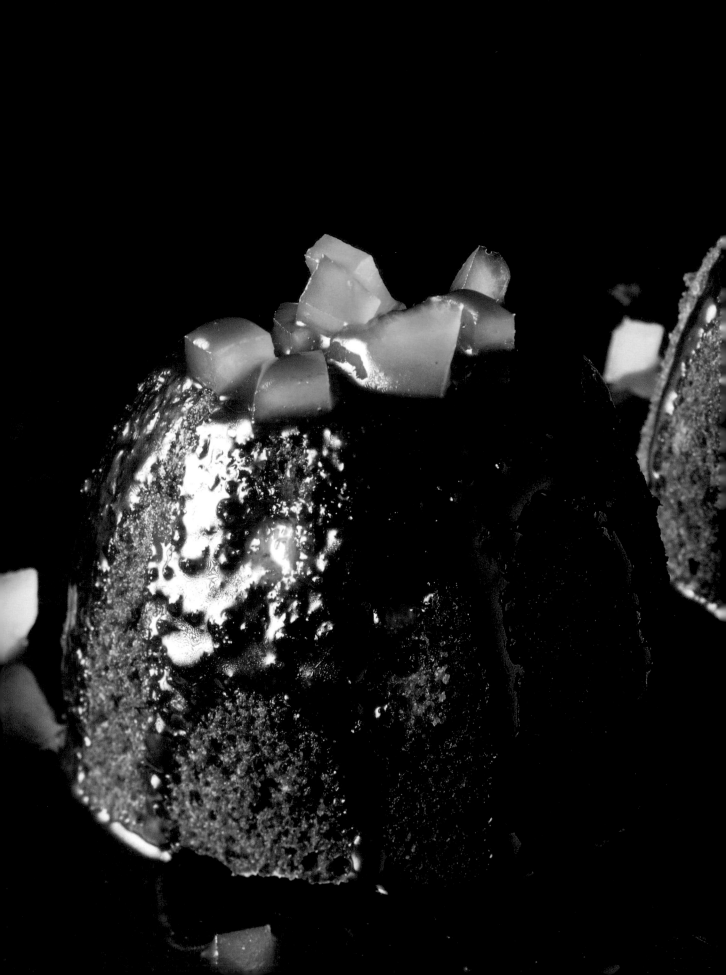

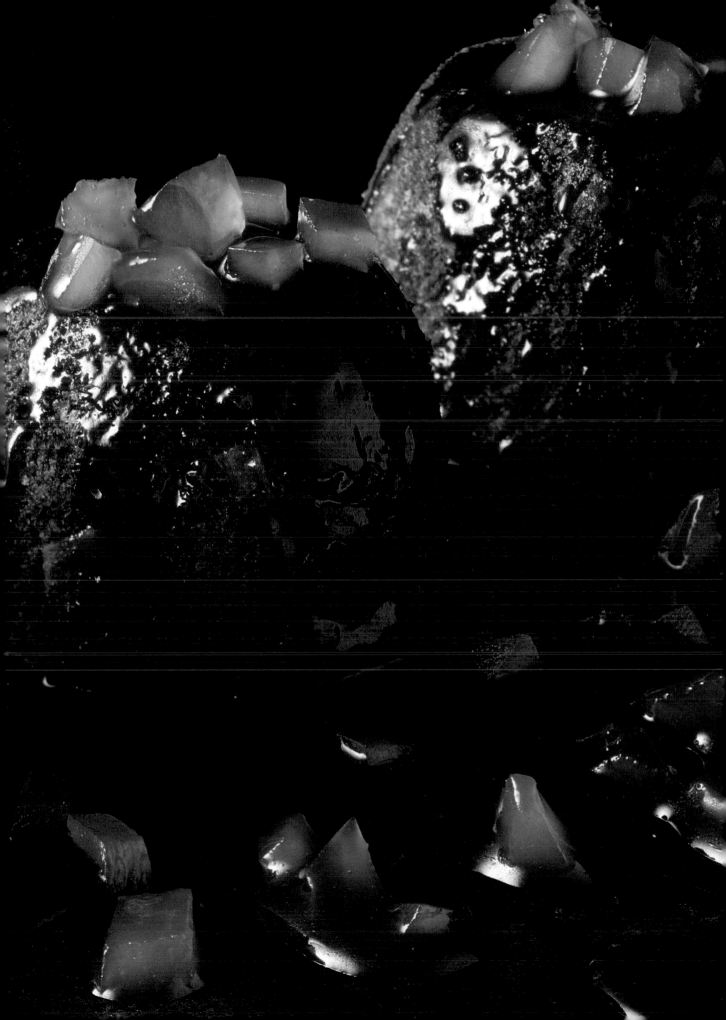

Apple Sponge Puddings
with Mincemeat Topping and Real Custard

Serves 6

Somehow it's more elegant to serve little individual puddings if you are entertaining. These are incredibly light and fluffy with chunks of apple that become soft and squidgey during the steaming. My thanks to Sister Lucy at St. Joseph's Rearsby for giving me the original recipe.

1 cup self-rising flour
1 stick butter, softened
½ cup superfine sugar
2 large eggs
1 medium Rome apple, chopped small
Grated zest of 1 lemon

3 heaping tablespoons mincemeat
*   (preferably homemade)*
1 tablespoon brandy

> *You will also need six ¾-cup aluminum pudding cups, well buttered,
> and a steamer, plus 6 pieces of aluminum foil measuring 6 × 8 inches.*

First of all sift the flour into a large bowl, then simply add the softened butter, superfine sugar and eggs, and beat, preferably with an electric mixer, until you have a soft, smooth, creamy mixture (about 2 minutes). After that, lightly fold in the chopped apple and half the lemon zest.

Next spoon the mincemeat into a small bowl and add the brandy and the other half of the lemon zest. Stir them together, then divide the mincemeat equally among the pudding cups and spoon the pudding mixture on top, smoothing it out with the back of a spoon. You'll need to leave a space of about ½ inch to allow the puddings to rise. Now place a square of foil on each pudding, making a pleat in the center, then fold in the edges of the foil all the way around the edge of the cup. Now place the steamer over a saucepan filled with boiling water. Put 3 puddings in, then loosely place a piece of crumpled foil on top and put the other 3 puddings on top of that. Now place a tight-fitting lid on the steamer and let the puddings steam for 1 hour, topping off the boiling water if it needs it. Before serving allow the puddings to stand for 15 minutes before turning them out onto warm serving plates. Serve with Real Custard Sauce (opposite).

NOTE: *If you want you can make this as one large pudding and steam for 2½ hours, using a 1-quart pudding basin.*

Real Custard Sauce

Makes 3¾ cups (enough for 6 people)

*P*roper custard is a treat for special occasions, and if you really want to push the boat out you can use heavy cream in place of light.

2¼ cups light cream
1 cup milk
1 vanilla bean

5 large egg yolks
3 tablespoons superfine sugar
2 teaspoons cornstarch

First of all take a saucepan and slowly heat the cream and milk together, with the vanilla bean added, until the liquid just reaches simmering point. Then take it off the heat and allow the vanilla to infuse for about 15 minutes.

Meanwhile, whisk the egg yolks, sugar and cornstarch together in a large bowl. After 15 minutes remove the vanilla bean (you can wipe it dry and use it again), then whisk the milk and cream gradually into the egg mixture. Now pour everything back into the pan and over a gentle heat, still whisking the whole time, allow the mixture gently to come back to a simmer—by which time it will have thickened. If it looks at all grainy, don't worry; it will always regain its smoothness when cooled and whisked. Serve the custard either warm or well chilled.

If you want to make it in advance and keep it hot, just put the custard in a bowl and place it over a pan of hot water with plastic wrap resting on the surface until you are ready to serve it.

Chocolate Bread and Butter Pudding

I have to thank Larkin Warren for her original recipe from her restaurant, Martha's Vineyard, which I have adapted. It is quite simply one of the most brilliant hot puddings ever invented. It's so simple but so good—and even better prepared two days in advance. Serve in small portions because it is very rich. Though I doubt if there will be any left over, it's also wonderful cold.

9 slices, good-quality day-old white bread, each ¼ inch thick
5 ounces good-quality dark unsweetened chocolate (see note on page 233)
2 cups heavy cream
¼ cup dark rum
½ cup superfine sugar

¾ stick butter
A good pinch of ground cinnamon
3 large eggs

TO SERVE:
Heavy cream, well chilled

You will also need a shallow ovenproof dish 7 × 9 × 2 inches, lightly buttered.

Begin by removing the crusts from the slices of bread, which should leave you with approximately 9 × 4-inch squares. So now cut each slice into 4 triangles. Next place the chocolate, heavy cream, rum, sugar, butter and cinnamon in a bowl set over a saucepan of barely simmering water, being careful not to let the bowl touch the water, then wait until the butter and chocolate have melted and the sugar has completely dissolved. Next remove the bowl from the heat and give it a really good stir to amalgamate all the ingredients.

Now in a separate bowl, whisk the eggs and then pour the chocolate mixture over them and whisk again very thoroughly to blend them together.

Then spoon about a ½-inch layer of the chocolate mixture into the base of the dish and arrange half the bread triangles over the chocolate in overlapping rows. Now pour half the remaining chocolate mixture all over the bread as evenly as possible, then arrange the rest of the triangles over that, finishing off with a layer of chocolate. Use a fork to press the bread gently down so that it gets covered very evenly with the liquid as it cools.

Cover the dish with plastic wrap and allow to stand at room temperature for 2 hours before transferring it to the fridge for a minimum of 24 (but preferably 48) hours before cooking. When you're ready to cook the pudding, preheat the oven to 350°F. Remove the plastic wrap and bake in the oven on a high rack for 30–35 minutes, by which time the top will be crunchy and the inside soft and squidgey. Leave it to stand for 10 minutes before serving with well-chilled cream poured over.

CHOCOLATE BREAD AND BUTTER PUDDING

Hot Citrus Pudding in Its Own Juices

Serves 6

This delightful hot pudding full of fresh citrus flavors is very light and fluffy and has the advantage of emerging from the oven in a pool of its own sauce. Then all it needs is some chilled heavy cream.

¾ stick butter, softened
¼ cup superfine sugar
3 large eggs, separated
⅔ cup self-rising flour
Grated zest and juice of 1 orange
Grated zest and juice of 1 lemon

Grated zest and juice of 2 limes
1 scant cup milk

To Serve:
Heavy cream, well chilled

You will also need a deep baking dish of 1½ quarts capacity, well buttered.

Preheat the oven to 350°F.

First take a large bowl and in it whisk the butter and sugar together until pale in color—it won't go light and fluffy, but don't worry, that's because there is more sugar than butter. After that beat the egg yolks and whisk them into the mixture a little at a time. Next sift the flour and lightly fold it into the mixture, alternating it with the citrus juices and zests, and lastly adding the milk.

Now in a clean bowl, and using a washed and dried spanking-clean whisk or electric mixer, whisk the egg whites to the soft-peak stage and lightly fold them into the mixture. Don't worry that it might look a little curdled at this stage—it's supposed to. Now pour the mixture into the prepared dish and bake it on the middle rack of the preheated oven for 50 minutes, by which time the top should be a nice golden brown color.

Although this pudding is meant to be served hot, it is just as nice cold. Mind you, I doubt if there will be any left over.

Chunky Marmalade Bread and Butter Pudding

Serves 4–6

Is there anyone, anywhere who doesn't like bread and butter pudding? If you're a devoted fan, then this is bread and butter pudding as you've always known it, but with the added flavor of Seville orange marmalade, chunky candied citrus peel and grated orange zest—a delightfully different combination, which produces another winning version of an old-time favorite. Bread and butter pudding is served a lot in restaurants nowadays, but none is as good as the homemade version, which for me has to have a crunchy top to contrast with a soft fluffiness inside. (See photograph on pages 240–41.)

½ stick butter, softened
6 slices good-quality white bread with
    crusts left on, each ½ inch thick
4 tablespoons dark chunky Marmalade
    (see page 242)
1¼ cups milk
⅓ cup heavy cream
3 large eggs

⅓ cup sugar
Grated zest of 1 large orange
1 tablespoon brownulated sugar
¼ cup candied mixed citrus peel, finely
    chopped

To Serve:
Crème fraîche or chilled heavy cream

You will also need a baking dish, 7 × 9 × 2 inches, lightly buttered.

Preheat the oven to 350°F.

First generously butter the slices of bread on one side, then spread the marmalade on 3 of these slices and put the other 3 slices on top (buttered side down) so you've got 3 rounds of sandwiches. Now spread some butter over the top slice of each sandwich and cut each one into quarters to make little triangles or squares.

Then arrange the sandwiches, buttered side up, overlapping each other in the baking dish and standing almost upright. After that whisk the milk, cream, eggs and sugar together and pour this all over the bread. Scatter the surface of the bread with the grated orange zest, brownulated sugar and candied citrus peel, then place the pudding on the high rack of the oven and bake it for 35–40 minutes until it's puffy and golden and the top crust is crunchy.

Serve the pudding straight from the oven while it's still puffy, with either crème fraîche or chilled cream.

CHAPTER TWELVE

Back to Home Baking

I WELL REMEMBER BOTH MY GRANDMOTHER AND MOTHER HAVING WEEKLY "baking days," an entire day spent in the kitchen producing cakes, apple pies and all sorts of tarts. All these would be cooled, then stored in large airtight containers, and each day at teatime out would come something like a piece of jam sponge, an almond or jam tart or some fluffy butterfly cakes.

Now this tradition has died out; we count calories one minute and eat snack bars the next. So here I want to indulge a little in the pleasures of my childhood and suggest that, although batch-baking might be ruled out by the pressures of our modern lives, you can still take just one free Saturday afternoon, closet yourself in the kitchen and immerse yourself in some very rewarding home baking. If there's no rush and no pressure it can actually be very relaxing—put on some music, listen to the radio, or just be silent with your thoughts. Then watch the smiles of pleasure as the house is filled with a delicious aroma and everyone gets a teatime treat.

American One-Crust Pie
with Spiced Apples and Raisins

Serves 6–8

This is without a doubt the easiest apple pie in the world. No special pie pans needed, no upper crust to be cut and fitted, no tiresome fluting of edges. It's also a beginner's dream because, somehow, the more haphazard the whole thing looks, the better.

FOR THE CRUST PASTRY:
1 ¾ cups flour
4 tablespoons shortening
½ stick butter, at room temperature
Cold water

FOR THE FILLING:
1 pound Rome apples, peeled, cored and sliced
8 ounces dessert apples (such as Granny Smith), peeled, cored and sliced

¼ teaspoon ground cloves
1 teaspoon ground cinnamon
¾ cup raisins
¼ whole nutmeg, grated
¼ cup brown sugar

FOR THE GLAZE:
1 small egg, separated
6 brownulated sugar cubes, crushed

You will also need a solid baking sheet.

Make up the pastry by sifting the flour into a large mixing bowl, then rubbing the shortening and butter into it lightly with your fingertips, lifting everything up and letting it fall back into the bowl to give it a good airing. When the mixture reaches the crumb stage, sprinkle in enough cold water to bring it together to a smooth dough that leaves the bowl absolutely clean. Give it a little light knead to bring it fully together, then place the pastry in a plastic bag in the fridge to rest for 30 minutes.

Meanwhile prepare the apples and all the other filling ingredients and mix them together in a bowl. After that, preheat the oven to 400°F.

Then roll the pastry out on a flat surface to a round of about 14 inches in diameter: As you roll it, give it quarter-turns so that it ends up as round as you can make it. (Don't worry about ragged edges—they're fine.) Now carefully roll the pastry around the rolling pin and transfer it to the center of a lightly greased baking sheet. To prevent the pastry getting soggy from the juice of the apples, paint it with the egg yolk over roughly a 10-inch inner circle—this forms a kind of waterproof coating.

Now simply pile the prepared fruit mixture in the center of the pastry, then turn in the edges of the pastry. If the pastry breaks, just patch it back again—it's meant to look ragged and interesting. Brush the pastry surface all around with the egg white, then crush the sugar cubes with a rolling pin and sprinkle over the pastry (the idea of using cubes is to get a less uniform look than with granulated sugar).

Pop the pie on the highest rack of the oven and bake for approximately 35 minutes, or until the crust turns golden brown. Remove from the oven and serve warm with chilled crème fraîche or ice cream.

Traditional Apple Pie with a Cheddar Crust and Mascarpone Nutmeg Ice Cream

Serves 8

This is a huge family apple pie, which I often call "More Apple Than Pie" as it has four pounds of apples in it. Putting Cheddar cheese in the crust gives it a lovely crisp, flaky texture without a strong cheese flavor. If you serve it still warm from the oven with some Mascarpone Nutmeg Ice Cream (see opposite) it tastes heavenly. (See photograph on pages 216–17.)

FOR THE PASTRY:
1¾ cups flour
½ stick butter, softened
¼ cup shortening
¾ cup coarsely grated mild Cheddar
3 tablespoons cold water

FOR THE FILLING:
2 pounds Rome apples
2 pounds dessert apples (such as Granny Smith)
1 tablespoon fine semolina
⅓ cup superfine sugar
12 whole cloves
1 large egg, beaten

You will also need a rimmed metal pie pan, 9 inches in diameter and 1¼ inches deep, with sloping sides, and a solid baking sheet.

Preheat the oven to 425°F.

First make the pastry. Sift the flour into a roomy bowl, holding the sifter up high to give it a good airing, then add the butter and shortening cut into small pieces, rubbing them into the flour with your fingertips until it reaches the crumbly stage. Now add the grated Cheddar and enough of the water to make a soft dough that leaves the bowl clean. Then turn it out onto a board, knead it briefly and lightly, then wrap it in plastic wrap and leave it to rest in the fridge for about 30 minutes.

Meanwhile peel, quarter and core the apples and then cut them into very thin slices straight into a bowl, mixing the two varieties together. Now is a good time to switch the oven on to preheat.

Next take a little less than half of the pastry and roll it out very thinly to approximately 12 inches in diameter to line the bottom and sides of the pie pan. Trim the edges and leave unused pastry trimmings aside. Then scatter the semolina over the bottom of the pastry and after that pile in the apple slices, building up the layers closely and scattering in the sugar and cloves as you go. Then press and pack the apples tightly.

Now roll the remaining pastry out, again very thinly, to make the top, this time 16 inches in diameter. Brush the rim of the bottom pastry with a little beaten egg and carefully lift the top over. Press the edges together to get a good seal all around, then trim, using a knife. Finally gather up the trimmings and reroll them to cut out into leaf shapes. Make a 1-inch-diameter hole in the center (to allow the steam to escape) and arrange the leaves on top. Now using the back of a small knife, "knock up" the edges, then flute them using your thumb and the back of the knife.

Finally brush the crust with beaten egg, then place the pie on the baking sheet and bake on the high rack for 10 minutes. After that reduce the temperature to 375°F and bake for a further 45 minutes or until it has turned a deep golden brown. Then remove the pie and allow it to stand for at least 20 minutes before serving.

Mascarpone Nutmeg Ice Cream

Makes 2½ cups

T his very easy ice cream is made with mascarpone and has a rich, velvety texture. The freezing process seems to draw out the aromatic flavor of the nutmeg superbly, making it an absolute winner with apple pie.

⅓ cup milk
½ whole nutmeg
2 large egg yolks
1 teaspoon cornstarch

⅓ cup superfine sugar
1¼ cups mascarpone (Italian cream cheese)
1 cup fromage blanc (8% fat)

You will also need a shallow plastic freezing container of approximately 1 quart capacity.

Begin by placing the milk in a small saucepan, then, using either a nutmeg grater or the fine side of an ordinary grater, grate the nutmeg into the milk. Then place it on low heat and let it come up to a gentle simmer. Meanwhile put the egg yolks, cornstarch and sugar in a large bowl and whisk these together until light and creamy.

Now pour the hot milk over the egg mixture, still whisking away, then return everything to the pan and bring it back to a gentle simmer, continuing to whisk the whole time to keep the mixture smooth. Then cover the pan and put aside to cool.

After that whisk the mascarpone and fromage blanc together in another bowl, then combine this with the egg custard mixture, and whisk again to combine thoroughly. Now pour the mixture into the freezing container, put a lid on and place in the coldest part of the freezer for 2 hours or until the edges are frozen. Then remove and, using an electric mixer, blend the edges into the softer middle. Put the lid on and return to the freezer until completely frozen (about 6 hours). If you're using an ice-cream maker, freeze-churn according to the manufacturer's instructions. In either case, about 1½ hours before serving, remember to remove the ice cream to the main body of the fridge to soften enough to scoop easily.

NEXT PAGE: TRADITIONAL APPLE PIE
WITH A CHEDDAR CRUST

Hot Cross Buns

Makes 12

Hot cross buns cannot be dashed off quickly—they are best made when you have set aside some time to lock yourself in the kitchen, switch on the radio and lose yourself in a rewarding session of yeast cookery. Kneading the dough and watching it rise is all very satisfying, and then your family can enjoy all that fruity, spicy stickiness! Hot cross buns are a special occasion in themselves, so serve them still slightly warm from the oven and spread with your best butter.

3 cups white flour
¼ teaspoon ground coriander
¼ teaspoon ground ginger
¼ teaspoon ground cloves
¾ teaspoon ground cinnamon
½ teaspoon freshly grated nutmeg
2 packages active dry yeast
¼ cup superfine sugar
1 cup currants
½ cup chopped candied mixed citrus peel
⅔ cup hot milk

¼ cup warm water
1 large egg, beaten
½ stick butter, melted

FOR THE CROSSES:
⅓ cup flour
1½ tablespoons water

FOR THE GLAZE:
2 tablespoons granulated sugar
2 tablespoons water

You will also need a greased baking sheet and a large plastic bag, lightly oiled.

First of all sift the flour, spices, cinnamon and nutmeg into a mixing bowl. Then sprinkle in the yeast and superfine sugar, followed by the currants and citrus peel. Mix everything together evenly. Then make a well in the center and pour in the milk and water, followed by the beaten egg and melted butter.

Now mix everything to a dough, starting off with a wooden spoon and then using your hands when the mixture becomes less sticky. Because it is never possible to be exact with the liquid, as flour can vary, if you need to add a spot more water, do so—or if you find the mixture is getting too sticky, sprinkle in a bit more flour.

Then transfer the dough to a clean surface and knead it until it feels smooth and elastic—this will take about 6 minutes. After that place the dough back in the bowl and cover the bowl with plastic wrap. Leave it in a warm place to rise—it will take about 1½ hours to double in size. If it takes longer than that, don't worry, just wait until the dough is double its original volume. Then, punching it down, reshape the dough.

Now divide it into 12 round portions and place them on the greased baking sheet, leaving plenty of room around each one. Use a sharp knife to make a cross on the top of each bun. Then leave them to rise again, covering them with the oiled plastic bag. This time they will take about 30 minutes.

While that's happening, preheat the oven to 425°F and make the crosses. Form a paste with the flour and water, then roll this out and cut it into ¼-inch strips. When the second rising time is up, brush the strips with water to make them stick and place them on top of the buns along the indentations you made earlier. Put the buns on a high rack in the oven and bake them for about 15 minutes.

While they are cooking, make the glaze by slowly melting together the sugar and water over a gentle heat until all the sugar has dissolved and you have a clear syrup. As soon as the buns come out of the oven, brush them immediately with the glaze while they are still warm. If you want to make them ahead of time, it's quite nice just to warm them through again in the oven before eating. If you want to freeze them, they do freeze well—just remember to put on the glaze after defrosting and then warm the buns through in the oven.

Cranberry and Orange One-Crust Pies

Serves 6

I seem to have a craze at the moment for cooking everything in individual portions. I love individual steamed puddings, and now I'm into making individual pies as well. These are dead simple to make and easy to serve, and the rich, luscious flavor of the cranberries is extremely good.

FOR THE FILLING:
6 cups fresh cranberries
½ cup sugar
Zest and juice of 1 orange
¼ teaspoon ground cloves
¼ teaspoon ground cinnamon
¼ teaspoon ground ginger
½ whole nutmeg, freshly grated
1 large egg yolk
9 teaspoons semolina

FOR THE PASTRY:
1⅓ cups flour
¾ stick butter
3 tablespoons cold water

FOR THE GLAZE:
1 large egg white, lightly beaten
6 sugar cubes, crushed

TO SERVE:
Sifted confectioners' sugar and crème
       fraîche

You will also need a solid baking sheet, lightly greased.

Preheat the oven to 400°F.

First of all prepare the cranberries by placing them in a saucepan with the sugar, orange zest and juice and the spices. Bring everything up to simmering point then reduce the heat, cook for about 10 minutes or until the cranberries are soft. Then remove them from the heat and leave them aside to cool.

If you are feeling lazy, make the pastry in a food processor, placing the flour and butter in the bowl and processing until you have fine crumbs. Then add the cold water and process until the pastry just comes together, then gather it up into a ball and place it in a plastic bag in the fridge for 30 minutes to rest.

After that remove the pastry and divide it into 6 equal-sized pieces. Roll each piece into roughly a 7-inch circle—it doesn't matter how uneven it is. Then paint a 3½-inch circle in the center with egg yolk and sprinkle 1½ teaspoons of semolina onto this circle. (The semolina is there to soak up any excess juices.)

Now divide the cranberries among the pastry circles, spooning them over the semolina and leaving a couple of tablespoons left over. Fold the edges of the pastry over them, leaving an uncovered area in the center. Now pop the leftover cranberries in to fill any gaps. Next brush the pastry all over with the beaten egg white and sprinkle with the crushed sugar cubes. Then very gently place the pies (a spatula is good for this) on a greased baking sheet and bake in the oven for about 15–20 minutes or until the pastry is golden brown.

Serve the pies warm from the oven with a dusting of confectioners' sugar—and I like to serve them with large quantities of crème fraîche.

Quick Apricot,
Apple and Pecan Loaf Cake

If you've never made a cake in your life before, I promise you that you can make this one—whether you're male, female, age 6 or 106, it really is easy, but it tastes so divine you would think it took oodles of skill. The only important thing to remember (as with all cakes) is to use the right size pan.

1½ cups pecans
A pinch of salt
1½ teaspoons baking soda
4 teaspoons ground cinnamon
1 cup whole wheat flour
¾ cup flour
1 stick butter, at room temperature
¾ cup brown sugar
2 large eggs, beaten

3 tablespoons milk
1 cup dried apricots, each chopped in half
1 medium cooking apple (about 1 cup),
    cut into ½-inch chunks

FOR THE TOPPING:
4 cubes brownulated sugar, roughly
    crushed
¼ teaspoon ground cinnamon

You will also need a 2-pound bread loaf pan measuring 3½ × 6½ inches, lightly buttered.

Preheat the oven to 350°F.

First of all when the oven has preheated, spread the pecans out on a baking sheet and toast them lightly for about 8 minutes, using a timer so that you don't forget them. After that remove them from the oven to a chopping board, let them cool a bit, then chop them roughly.

Meanwhile, take a large mixing bowl and sift the salt, baking soda, cinnamon and both flours into it, holding the sieve up high to give the flour a good airing and adding the bran from the sieve to the bowl as well. Then simply add all the rest of the ingredients except the fruit and pecans. Take an electric mixer, begin to beat the mixture on a slow speed, then increase the speed to mix everything thoroughly till smooth before lightly folding in the apricots, apple and pecans.

When it's all folded in add a drop more milk if necessary to make a mixture that drops easily off the spoon when you give it a sharp tap, then pile the mixture into the loaf pan, level the top and sprinkle on the crushed sugar and cinnamon. Bake in the center of the oven for 1¼–1½ hours or until the cake feels springy in the center.

After that remove it from the oven and let it cool for about 5 minutes before turning it out onto a wire rack. Let it get completely cool before transferring it to a cake tin, which may not be needed if there are people around, as this cake tends to vanish very quickly!

A Return
to the Black Forest

*T*hough much debased by many frozen versions, the original Black Forest cake, way back in the sixties, was a delight: a soft, light concoction made with seriously dark chocolate and sour cherries. So here it is—still using the lightest batter (no flour), baked flat, then rolled around a luscious filling and decorated with chocolate curls.

FOR THE FILLING:
8 ounces good-quality dark unsweetened
   chocolate (see note on page 233)
2 tablespoons water
2 large eggs, separated
1 1½-pound jar pitted sour cherries
2 tablespoons cherry brandy
1 cup heavy cream

FOR THE CAKE:
6 large eggs, separated
⅔ cup superfine sugar
¼ cup cocoa powder, sifted

FOR THE TOPPING:
3½ ounces good-quality dark
   unsweetened chocolate
1 tablespoon sour-cherry jam
A little cocoa powder for dusting

You will also need a jelly roll pan 13 × 9 × ½ inch, lined with parchment paper, cut and folded to give a depth of at least 1½ inches.

Preheat the oven to 350°F.

You can make the chocolate filling well ahead of time. To do this, break the pieces of chocolate into a bowl and add the water. Now place the bowl over a saucepan of barely simmering water, making sure the bowl isn't actually touching the water. Then remove the pan from the heat and wait for the chocolate to melt before beating it with a wooden spoon until smooth.

Next beat the egg yolks, first on their own and then into the warm chocolate mixture. As soon as the mixture has cooled, whisk the egg whites to the soft-peak stage, then gently cut and fold them into the chocolate mixture. Cover the bowl with plastic wrap and leave it in the fridge until you're ready to use it, but for a minimum of 1 hour.

Drain the cherries in a sieve, discard the syrup, then place them in a shallow dish, spoon over the cherry brandy and leave aside till needed.

To make the cake, first place the egg yolks in a bowl and beat them with an electric mixer until they begin to thicken. Then add the superfine sugar and continue to beat, but be careful not to overdo this, as it can eventually become too thick—stop when it falls off the beaters in ribbons. Now fold in the sifted cocoa powder. Then, using a spanking-clean bowl and carefully washed and dried beaters, beat the egg whites to the soft-peak stage. Then take 1 large spoonful, fold it into the chocolatey mixture to slacken it, and gently cut and fold in the rest of the egg whites.

Now pour the mixture into the prepared pan and bake the cake on the middle rack of the oven for about 20 minutes or until it's springy in the center. It will look very puffy, but a little finger gently pressed into the center should reveal that it is cooked. It's important not to overcook it; otherwise it will be difficult to roll.

Remove it from the oven and don't panic as it sinks down, because this is quite normal. Leave it until it's absolutely cool, then turn it out on a sheet of parchment paper that has been lightly dusted with sifted cocoa powder. Then carefully peel away the baking parchment.

Drain the cherries again in a sieve placed over a bowl to catch the liqueur and sprinkle all but 1 tablespoon of the liqueur all over the cake. Next remove the chocolate filling from the fridge and, using a small metal spatula, spread it carefully and evenly all over the surface of the cake. Next whip the cream softly, and spread this all over the chocolate filling, leaving a good 1-inch border all around to allow for it spreading, then lightly press the cherries into the cream.

Rolling this cake up is going to be a lot easier than you think. All you do is take hold of one edge of the parchment paper beneath it, lift it and, as you lift, the cake will begin to come up. Just gently roll it over, pulling the paper away as it rolls. If the cake itself cracks as you roll it, this is not a problem—it's all going to get covered in chocolate anyway!

Now to make the chocolate curls for the topping—don't worry, it's much easier than it sounds—all you do is melt the chocolate as before, taking great care not to overheat it, then pour it onto an upturned plate 6 inches in diameter. Then place in the fridge for about 45 minutes until it's set. The chocolate should be firm when you touch it. If it's too soft it won't make nice curls.

To make the curls use a cheese slicer, or a very sharp knife will do if you hold the blade with both hands. Start at one end and just pull the slicer or knife along the surface of the chocolate toward you until curls form. As you make the curls, place them in a plastic container, as they're much easier to handle later on if they're well chilled. Put the container in the fridge.

Now you can decorate the cake: Spoon the cherry jam into a small saucepan, add the reserved tablespoon of liqueur from the cherries, warm it gently and then brush it all over the surface. Place the chocolate curls all over that. Finally, sift over a little cocoa powder to dust the surface lightly.

Four-Nut
Chocolate Brownies

If you've never made brownies before, you first need to get into the brownie mode, and to do this stop thinking "cakes." Brownies are slightly crisp on the outside but soft, damp and squidgey within. I'm always getting letters from people who think their brownies are not cooked, so once you've accepted the description above, try and forget all about cakes.

¼ cup each macadamias, brazils, pecans
    and hazelnuts
2 ounces good-quality dark unsweetened
    chocolate (see note on page 233)
1 stick butter

2 large eggs, beaten
1 cup granulated sugar
½ cup flour
1 teaspoon baking powder
¼ teaspoon salt

You will also need a well-greased cake pan measuring 8 inches square, lined with
parchment paper, allowing the paper to come 1 inch above the cake pan.

Preheat the oven to 350°F.

Begin by chopping the nuts roughly, not too small, then place them on a baking sheet and toast them in a preheated oven for 8 minutes exactly. Please use a timer here; otherwise you'll be throwing burned nuts away all day! While the nuts are cooking, put the chocolate and butter together in a large mixing bowl fitted over a saucepan of barely simmering water, making sure the bowl doesn't touch the water. Allow the chocolate to melt, then beat it until smooth, remove it from the heat and simply stir in all the other ingredients until thoroughly blended.

Now spread the mixture evenly into the prepared cake pan and bake on the center rack of the oven for 35–40 minutes or until it's slightly springy in the center. Remove the pan from the oven and leave it to cool for 10 minutes before cutting into roughly 16 squares. Then, using a metal spatula, transfer the squares onto a wire rack to finish cooling.

FOUR-NUT CHOCOLATE BROWNIES

Deep Lemon Tart

I once spent a great deal of time trying every sort of lemon tart imaginable in order to come up with the definitive version. And here it is—thicker than is usual and with, quite rightly I think, much more filling than pastry. If you want to serve it warm you can prepare everything in advance and pour the filling in just before you bake it.

FOR THE PASTRY CRUST:
1 ⅓ cups flour
⅓ cup plus 1 tablespoon confectioners'
    sugar
¾ stick butter, softened
1 large egg, separated
1 tablespoon water

FOR THE FILLING:
6 lemons (plus more if needed to provide
    1 ¼ cups juice)
6 large eggs
¾ cup superfine sugar
1 cup heavy cream

TO SERVE:
A little confectioners' sugar and crème
    fraîche

*You will also need a deep, fluted quiche pan with a loose base 9 inches in diameter
and 1 ½ inches deep, lightly oiled.*

The best way to make the pastry is in a food processor. To do this add all the pastry ingredients (except the egg white) to the bowl and process until it forms a firm dough. Then turn it out and knead lightly before placing in a plastic bag and leaving in the fridge for 30 minutes to rest. To bake the pastry crust, preheat the oven to 400°F and place a solid baking sheet inside to preheat as well. Now roll out the pastry as thinly as possible and carefully line the quiche pan, pressing the pastry around the bottom and sides so that it comes about ¼ inch above the edge of the pan. Then prick the crust with a fork and brush it all over with the egg white, which you should lightly beat first.

Bake on the baking sheet on the middle rack for 20 minutes, then, as you remove it, turn the temperature down to 350°F.

To make the filling, grate the zest from 6 lemons, and squeeze enough juice to give 1¼ cups. Now break the eggs into a bowl, add the sugar and whisk to combine, but don't overdo it or the eggs will thicken. Next add the lemon juice and zest, followed by the cream, and whisk lightly. Now pour it all into a 1-quart pitcher.

The easiest way to fill the tart is to place the pastry crust on the baking sheet in the oven, and then pour the filling straight into the pastry (this avoids having to carry the tart to the oven and spilling it). Bake for about 30 minutes or until the tart is set and feels springy in the center. Let it cool for about 30 minutes if you want to serve it warm. It's also extremely good chilled. Either way, dust it with confectioners' sugar just before serving and serve with well-chilled crème fraîche.

Prune, Apple and Armagnac Cake
with Almond Streusel Topping

This is a cake that borders on being a dessert, and it would be my choice for a celebration winter supper party, served warm with crème fraîche or whipped cream. If you are not a lover of Armagnac, the prunes also taste good soaked in port or Amaretto liqueur.

FOR THE PRUNES:
12 ounces large pitted prunes
⅓ cup superfine sugar
⅔ cup water
⅓ cup Armagnac

FOR THE STREUSEL TOPPING:
⅔ cup self-rising flour, sifted
¼ stick butter, softened
½ cup brownulated sugar
½ tablespoon cold water
½ cup almonds, halved lengthwise and
   slivered very finely

FOR THE CAKE:
⅔ cup self-rising flour
½ teaspoon baking powder
½ stick butter, softened
⅓ cup ground almonds
¼ cup superfine sugar
1 large egg
2 tablespoons milk
⅓ cup diced Rome apple

TO FINISH:
Confectioners' sugar

You will also need an 8-inch cake pan with a loose base, greased and lined with parchment paper.

Preheat the oven to 350°F.

Although the prunes are not supposed to need soaking, I prefer to soak them just the same (the advantage is having them pitted). Start the recipe the night before you want to serve the cake by placing the prunes in a saucepan along with the sugar and water, and simmer them very gently for 15 minutes. After that drain them, discarding the cooking liquid, then place them in a bowl, add the Armagnac, stir well, cover and leave overnight.

When you're ready to make the cake, begin with the streusel topping: Place the sifted flour and butter in a bowl and rub the butter in until the mixture becomes crumbly. Then add the sugar, mixing it in evenly, and after that sprinkle in the cold water and fork the mixture until it is coarse and lumpy. Now leave it aside with the almonds.

The cake mixture is very simple indeed—all you do is sift the flour and baking powder into a bowl, add the rest of the ingredients (except for the apple), then, using an electric mixer or a wooden spoon and some old-fashioned elbow grease, beat the mixture together until smooth. After that, fold in the apple, then spoon the mixture into the prepared cake pan.

Now arrange the prunes all over the mixture, then fork the streusel topping over them and finally sprinkle the shredded almonds evenly over the surface. Place the cake on the center rack of the oven, bake it for 1 hour and remove it from the oven. Then leave it in the cake pan for 30 minutes before turning it out to cool on a wire rack. Just before serving sift the confectioners' sugar over the surface.

Iced Lemon Curd Layer Cake

You couldn't get a more lemony recipe than this: layers of lemon-flavored sponge, filled with homemade lemon curd and then a lemon icing for the finishing touch. It's wonderful.

1⅓ cups self-rising flour, sifted
1 teaspoon baking powder
1½ sticks butter, at room temperature
¾ cup superfine sugar
3 large eggs
Grated zest of 1 lemon
1 tablespoon lemon juice

FOR THE LEMON CURD:
⅓ cup superfine sugar

Grated zest and juice of 1 large juicy
    lemon
2 large eggs
½ stick unsalted butter

FOR THE ICING:
Zest of 1 large lemon
½ cup confectioners' sugar, sifted
2–3 teaspoons lemon juice

  Prepare two 7-inch nonstick cake pans, 1½ inches deep, by greasing them, lining the bottoms
with parchment paper and greasing the paper too.

Preheat the oven to 325°F.

Just measure all the cake ingredients into a mixing bowl and beat—ideally with an electric mixer—till you have a smooth, creamy consistency. Then divide the mixture evenly between the 2 cake pans and bake them on the center rack of the oven for about 35 minutes or until the centers feel springy when lightly touched with a little finger.

While the cakes are baking, make the lemon curd. Place the sugar and grated lemon zest in a bowl, whisk the lemon juice together with the eggs, then pour this over the sugar. Then add the butter, cut into little pieces, and place the bowl over a pan of barely simmering water. Stir frequently till thickened—about 20 minutes. You don't have to stay with it—just come back from time to time to give it a stir.

When the cakes are baked, remove them from the oven and after about 30 seconds turn them out onto a wire rack. When they are absolutely cool—and not before—remove the parchment paper, then carefully cut each cake horizontally in half, using a sharp serrated knife. Now spread the curd thickly to sandwich the sponges together.

To make the icing, begin by removing the zest from the lemon—it's best to use a zester to get long, curly strips. Then sift the confectioners' sugar into a bowl and gradually stir in the lemon juice until you have a soft, runny consistency. Allow the icing to stand for 5 minutes before spreading it on top of the cake with a knife, almost to the edges, and don't worry if it runs a little down the sides of the cake. Then scatter the lemon zest over the top and leave it for 30 minutes for the icing to firm up before serving.

ICED LEMON CURD LAYER CAKE

Polenta and Ricotta Cake
with Dates and Pecans

This is a very unusual cake, quite different in flavor and texture from anything else. It's Italian in origin, and polenta gives it a sandy texture, while at the same time ricotta cheese and Amaretto liqueur give a wonderful moistness. It also freezes very well, but as you won't have any left over you might as well make two—it's so easy!

1 cup chopped dates

3 tablespoons Amaretto

½ cup pecans, roughly chopped

1⅓ cups polenta

1½ cups self-rising flour

2 teaspoons baking powder

1 tablespoon ground cinnamon

1 cup superfine sugar

1¼ cups ricotta cheese

1 stick butter, melted

Scant 1 cup tepid water

1 tablespoon brownulated sugar

You will also need an 8-inch loose-based cake pan lined with parchment paper.

Preheat the oven to 325°F.

First of all place the dates in a small bowl, pour the liqueur over them and leave them to soak for 15 minutes. Then place the pecans on a baking tray and toast them for 8 minutes—use a timer so they don't get overcooked. Now to make the cake, take a large mixing bowl and first sift in the polenta, flour, baking powder and cinnamon. Keep the sieve held high to give the flour a good airing, then add the grains from the sieve to the rest.

Next add the superfine sugar, ricotta, melted butter and water and beat with an electric mixer until everything is thoroughly blended (about 1 minute). After that, thoroughly fold in the nuts, the dates and the liqueur in which they were soaking. Spoon the mixture into the prepared cake pan and smooth the top with the back of a spoon. Now scatter the brownulated sugar evenly over the surface, then pop the cake into a preheated oven on the middle rack, where it will take between 1¾ and 2 hours to cook. When it's cooked it will feel springy in the center when you make a very light depression with your little finger. If it's not cooked give it another 10 minutes and then do another test.

When the cake is ready remove it from the oven, allow it to cool in the cake pan for 15 minutes, then remove it from the pan and leave it to cool completely on a wire rack. Store in an airtight container.

Rich Fruit Buttermilk Scones

Makes 12 scones

These tempting little scones are so quick and easy to make that you can have them on the table in less than half an hour after you first thought about making them. Don't worry if you don't have buttermilk; just use ordinary milk.

1 ¾ cups self-rising flour
⅓ cup superfine sugar
¾ stick butter, at room temperature
½ cup mixed dried fruit

1 large egg, beaten
3–4 tablespoons buttermilk
A little extra flour for dusting tops

You will also need a lightly greased baking sheet and a 2-inch pastry cutter.

Preheat the oven to 425°F.

Begin by sifting the flour into a bowl and sprinkling in the sugar, then rub the butter in lightly until the mixture looks crumbly. Now sprinkle in the dried fruit, pour in the beaten egg and add 3 tablespoons of the buttermilk. Start to mix the dough with a knife and finish off with your hands—it should be soft but not sticky, so add more milk, a teaspoon at a time, if the dough seems too dry.

Next form the dough into a ball and turn it out onto a lightly floured working surface. Now roll it out very lightly to a round at least 1 inch thick, then cut the scones out by placing the cutter on the dough and giving it a sharp tap. Don't twist the cutter, just push the dough out, then carry on until you are left only with trimmings—roll these and cut an extra scone. Then place the scones on the lightly greased baking sheet and dust lightly with the extra flour.

Bake the scones in the top half of the oven for 10–12 minutes or until they are well risen and golden brown. After that remove them to a wire rack and serve very fresh, split and spread with butter.

N O T E : *Scones do not keep well so are best eaten on the day they're made. Any left over, however, will freeze perfectly well.*

Feta, Olive
and Sun-Dried Tomato Scones

Makes 12

These are lovely served as a snack or savory at teatime. They also go very well as a companion to any of the soups in the first chapter for lunch.

1⅓ cups self-rising flour
½ cup whole wheat flour
¼ teaspoon baking powder
¼ teaspoon cayenne pepper
¼ teaspoon ground mustard
2 tablespoons extra virgin olive oil
⅓ cup sun-dried tomatoes, chopped,
   drained of oil (discard all but
    1 tablespoon)
1½ teaspoons chopped, fresh thyme

¾ cup feta cheese, cubed small
10 black olives, pitted and roughly
   chopped
1 large egg
2 tablespoons milk

FOR THE TOPPING:
Milk for brushing
½ cup crumbled feta cheese

You will also need a 2-inch pastry cutter and a lightly greased baking sheet.

Preheat the oven to 425°F.

First sift the flours and baking powder into a large, roomy bowl, add any bran left in the sieve, then add the cayenne and mustard and, using a knife, work in the olive oil, plus the oil from the sun-dried tomatoes. When the mixture looks like lumpy breadcrumbs stir in the chopped thyme, cubed feta, sun-dried tomatoes and olives.

Now in a separate bowl beat the egg with the milk and add half this mixture to the other ingredients. Using your hands, bring the mixture together to form a dough, adding more of the egg and milk as it needs it—what you should end up with is a dough that is soft but not sticky.

Now on a floured board, roll the dough out to a depth of 1 inch. Then stamp out the scones using a 2-inch cutter, either plain or fluted. Put the cut-out pieces on a baking sheet and brush them with the milk. Finally top each scone with crumbled feta, and put the sheet on the highest rack of the oven to bake for 12–15 minutes or until they've turned a golden color. Then remove them to a wire rack until they are cool enough to eat.

Ingredients Update

One of the tasks of the cookery writer is to keep up to date with new ingredients and then pass on the information so that hopefully everyone everywhere will be able to get hold of them and be able to use them. This does initially cause disappointment because when a new ingredient is mentioned on television there can be such a rush for it and it can sell out, or it may not be widely available anyway. I feel it's worth the initial problem because eventually the more we ask for things, the more they become available. The following is a list of ingredients in this book that you may particularly want to look out for.

Puy Lentils

Unlike other legumes, lentils do not need presoaking. We have included these tiny gray lentils in quite a few recipes as they retain their shape and texture when they're cooked without going mushy. Add them to a little sautéed onion and garlic, braise with wine or cider and serve as an accompaniment to meat or fish, or they're also very good in a salad. (See Warm Lentil Salad with Walnuts and Goat Cheese, page 33; and Broiled Chicken with Lemon, Garlic and Rosemary Served with Puy Lentils, page 82.)

Flageolet and Cannellini Beans

The tiny green unripe flageolets and the fully grown cannellini have a wonderful flavor. They are cheap, they help to bulk out meat and they are also very nutritious and filling. The other advantage is they are very good at absorbing the flavors of the dish (see Braised Lamb with Flageolet Beans, page 110, or Oxtail Braised in Guinness with Cannellini Beans, page 119). If you're serving these, there's no need to serve either rice or potatoes.

Dried Porcini Mushrooms

They may seem a little expensive, but these Italian dried mushrooms have a wonderfully intense concentrated flavor, and you'll find very little goes a long way. They are always soaked first in a little boiling water, which it self becomes infused with the flavor, so this can either be used in the recipe or kept aside for stock. Because we can rarely get hold of wild mushrooms, porcini are a must for every pantry.

Pancetta

Pancetta is Italian cured fatty bacon, smoked or unsmoked, with a very fine concentrated bacon flavor. Pancetta Coppata is unsmoked and rolled up with a bit of shoulder ham, giving the round slices. I use this a lot as it gives a much deeper flavor than bacon—it's fantastic in Spaghetti alla Carbonara (see page 31). Supermarkets now sell the sliced pancetta and also small cubes. In an Italian deli you can buy it in one piece.

Chocolate

If you want to make the best chocolate dessert in the world, I've got the recipes, but you need to get the best chocolate. Look for continental deluxe unsweetened dark chocolate, such as Ghirardelli or Lindt. (I check the amount of cocoa solids—75% is the best, as this gives all the concentrated flavor of chocolate. Once you've used it you'll never go back to the normal chocolate with only 51%. Unfortunately, brands found in the United States do not typically list the amount of cocoa solids.)

Ricotta

Ricotta is Italian wheyed cheese, mostly used in fresh unripe form. It's white and creamy, with a slightly acidic dairy flavor that has a sweet edge. We've used it in Polenta and Ricotta Cake with Dates and Pecans, page 230; Lemon Ricotta Cheesecake with a Confit of Lemons, page 188; Vegetarian Moussaka with Ricotta Topping, page 102; and Crêpe Cannelloni with Spinach and Four Cheeses, page 89.

Fontina

This is a beautiful cheese for cooking—it comes from the Alpine meadows of Valle d'Aosta in Italy. It's made from unpasteurized cows' milk and has all the melting quality of mozzarella but with a richer, creamier flavor. The texture is rather like Swiss Gruyère, glossy and springy with random holes. We have used this in Roasted Pumpkin Soup with Melting Cheese, page 14.

Cranberries

If I was teased about limes in the *Summer Collection,* I'm probably in for the same here, as I really don't feel we pay enough attention to cranberries. When the last of the autumn fruits have disappeared, November brings in a fresh crop of these dazzling scarlet berries with their rich juice and sharp flavor. So instead of just confining them to the Christmas turkey I have included them in several recipes for you to try. We've also had great fun testing their freshness—to do this you bounce them, and the higher they bounce the fresher they are!

Polenta

This is a very fine golden cornmeal from Italy that can be used on its own to make a type of maize porridge—a popular Italian staple. We have used it in Polenta and Ricotta Cake with Dates and Pecans, page 230, which really does give a *different* texture. Polenta also makes a great alternative to flour both for cooking and as a coating instead of breadcrumbs.

Suet

Suet, the white fatty casing that surrounds the kidneys, can be bought from the butcher. You may ask the butcher to shred the suet for you, or you can do it yourself: First remove the thin skin, then grate the suet as you would grate cheese, either with a grater or in a food processor. You can store suet in a tightly closed jar, refrigerated, for up to three months.

Sun-Dried Tomato Paste

This has all the deep concentrated flavor of sun-dried tomatoes in a dense textured paste that adds a lovely tomatoey flavor when added to recipes. I now use it quite often instead of the regular tomato paste. It should be becoming more widely available, but again we need to keep asking.

More Crème Fraîche

No, I haven't got shares in it, but because it's such a wonderful ingredient and has slightly less fat than heavy cream, more flavor and a longer shelf life, I tend to use it most of the time. But if you prefer you can replace it with heavy cream in recipes.

Oriental Ingredients

Japanese

• Mirin is a sweet rice cooking wine, quite mild.

• Sake is a fortified rice wine, stronger and more powerful.

• Japanese rice vinegar is much softer and mellower than Chinese.

• Daikon, known as mooli radish, has twice the vitamin content of red radishes with a fresh peppery taste. It's long and white and is mostly grated. (See Teriyaki Steak on page 174.)

• Sansho pepper spice comes from the jacket of the prickly ash seed.

• Kikkoman soy sauce is a traditionally matured soy sauce, containing only toasted wheat soy beans, water and salt.

Chinese

• Five-spice powder is a combination of star anise, fagara, cassia, fennel seed and cloves.

• Dried shrimp, available from Oriental food shops, are tiny dried pink shrimp with a lovely concentrated shrimp flavor.

• Rice noodles are transparent noodles made from rice and need no cooking, just soaking.

• Star anise is a pretty star-shaped spice that has a very pungent aniseed flavor, so a little goes a long way.

Thai

• Fish sauce looks like medium sherry and is now becoming more widely available.

• Shrimp paste, available from Thai shops, is not pleasant to look at or to smell, but a little gives all the authentic flavor of Thai cooking.

• Kaffir lime leaves are small shiny leaves that come in twos like twins. These may be found in specialty supermarkets.

• Birdseye chilies: extremely hot! For non-Thais only a few are needed.

• Palm sugar is a soft mellow sugar, but our light brown sugar can be used to replace it.

• Galangal is a first cousin of ginger and has a mild peppery flavor. It is also known as Thai ginger.

CHAPTER THIRTEEN

Marmalades and Other Preserves

EVERY SUNDAY BEGINS FOR ME WITH A SMALL BUT VERY SIGNIFICANT LUXURY: really good marmalade on bread or toast. It makes a very cheery start to the day. And I emphasize really good marmalade, by which I mean proper homemade marmalade, which really is one of the world's great luxury foods. For, however good the store-bought versions are, they can never match what can be made at home from just three simple ingredients—Seville oranges, water and sugar.

Why Seville oranges? Because they are bitter. If you cook sweet oranges with an equal amount of sugar, what you get is overpowering sweetness with only a background of orange flavor. On the other hand, when you combine the bitter ones with sugar, the predominant flavor is that of oranges. The Seville orange season is short, from December to February, so it's best to make enough marmalade for the whole year while they're available. But if you don't have the time, you can still stock up, as Sevilles do freeze perfectly well.

I have included two other marmalade recipes in this chapter, to ring the changes. I've also discovered three exciting new chutneys and a variation on Christmas mincemeat, using cranberries, which has now become my standard recipe.

Spiced Cranberry Chutney

Makes 1 quart

ecause the cranberry season is so short, it is a good idea to preserve some for later, and this cranberry and orange chutney makes a wonderful pantry ingredient to use with pork, ham or cold cuts. It also has a fantastic color, which adds a bit of brightness to a dull January day.

1 teaspoon coriander seeds
1¼ cups red wine vinegar
¾ cup cider vinegar
1¾ cups granulated sugar

1 medium orange
6 whole cloves
4 cups fresh cranberries

You will also need 2 sterilized mason-type jars (see Note) of ½ quart capacity, with lids.

First heat a large saucepan until it gets really hot on the bottom, then add the coriander seeds, shaking them around and watching them carefully. When they get hot and slightly brown they will start to "jump" and dance, and this will draw out their flavor. Then transfer them to a mortar and pestle and crush them coarsely. Now turn the heat to low, pour the wine vinegar and cider vinegar into the pan and stir, then add the sugar and cook, stirring with a wooden spoon until all the sugar has dissolved. While that is happening, pare off the outer zest of the orange with a potato peeler and then cut into fine shreds, and squeeze the juice from the orange and reserve it.

Now test to see if the sugar has dissolved by coating the back of a wooden spoon. If it has, bring the liquid back to a simmer and add the orange zest and juice, cloves, coriander and cranberries. Stir well, then simmer gently without a lid for 1 hour, stirring occasionally to prevent the mixture sticking to the bottom. Be gentle with the stirring to avoid bursting berries—some will burst during the cooking, but the chutney looks more attractive if the majority of berries remain whole in the jars.

When the cooking time is up remove the pan from the heat and leave the contents to stand for 30 minutes. By this time it will be cool enough to handle and the chutney can be ladled into sterilized jars, sealed and, when completely cooled, labeled. Don't be tempted to eat the chutney for at least a month, as it takes that long for it to mellow and develop.

NOTE: *To prepare the jars, stand them on a rack in a large kettle. Add water to cover, bring to a full rolling boil, cover the kettle and boil for 10 minutes.*

Mango Chutney

Makes about 3¼ pints—1½ quarts

It gets more and more difficult to find mango chutney that has really visible chunks of mango all through it. So, because it is very easy to make, here is a recipe that includes large luscious chunks of mango. It is really good served with cold ham, poultry or game—or, of course, any kind of curry.

*8 mangoes, slightly underripe, total
    weight approximately 6 pounds*
3 cups light brown sugar
1 teaspoon cumin seeds
2 heaping teaspoons coriander seeds
12 cardamom pods
1 teaspoon cayenne pepper

1 teaspoon ground turmeric
½ cup fresh grated gingerroot
1 teaspoon ground cloves
2 pints malt vinegar
*8 cloves garlic, crushed with 4 teaspoons
    salt with a mortar and pestle*
2 Spanish onions, finely chopped

*You will also need a preserving pan or large wide saucepan, and 3 half-quart mason-type jars,
sterilized as described in Note on page 237.*

Begin this recipe a day ahead by preparing the mangoes. The easiest way to do this is to peel them using a potato peeler, then, with a small sharp paring knife, cut wedges out of them, each about ½ inch thick. This is very easy: Cut through to the large stone as if you were segmenting an orange—do it over a large bowl and let the pieces drop into it. If any of the flesh remains clinging to the stone, scrape it off to join the rest of the mangoes. Then sprinkle the brown sugar over the fruit in the bowl, turning it lightly to distribute the sugar evenly, then cover with plastic wrap and leave it in a cool place overnight.

Next day begin by preheating a small skillet, then dry-roast the cumin, coriander and cardamom pods for a couple of minutes to draw out their full flavor. Then crush them with a mortar and pestle—the cardamom pods will separate from the seeds, but put everything (pods as well) into the preserving pan together with all the other ingredients, including the mangoes and their syrup. Now bring everything up to a gentle simmer and let it simmer for about 3 hours, stirring from time to time, until the mangoes become translucent and the liquid has almost evaporated, leaving behind a thick syrup. You will need to do a bit more stirring from time to time at the end to prevent it sticking.

After that remove the chutney from the heat, let it cool for 15 minutes, then ladle it into warm sterilized jars, using a funnel. Seal while the chutney is still hot, and label when cool. Now you're going to have to forget all about it for 8 weeks so that it can mellow and mature.

Lemon and Lime Marmalade

Makes 5 half-quart jars

This is a very refreshing marmalade, good wake-up food on a dull morning. Its other advantage is that it can be made at any time of the year. Although this does need fast-boiling, the quantity is small enough for a modern stovetop (see page 242).

1½ quarts water
6 large thin-skinned lemons

6 limes
6 cups granulated sugar

You will also need a large saucepan or preserving pan of 5 quarts capacity, a piece of string, and a piece of cheesecloth 12 inches square. Jars should be sterilized as described in Note on page 257. You will need about 4 saucers to test for setting point.

Begin by measuring the water into a preserving pan, then cut the lemons and limes in half and squeeze the juice out of them. Add the juice to the water, and place the seeds and any bits of pith that cling to the juicer on the square of cheesecloth (laid over a dish or cereal bowl first). Now cut the lemon and lime peel into quarters with a sharp knife, and then cut each quarter into thinnish shreds. As you cut, add the shreds to the water, and any seeds or spare pith you come across should go onto the cheesecloth. The pith contains a lot of pectin, so don't discard any, and don't worry about any pith and peel that clings to the shreds—it all gets dissolved in the boiling.

Now tie the seeds, etc., up loosely in the cheesecloth to form a little bag, and tie this onto the handle of the pan so that the bag is suspended in the water. Then bring the liquid up to simmering point and simmer gently, uncovered, for 2 hours or thereabouts until the peel is completely soft—test a piece carefully by pressing it between your finger and thumb. Toward the end of the simmering time preheat the oven to 325°F. Pour the sugar into a roasting pan lined with foil and place it in the oven to warm gently for 10 minutes. At this point pop the saucers into the freezer.

Next remove the bag of seeds and leave it to cool on a small plate. Then pour the sugar into the pan and stir it now and then over a low heat until all the crystals have dissolved (check this carefully; it's important). Now increase the heat to very high, and squeeze the bag of seeds over the pan to extract all of the sticky, jellylike substance that contains the pectin. As you squeeze you'll see it ooze out. You can do this by placing the bag between 2 small plates or using your hands. Then stir or whisk it into the rest.

As soon as the mixture reaches a really fast boil, start timing. Then after 15 minutes take the pan off the heat and spoon a little of the marmalade onto one of the cold saucers from the freezer, and let it cool back in the fridge. You can tell—when it has cooled—if you have a "set" by pushing the mixture with your little finger: If it has a really crinkly skin, it is set. If not, continue to boil the marmalade and give it the same test at about 10-minute intervals until it does set.

After that remove the pan from the heat (if there's a lot of scum, most of it can be dispersed by stirring in ½ teaspoon of butter, and the rest can be spooned off). Leave the marmalade to settle for 20 minutes before potting into jars. Label when completely cooled.

Dark Chunky Marmalade

Makes 7½ pints–3 quarts

The problem with twentieth-century marmalade-making is that today's stovetops don't always oblige when it comes to getting large amounts of marmalade up to what old-fashioned cooks called a rolling boil, without which traditional marmalade stubbornly refuses to set. So when, in 1994, I tasted one of the best marmalades ever, I was thrilled to learn that the friend who had made it had cooked it long and slow—which solves the dilemma completely. Here is my version of Mary McDermot's original recipe, and it's the best I've ever tasted.

3 pounds Seville oranges   2½ quarts water
2 lemons   6 pounds granulated sugar

> You will also need a preserving pan, a piece of cheesecloth (15 inches square), a nylon sieve, some foil and jars sterilized as described in Note on page 237 and some small flat plates.

This recipe is extremely easy as long as you remember that it happens in *two* stages. So ideally begin the recipe one afternoon or evening and finish it the following morning.

So for stage 1: Lightly scrub the fruit, then place it in the preserving pan, add the water and bring it all up to a gentle simmer. Now take a large piece of double foil, place it over the top of the pan and fold the edges firmly over the rim. What needs to happen is for the fruit to very gently poach without any of the liquid evaporating. This initial simmering will take 3 hours.

After this remove the preserving pan from the heat and allow everything to get cool enough to handle. Then place a large colander over a bowl and, using a slotted spoon, lift the fruit out of the liquid and into this, reserving the poaching liquid. Now cut the oranges in half and scoop out all the inside flesh and seeds as well, straight into a medium-sized saucepan. Reserve the peel. Next do the same with the lemons but discard the peel. Now add 2½ cups of the poaching liquid to the fruit pulp, then place the saucepan over a medium heat and simmer for 10 minutes. Have ready a large nylon sieve lined with cheesecloth, and place it over a bowl, then strain the contents of the saucepan through the sieve. Leave it all like this while it cools and drips through.

While you are waiting for it to cool is a good time to deal with the orange peel. Cut the halves of peel into quarters then into chunky strips—the thickness is up to you, according to how you like your marmalade. Add these back into the reserved liquid in the preserving pan.

When the pulp is cool what you need to do next is gather up the corners of the cheesecloth and twist it into a ball, then, using your hands, squeeze all of the pectin-

PREVIOUS PAGE: CHUNKY MARMALADE BREAD AND BUTTER PUDDING (SEE PAGE 211) MADE WITH DARK CHUNKY MARMALADE

rich juices into the preserving pan. Don't be fainthearted here—squeeze like mad so that every last bit of stickiness is extracted and you're left only with the pithy membranes of the fruit, which you can now discard. When you have added the strained pectin, just leave all of this overnight, loosely covered with a clean cloth.

Stage 2: The following day, preheat the oven to 325°F. Then empty the sugar into a large roasting pan lined with foil, then place it in the oven and allow it to warm gently for 10 minutes. Then place the preserving pan and its contents over a gentle heat and as soon as it starts to warm through, add the warmed sugar to the pan.

Now, using a large wooden spoon, stir the marmalade, keeping the heat gentle, until all the sugar has fully dissolved. What you must *not* do is let the marmalade boil until all the sugar is completely dissolved. Keep looking at the back of the wooden spoon as you stir, and when you are sure there are no more crystals left turn up the heat and let the marmalade bubble away gently—it can take 3–4 hours for it to darken and develop its lovely rich flavor.

When the marmalade has been cooking for 2½ hours place some small flat plates in the fridge. Then, to test for a set, after 3 hours draw the pan from the heat and spoon a teaspoonful of marmalade onto a chilled plate. Allow it to cool for a minute back in the fridge, then push it with your little finger—if a crinkly skin forms, it has reached setting point. If not, continue cooking and do more testing at 15-minute intervals. When it has set, leave the marmalade to cool for 30 minutes before ladling through a funnel into warm sterilized jars. Seal the jars while they are hot, then label the next day when cold. Then, as soon as possible, make the Chunky Marmalade Bread and Butter Pudding on page 211. It's utterly divine!

Homemade Christmas Mincemeat with Cranberries

Makes five 2½-cup jars

This is my own traditional recipe, but by replacing some of the apple with cranberries it is sharper and slightly different. This recipe always comes with a warning: Once you have tasted homemade mincemeat you will never buy it again. In the past people used to have problems storing mincemeat because the high proportion of fruit oozed too much juice, and the juice started to ferment. In this recipe the mincemeat is placed in a barely warmed oven to let the suet melt gradually, and as this happens, it coats all the fruits and seals in all the juices.

4 cups fresh cranberries
8 ounces Rome apples, cored and chopped
    small
2 cups shredded beef suet
3 cups raisins
2 cups golden raisins
2 cups currants
8 ounces candied mixed citrus peel,
    finely chopped
1¼ cups dark brown sugar

Grated zest and juice of 2 oranges
Grated zest and juice of 2 lemons
⅓ cup almonds, cut into slivers
1¼ teaspoons ground coriander
1¼ teaspoons ground ginger
1¼ teaspoons ground cloves
½ teaspoon ground cinnamon
A good grinding of fresh nutmeg
6 tablespoons brandy

You will also need 5 half-quart mason-type preserving jars, sterilized as described on page 237.

All you do is combine the above ingredients, except for the brandy, in a large oven-proof ceramic mixing bowl, stirring them and mixing them together very thoroughly indeed. Then cover the bowl with a clean cloth and leave the mixture in a cool place overnight or for 12 hours, so the flavors have a chance to mingle and develop. After that preheat the oven to 225°F, cover the bowl loosely with foil and place in the oven for 3 hours.

Then remove the bowl from the oven and don't worry about the appearance of the mincemeat, which will look positively swimming in fat—that's how it should look. As it cools, stir it from time to time so that everything gets a coating of melted suet. When the mincemeat is quite cold, stir in the brandy, then pack in sterilized jars, cover with waxed discs and seal. It will keep in a cool, dark cupboard indefinitely, but I think it is best eaten within a year of making.

NOTE: *Vegetarians can make this mincemeat happily, using vegetarian suet.*

Fresh and Sun-Dried Tomato Chutney

Makes four ½-quart or eight 1-cup jars

One of the delights of the winter months is being able to taste some of the fruits of summer. So it's good to find a little bit of space for pickling and chutney-making in the autumn. This one's an absolute winner, great for jazzing up sausages or hamburgers, and we love it spread on top of cheese for sandwiches—it also has a great affinity with any kind of toasted cheese.

8 ounces dry-packed sun-dried tomatoes
1 tablespoon coriander seeds
½ tablespoon mustard seeds
4 pounds fresh tomatoes, halved (no need to skin or seed)
4 large cloves garlic

4 fresh red chilies, halved lengthwise with seeds left in
4 large onions, quartered
2 large red bell peppers, seeded
¾ cup dark brown sugar
2½ cups cider vinegar
1 tablespoon salt

You will also need a small preserving pan and jars as above, sterilized as described in Note on page 237.

First of all rinse the sun-dried tomatoes under running water to remove any dust or grit, then put them in a bowl and cover them with hot, not boiling, water and leave them to soak for about 20 minutes. Then heat a small heavy-bottomed skillet and dry-roast the coriander and mustard seeds over a medium heat, turning and stirring them around for 2 minutes to draw out their flavor. Then crush them together with a mortar and pestle—not very much; they just need to be broken up.

Making the chutney is going to be a lot easier if you have a food processor. In the past an old-fashioned mincer was used for chutneys; now a processor is even faster, but if you have neither then you just need to chop everything uniformly small.

First drain the sun-dried tomatoes, add these to the processor, switch on and chop till roughly ¼ inch in size. Then add the fresh tomatoes and process briefly until they are the same size. Now pour everything into the preserving pan and reposition the processing bowl and blade. Then add the garlic, chilies, onions and red bell peppers and process these to approximately the same size. Then transfer them to join the tomatoes and add the spices, brown sugar, cider vinegar and salt.

Bring everything up to simmering point, stirring all the time, then when you have a gentle simmer, turn the heat low and let it simmer very gently uncovered for about 3–3½ hours. It doesn't need a great deal of attention—just come back now and then and give it a stir to prevent it sticking.

The chutney is ready when all the liquid has been absorbed and the mixture has thickened to a nice soft consistency. The way to test for the right moment is by using a wooden spoon to make a trail all the way across the top of the chutney—if the trail fills with juice, it's not ready. When the spoon leaves a trail that does not fill with the vinegary juices, the chutney is ready.

You need to watch this carefully at the end because undercooking will make the chutney too sloppy, and overcooking will make it dry. When the chutney is ready, allow it to cool a little and spoon it into hot sterilized jars. Cover with a waxed disc, seal it down when hot, but don't put the label on until it's completely cool. Store the chutney in a cool dark place for 6–8 weeks before using.

Equipment Update

After every TV series I always get inundated with letters from people wanting to know about the various items of equipment used. So the following notes may be useful:

Really Solid Roasting Trays and Pans

In Britain, the really solid roasting tray campaign is still under way. Since the *Summer Collection* more and more of them are being sold and hopefully extinguishing forever the flimsy, buckling varieties. (Fortunately, roasting pans in the United States are much sturdier.) If you invest in the right one it will last you a lifetime. We have persuaded one supplier—Mermaid—to manufacture a solid Yorkshire pudding pan.

Quality Skillets

The very best solid skillets available now are made by a firm called Morso. They are black with wooden handles and are of superb quality, and there's no coating, which means no nasty peeling and flaking if the heat is too high. Morso also makes ovenproof skillets, which are perfect for things like Red Onion Tarte Tatin.

Mini Sauce Whisk

This is very good for making emulsions and for whisking vinaigrettes just before serving. Also brilliant for getting lumps out of sauces.

Wire Roasting Racks

Wire roasting racks to fit in roasting pans. Especially good for duck recipes, so the bird doesn't sit in its own fat.

Pudding Basin

A metal pudding mold (similar to a Jell-O mold) with a flat lid. It can also have a tube in the center, like a bundt pan.

Crêpe Pan

This is inexpensive and worth keeping just for making crêpes. There is also a crêpe pan handle holder available, to protect your hands from the heat.

Palette Knife

Serrated palette knife. I have been using one made by Victorinox for years and it is still my favorite knife.

Mandoline

The one I use is a Japanese invention and is great for slicing things very thinly in a lot less time than it takes trying to do it with a knife.

Copper Pans

Copper pans with stainless steel linings are simply wonderful for sauces. There is also now an excellent aluminum version. I used both in the TV series.

Suppliers

American Spoon Foods
P.O. Box 566
Petoskey, MI 49770
(616) 347-1739
Flours, preserves, dried berries, nuts, honeys

Aux Delices des Bois
14 Leonard Street
New York, NY 10013
(212) 334-1230
Seasonal fresh wild mushrooms and specialty produce imported from France

Balducci's
424 Sixth Avenue
New York, NY 10011
(800) 225-3822
Gourmet and specialty foods

Bridge Kitchenware
214 E. 52nd Street
New York, NY 10022
(212) 688-4220
Every kind of bakeware, ramekins, soufflé dishes

D'Artagnan
300-419 St. Paul Avenue
Jersey City, NJ 07306
(800) 327-8246
Game, poultry, fresh fois gras, homemade pâtés

Egg Farm Dairy
2 John Walsh Boulevard
Peekskill, NY 10566
(914) 734-7343
Fresh butter, crème fraîche

Gourmand of California
5873 Blackwelder Street
Culver City, CA 90230
(310) 839-9222
Imported chocolate, gourmet groceries

Katagiri & Co.
224 E. 59th Street
New York, NY 10022
(212) 755-3566
Japanese specialty foods

Browne Trading Co.
260 Commercial Street
Portland, ME 04101
(207) 775-3118
Maine fish, seafood

Peppercorn Gourmet
1235 Pearl Street
Boulder, CO 80302
(303) 449-5847
Oriental and gourmet cookware, spices, foods

M. Slavin and Sons Fish, Ltd.
122 Thatford Avenue
Brooklyn, NY 11212
(718) 346-6734
All kinds of fresh fish and seafood

Spice Merchant
P.O. Box 524
Jackson Hole, WY 83001
(307) 733-7811
Oriental spices

Williams-Sonoma
P.O. Box 7456
San Francisco, CA 94120
(800) 541-2233
Specialty foods, gourmet cookware

Zabar's
2245 Broadway
New York, NY 10024
(212) 787-2000
Specialty foods, cookware, small appliances

Index

Page numbers in *italic* refer to the photographs.

254 ᕁ

About the Author

DELIA SMITH is without a doubt the most popular, best-loved cook in the United Kingdom. With more than ten million copies of her books in print, she is Britain's all-time bestselling cookbook author. She is the food editor of one of England's most prestigious periodicals (Sainbury's *The Magazine*) and is married to the writer and editor Michael Wynn Jones. They live in Suffolk, England.

About the Type

THIS BOOK was set in Sabon, a typeface designed by the well-known German typographer Jan Tschichold (1902-74). Sabon's design is based upon the original letter forms of Claude Garamond and was created specifically to be used for three sources: foundry type for hand composition, Linotype, and Monotype. Tschichold named his typeface for the famous Frankfurt typefounder Jacques Sabon, who died in 1580.